Fountas & Pinnell

Leveled Literacy Intervention

LLI Green System Guide

LLI Green System • Levels A–K • Lessons 1–130

Irene C. Fountas & Gay Su Pinnell

Heinemann, Portsmouth, NH

Heinemann

361 Hanover Street
Portsmouth, NH 03801–3912
www.heinemann.com

Offices and agents throughout the world

Copyright © 2017, 2009 by Irene C. Fountas and Gay Su Pinnell

All rights reserved. No part of this book may be reproduced in any form or by any electronic or mechanical means, including information storage and retrieval systems, without permission in writing from the publisher, except by a reviewer, who may quote brief passages in a review; and with the exception of reproducibles (identified by the Texts and Lessons for Content-Area Writing copyright line), which may be photocopied for classroom use.

> *Heinemann's authors have devoted their entire careers to developing the unique content in their works, and their written expression is protected by copyright law. We respectfully ask that you do not adapt, reuse, or copy anything on third-party (whether for-profit or not-for-profit) lesson sharing websites.*
>
> —**Heinemann Publishers**

"Dedicated to Teachers" is a trademark of Greenwood Publishing Group, Inc.

Library of Congress Cataloging-in-Publication Data
Names: Fountas, Irene C., author. | Pinnell, Gay Su, author.
Title: Fountas & Pinnell leveled literacy intervention LLI green system guide / Irene C. Fountas & Gay Su Pinnell.
Other titles: Fountas and Pinnell leveled literacy intervention LLI green system guide
Description: Portsmouth, NH : Heinemann, 2017. | Includes bibliographical references.
Identifiers: LCCN 2017005353 | ISBN 9780325088426 (alk. paper)
Subjects: LCSH: Language arts (Elementary)—Handbooks, manuals, etc. | Language arts (Middle school)—Handbooks, manuals, etc. | Reading (Elementary)—Handbooks, manuals, etc. | Reading (Middle school)—Handbooks, manuals, etc.
Classification: LCC LB1576 .F6628 2017 | DDC 372.6/044—dc23
LC record available at https://lccn.loc.gov/2017005353

ISBN 978-0-325-08842-6

Editor: Debra Doorack
Production: Angel Lepore
Cover: Monica Ann Crigler, Ellery Harvey
Interior design: Lisa Fowler
Typesetter: Gina Poirier Design
Manufacturing: Erin St. Hilaire

Printed in Humen, China 21022407
6 7 8 9 RRD 24 23 22 21
December 2021 Printing

CONTENTS

Section 1: The *Leveled Literacy Intervention Green System* ... 1

LLI: Fifteen Keys to a Successful Intervention Design ... 1
The Critical Role of a Gradient of Text ... 3
Leveled Literacy Intervention Within a Comprehensive Educational System ... 4
Who Benefits from *LLI*? ... 4
    LLI for the First Years of School ... 5
    LLI for English Language Learners ... 5

The *LLI* Systems ... 8
    Orange System (Levels A–E) ... 9
    Green System (Levels A–K) ... 9
    Blue System (Levels C–N) ... 9
    Red System (Levels L–Q) ... 9
    Gold System (Levels O–T) ... 9
    Purple System (Levels R–W) ... 9

***LLI* System Components** ... 10
    System Guide ... 12
    Lesson Guide ... 12
    Books ... 12
    Writing Books ... 14
    Take-Home Bags ... 14
    Take-Home Books ... 14
    Student Folders ... 14
    Lesson Folders ... 14
    Student Whiteboards ... 14
    Fountas & Pinnell Prompting Guide, Part 1 for Oral Reading and Early Writing, K–8 ... 15
    Fountas & Pinnell Prompting Guide, Part 2 for Comprehension: Thinking, Talking, and Writing, K–8 ... 15
    Professional Book: *When Readers Struggle: Teaching That Works, A–N* ... 15
    LLI Ready Resources ... 15
    Online Resources ... 16
    Fountas & Pinnell Online Data Management System (ODMS) for *LLI* ... 16
    Professional Development and Tutorial Videos ... 16
    F&P Calculator/Stopwatch ... 17
    Optional Purchases for *LLI* System ... 17

| Section 2 | Implementing the *LLI Green System* | 19 |

Initial Assessment of Children	19
Finding Children's Instructional Reading Levels	19
Using the *Fountas & Pinnell Benchmark Assessment System 1*	19
Using Other Benchmark Assessment Systems	20
Alternative Assessments	20
Assessment Using Leveled Books	20
Selecting Children for the Intervention	21
Forming *LLI* Groups	21
Regrouping Children	23
Management of *LLI* Groups	23
Scheduling *LLI* Groups	23
Entering the System	24
Coordinating *LLI* Lessons with Classroom Instruction	24
Amount of Time in the System	25
Exiting the System	25
Getting Organized for Teaching	25
A Space for Teaching	25
Selecting a Table	25
Planning and Organizing for *LLI* Lessons	25

| Section 3 | *LLI Green System* Lesson Overview | 29 |

Lesson Guide Organization	29
The Lesson Frameworks	29
Overview of Getting Started Lessons	30
Overview of Odd-Numbered Lessons	36
Overview of Even-Numbered Lessons	42
Overview of *The Literacy Continuum*	48

| Section 4 | Teaching in the *LLI Green System* | 53 |

Key Aspects of Teaching *LLI* Lessons	53
Reading Texts in *LLI* Lessons	53
Writing Texts in *LLI* Lessons	54
Phonics and Word Work in *LLI* Lessons: Letters, Sounds, and Words	55
Oral Language Learning in *LLI* Lessons	55
Teaching with the *LLI* Lessons	55

Section 4	*continued*	53

Teaching the Getting Started Lessons 56
    Part 1: Reading (5 minutes) 57
    Part 2: Phonics/Word Work (5 minutes) 57
    Part 3: Reading a New Book (8 minutes) 57
    Part 4: Writing About Reading (7 minutes) 57
    Part 5: Letter/Word Work (5 minutes) 57

Teaching Standard Lessons (Odd-Numbered) 57
    Part 1: Rereading Books (5 minutes) 58
    Part 2: Phonics/Word Work (5 minutes) 58
    Part 3: Reading a New Book (15 minutes) 58
    Part 4: Letter/Word Work (5 minutes) 60

Teaching Standard Lessons (Even-Numbered) 60
    Part 1: Rereading and Assessment (5 minutes) 60
    Part 2: Phonics/Word Work (5 minutes) 61
    Part 3: Writing About Reading (15 minutes) 61
    Part 4: Reading a New Book (5 minutes) 62
    Optional Letter/Word Work 62

Section 5	Instructional Procedures and Teaching Materials for *LLI*	63

Instructional Procedures in *LLI* 63
    Instructional Procedures for Reading/Comprehension 63
    Instructional Procedures for Phonics/Word Work 65
    Instructional Procedures for Working with High-Frequency Words 69
    Working with Words in Text 71
    Introducing New Words to Learn 72
    Instructional Procedures for Writing About Reading 72
    Using *The Literacy Continuum* to Guide Instruction 75

Using *Prompting Guide, Part 1* in *LLI* Lessons 76

Using *Prompting Guide, Part 2* in *LLI* Lessons 76

Working with Series Books in *LLI* Lessons 76

Relationship Between Teacher Support and Child Control in *LLI* 77

Instructional Tools for *LLI* 77
    Alphabet Linking Chart 80
    13 Consonant Clusters and Digraphs Charts 80
    Fold Sheets 81
    Letter and Word Games 81
    Letter Minibooks 82
    Magnetic Letters 83
    My ABC Book 83

Section 5 *continued*

My Poetry Book	84
My Writing Book	84
Name Chart	85
Name Puzzle	85
Oral Games	85
Sentence Strips	86
Lap Books	86
Table Charts	86
Verbal Path for Letter Formation	87

Section 6 Assessment and Record Keeping in the *LLI System* 89

Continuous Assessment ... **89**
Administering the Reading Record Using the Recording Form ... **90**
Oral Reading ... **91**
   Coding Reading Behaviors on a Recording Form ... 91
   Assessing Fluency ... 91
   Calculating Accuracy ... 93
   Self-Correction Ratio ... 93
Talking About Reading ... **93**
   The Comprehension Conversation ... 93
   Scoring the Comprehension Conversation ... 94
Analyzing Oral Reading Behaviors ... **96**
   Sources of Information Neglected and Used ... 96
   Self-Correction Behavior ... 96
   Analyzing Strategic Actions ... 97
Using *The Literacy Continuum* to Monitor Progress and Guide Teaching ... **97**
Record-Keeping Forms ... **98**
   Lesson Record Form ... 98
   Intervention Record ... 100
   Student Achievement Log ... 100
   Communication Sheet—Individual ... 101
   Communication Sheet—Group ... 101
   Letter/Word Record ... 102
   Flip Record ... 102
   Writing Samples in *My Writing Book* ... 102
   Reading Records for Progress Monitoring ... 103
   Reading Graph and Reports ... 103
   Student Folder ... 104
Change over Time in Children's Progress ... **104**

Section 7: Professional Development for *LLI* — 105

Resources to Support Your Teaching 105
Frequently Asked Questions About Using *LLI* 109
- Implementing the *LLI Green System* 109
- Scheduling 109
- Selection 110
- Attendance/Exiting the Intervention 110
- Grouping 111
- Lesson Time 111
- Levels 112
- Teaching Decisions 112
- Assessment 114
- Parents 115

Appendix — 117

Appendix A, *LLI Green System* Book Chart 118

Appendix B, *LLI* Series Books 121

Appendix C, Text Analysis for Books in the *LLI Green System* 128

Appendix D, Master Plan for Word Work in the *LLI Green System* 129

Appendix E, New High-Frequency Words in the *LLI Green System* 155

Appendix F, F&P Calculator/Stopwatch Directions 158

Appendix G, *LLI* as a Complement to Reading Recovery® 159

Appendix H, Glossary 160

Appendix I, Bibliography 175

section 1

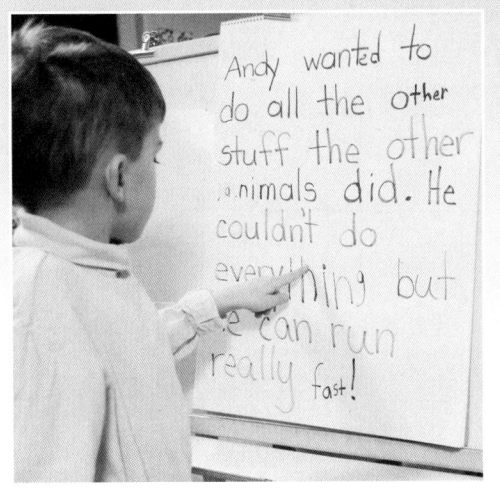

The *Leveled Literacy Intervention Green System*

▶ *LLI:* **Fifteen Keys to a Successful Intervention Design**

Powerful early intervention can change the path of a child's journey to literacy. Children who experience difficulty in the early grades fall further and further behind their peers (Stanovich 1986). Research shows that children who read below grade level at the end of grade 1 are likely to continue to read below grade level (Juel 1988). Many are retained at grade level or receive supplementary help throughout schooling. Others drop out of school as soon as they qualify. A growing body of research shows that reading difficulties are preventable with effective intervention programs (Demers 2012; Ransford-Kaldon, Ross, Lee, Sutton Flynt, Franceschini, and Zoblotsky 2013; Peterman, Grehan Ross, Gallagher, and Dexter 2009; Ward 2011; What Works Clearinghouse, ies.ed.gov/ncee/wwc/FWW).

Leveled Literacy Intervention is a scientifically based system that is designed to prevent literacy difficulties rather than correct long-term failure. It has been highly successful in achieving its goal of cutting

Closing the Gap: Grade 1 *LLI* Students Making Accelerated Progress

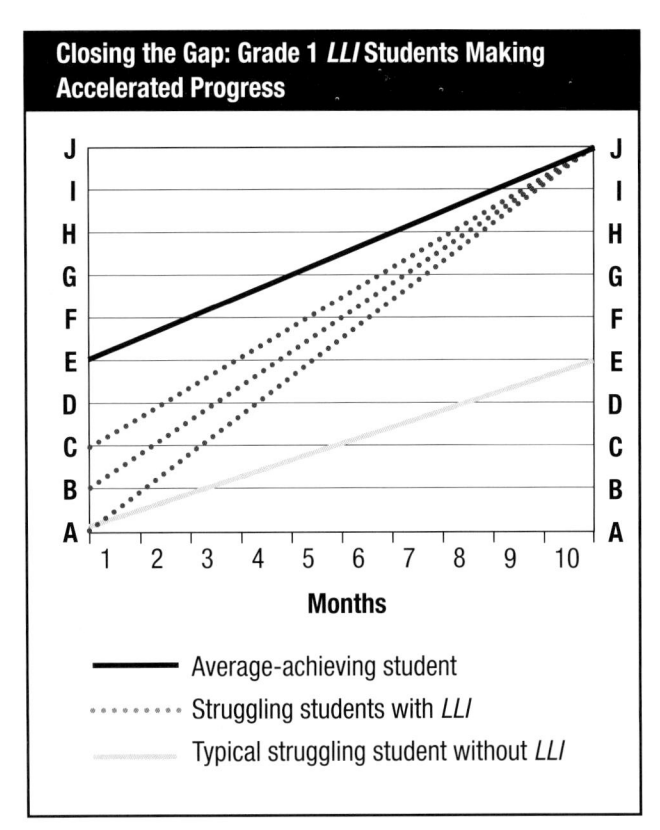

— Average-achieving student
······ Struggling students with *LLI*
— Typical struggling student without *LLI*

FIGURE 1.1 The *Leveled Literacy Intervention System* accelerates the rate at which children achieve grade-level performance.

across the path of literacy failure and bringing children to grade-level performance in tens of thousands of schools. *Leveled Literacy Intervention* has the following key characteristics:

- *LLI* is designed to **supplement**, not substitute for, the small-group instruction that children receive in the classroom.

- *LLI* lessons are provided **daily** and are of sufficient length to assure reinforcement of new learning and to support accelerated progress. The 30-minute lesson provides instruction in reading, writing, and phonics/word study.

- *LLI* lessons for the *Orange, Green,* and *Blue* Systems are provided to a small group, with a strong recommendation for **three children in the group.** The size of the group assures close observation and the intensive teaching interactions that promote individual learning and allow children to make faster progress.

- *LLI* is a **short-term intervention**. The *LLI Green System* is designed to provide an average of 14–18 weeks of lessons to bring children to grade-level performance. The *LLI Green System* provides enough lessons (130) for 26 weeks, but most children will not need a program of that length. As one group exits, a new group enters the teaching slot, allowing for six or more children to be served in each 30-minute teaching slot for the year.

- *LLI* provides a well-defined **framework for lessons** within which teachers make decisions specific to observations of the children's needs. The lessons include reading texts, writing, and phonics. Children learn the routines for each of the regular elements of the lesson so lessons are efficient.

- Lessons are **fast-paced**. The lessons are designed to move quickly within suggested time frames for each segment. Instead of "slowed down" teaching, children are highly engaged in experiences in which they find success.

- Reading focuses on deep **comprehending of texts**. Children read several books in every lesson. The teacher supports comprehension throughout the reading of the text and is provided a list of key understandings for each book.

- Writing focuses on building **early writing strategies.** Children learn how to compose, construct, and develop essential strategies for writing in the classroom. They learn how to use sound analysis, important spelling skills, and early writing conventions.

- Fluency is an important goal of *LLI* instruction. Lessons include **attention to fluent, phrased reading,** as well as fluency in writing. In order to be perceived as successful by classroom peers (as well as to process print effectively), readers and writers need to read smoothly and write quickly. It is especially important for low-achieving children to become fluent in literacy—before they become discouraged and perpetuate slow processing.

- Collections of **high-quality texts** have been created specifically for each *LLI* system. Written by children's authors and illustrated by well-known illustrators, the texts are designed to engage young readers with high-quality fiction and nonfiction selections. They have been systematically crafted to build phonics and word analysis skills are and arranged along a careful gradient of text characteristics (see Figure 1.2). Across a series of texts at each level of *LLI*, readers have the advantage of processing a new text every day. Every other day the reader is given a book that is easier than the instructional level (two levels below) to support confidence, fluency, and fast word solving. Children have the opportunity to read texts that are challenging and stretch the processing system as well as easy texts that build confidence. The Word Analysis charts (found in the Online Resources at resources.fountasandpinnell.com) provide a detailed analysis of the decoding, syntax, and vocabulary challenges for each book. See the Master Plan for Word Work in the *LLI Green System* (Appendix D, pp 129) for a detailed analysis of the phonics and word work goals in each lesson.

- The lessons include **systematic phonics**. A component of every lesson focuses on key aspects of phonics learning—phonological awareness, letter knowledge, letter-sound relationships, spelling patterns, high-frequency words, vocabulary, word structure, and word-solving actions (that is the fast application of phonics knowledge while processing print).

- *LLI* includes initial and ongoing **assessments, progress-monitoring,** and **record-keeping instruments** that are practical and that continuously inform teaching. The assessments will help you determine appropriate reading levels for grouping and provide useful information for daily teaching. Forms are provided for taking reading records on each child about once per week.

- *LLI* provides a high level of **professional development** within and outside lessons. You will notice the professional understandings provided in each lesson, including the analysis of book characteristics, support for teaching English language learners, assessment suggestions, and references to professional resources. The professional book *When Readers Struggle: Teaching That Works, A–N* (included in the *Green System*) is designed to provide strong support for teacher knowledge and decision-making in the lessons. In addition, Professional Development and Tutorial videos are included, and lessons also suggest other resources.

- *LLI* provides a strong **classroom connection**. Children take books to read, word activities to review, and writing to reread in their classrooms. Efficient record-keeping documents can be shared between the intervention and classroom teachers.

- *LLI* provides a strong **home connection**. When children have more opportunities to share their successes in the home, their self-esteem is enhanced. In addition, they gain valuable reading and writing practice. Children have many opportunities to take home phonics materials and writing. Take-home books and parent letters in multiple languages are provided to the children at the end of every lesson.

Finally, in any effective teaching, attention must be paid to children's home language and its relation to literacy. Each *LLI* lesson provides a list of lesson-specific suggestions that will help teachers adjust instruction to make it more powerful for English language learners.

▶ The Critical Role of a Gradient of Text

Leveled Literacy Intervention is based on the F&P Text Level Gradient™. Created and refined as a teaching and assessment tool over the past twenty years, the gradient consists of twenty-six points on a scale of reading difficulty (Figure 1.2). Each point on that gradient, from the easiest level A to the most challenging at level Z (Z+ in special cases), represents a small but significant increase in difficulty over the previous level. In the *LLI Green System*, the leveled books begin at level A and continue through level K, with a total of 130 lessons. Each new level of text makes increasing demands on the reader, but the demands and resulting changes are gradual. By engaging in intensively supportive lessons on each level, readers have the opportunity to expand their reading and writing abilities. With the support of instruction, they stretch themselves to read

F&P TEXT LEVEL GRADIENT™

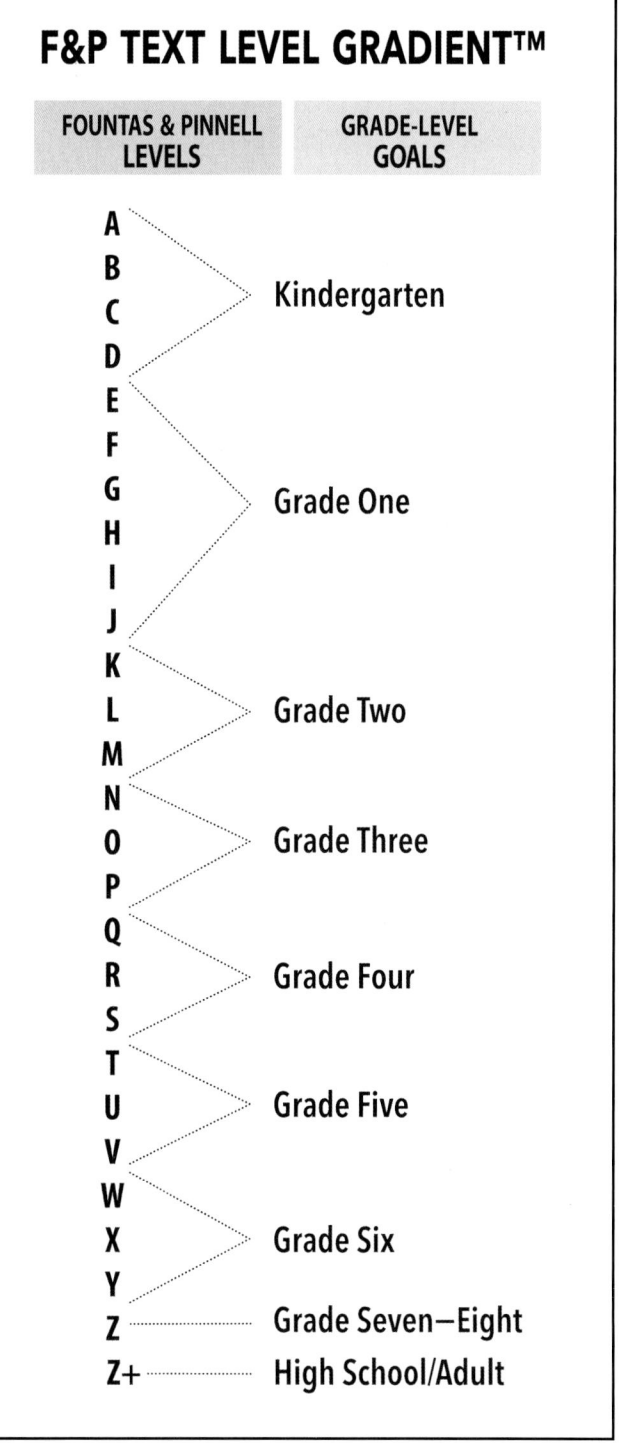

FOUNTAS & PINNELL LEVELS	GRADE-LEVEL GOALS
A, B, C, D, E	Kindergarten
F, G, H, I, J	Grade One
K, L, M	Grade Two
N, O, P	Grade Three
Q, R, S	Grade Four
T, U, V	Grade Five
W, X, Y	Grade Six
Z	Grade Seven–Eight
Z+	High School/Adult

FIGURE 1.2 F&P Text Level Gradient™

LLI lessons are designed for children who find reading and writing difficult.

more complex texts with accuracy, fluency, and comprehension—and to write with more complexity. With these goals in mind, children effectively engage in the reading and writing process every day.

We use the term *level* in the Text Level Gradient and throughout *LLI* because leveled books are a key component in helping children become competent readers who can access texts of increasing complexity. Each book is carefully designed, analyzed, and sequenced to provide enough support and a small amount of challenge so the reader can learn through the text and make small steps toward grade-level goals.

While readers are progressing along the text gradient, they receive specific instruction in phonics and word work; but it is the daily opportunity to *apply* what they know to reading and writing continuous text that enables children to make accelerated progress. Additionally, you provide explicit instruction in comprehension as the children discuss the texts, and you intentionally draw their attention to aspects of a text that they need to understand.

Key understandings for each text are indicated in the lessons and on the Recording Forms used for conducting reading records in even-numbered lessons. You will want to monitor children's comprehension closely as they respond to texts. These reading records make it possible to monitor progress systematically, over time. Assessment of phonics and word analysis, writing, reading, and comprehending are built into each lesson.

The F&P Text Level Gradient™ is the foundation for the creation of *The Fountas & Pinnell Literacy Continuum: A Tool for Assessment, Planning, and Teaching*, which provides a level-by-level description of the demands of the texts on readers at each level as well as the corresponding competencies to teach for, assess, and reinforce. You will find the specific competencies on a continuum of behaviors and understandings to notice, teach for, and support at the end of each level in the *LLI Green System Lesson Guides*.

▶ *Leveled Literacy Intervention* Within a Comprehensive Educational System

LLI is a critical and powerful part of a comprehensive literacy system. Districts and schools can incorporate *LLI* into their present system, with the following goals in mind:

- ❑ Help a large number of children enter the world of literacy and continue to expand their reading and writing abilities.
- ❑ Help teachers learn the value of a well-selected sequence of texts.
- ❑ Help teachers plan and implement efficient and effective small-group lessons.
- ❑ Suggest language that will help teachers internalize precise ways of teaching that they can apply in many instructional settings.
- ❑ Create a system within which multiple needs, at many levels, can be met.

Ultimately we expect coherent, many-layered systems that embrace highly effective classroom teaching alongside multiple interventions—some highly individualized and others supportive in systematic ways—to help all children who are having difficulty learning to read and write (see Figure 1.3). We strongly recommend *LLI* as a component of a comprehensive system.

▶ Who Benefits from *LLI*?

LLI is designed to be used with small groups of children who need intensive support to achieve grade-level competencies. *LLI* also provides strong support for children who are acquiring English as an additional language and are receiving classroom reading

A Many-Layered System of Literacy Intervention

Grade Level	All Students Need:	Struggling Readers (including Special Education and ELL) Need:
K	Good Classroom Teaching	*LLI* through Level E
1	Good Classroom Teaching	Reading Recovery®, if available
		LLI through Level K
2	Good Classroom Teaching	*LLI* through Level N
3	Good Classroom Teaching	*LLI* through Level Q
4	Good Classroom Teaching	*LLI* through Level T
5	Good Classroom Teaching	*LLI* through Level W
6	Good English Language Arts Classroom Teaching	Identified Intervention
7–12	Good English Language Arts Classroom Teaching	Identified Intervention

FIGURE 1.3 A Many-Layered System of Literacy Intervention

instruction in English. You may also decide to include children who are identified as having special needs if the content of the *LLI* intervention meets the educational program specifications for the child.

LLI for the First Years of School

LLI is particularly important for the lowest-achieving children in kindergarten. It serves as an important prevention program for literacy difficulties in subsequent years of schooling. We suggest that classroom teachers engage kindergarten children in rich literacy opportunities including interactive read-aloud, shared reading, interactive writing, and writing workshop for several months prior to selecting them for the *LLI Orange System*. The *Orange System* may be used with older children from the beginning of the school year.

Even with many high-quality literacy opportunities, some children show extreme difficulty in early literacy learning. *LLI* can give kindergarten children a boost so they can begin grade one (P2)* at the same level as their peers. The child's success in first grade will be a strong predictor of literacy success throughout schooling.

Ideally, in grade 1 both the *LLI Green System* and Reading Recovery are available. We take the most needy children into the one-to-one intervention immediately, and serve others in small groups. Because both are short-term interventions, smooth transitions can be made in and out of intervention throughout the year. In this way, *LLI* can serve as a powerful complement to Reading Recovery® (see Appendix G, page 159.)

LLI for English Language Learners

Each lesson in *LLI* provides specific suggestions for supporting English language learners who are selected for the program (also see *When Readers Struggle: Teaching That Works, A–N*). Use your district criteria for language proficiency to determine eligibility for reading instruction in English. English language learners will benefit greatly from the daily conversation with an adult and interaction with a very small group of children. They will also benefit from reading the large amount of continuous text provided in *LLI*. Through reading, talking, and writing about reading, they extend their knowledge of the structure of English and expand oral vocabulary. The *LLI* lesson structure is ideal for these children because of the opportunities for increased language modeling—oral language surrounds every element of the lesson. In addition, the group size and instructional approaches allow for decision-making based on the specific strengths and needs of each child.

---

*In many countries outside the United States, grade levels are designated as Primary 1 (kindergarten), Primary 2 (grade 1), Primary 3 (grade 2), and Primary 4 (grade 3).

If children cannot follow your instructions or participate fully in the activities of the group, you may want to give them whatever language support your district offers before placing them in an *LLI* group. Each lesson in the *LLI* program provides specific suggestions for supporting English language learners who are selected for the program. In addition, you can keep some general suggestions in mind as you work across lessons. Below, we list suggestions in four categories: oral language, reading, writing, and phonics. These ideas will be helpful as you work with English language learners as well as with other children who can benefit from extra support. You will also find specific suggestions in every lesson, in *When Readers Struggle: Teaching That Works, A–N*, and in *Guided Reading: Responsive Teaching Across the Grades*.

SUPPORTING ORAL LANGUAGE

- Make instruction highly interactive, with a great deal of oral language surrounding everything children are learning.
- At the same time, use short, simple (although natural-sounding) sentences instead of long and involved ones that children will find hard to follow. Support meaning with nonverbal signals.
- Have the children repeat sentences, if needed.
- When introducing books, use the language of the text in a conversational way and have children repeat the language several times to help them remember the syntax.
- Show children what you mean when you give directions. You may need to act out certain sequences of action and have children repeat those actions while you coach them. Have them repeat directions to each other or say them aloud as they engage in the activity. Support them during their first attempts rather than expecting independence immediately.
- Give English language learners more "wait and think" time. You could say, "Let's think about that for a minute" before calling for an answer. Demonstrate to children how you think about what you are going to say.
- Paraphrase and summarize for children. Repeat the directions or instructions several different ways, watching for feedback that they understand you.
- Remember that typical English language learners usually understand more than they can say. Ask children if they understand, and repeat if needed.
- Expand children's sentences in a conversational way during discussion rather than correcting them.

SUPPORTING READING

- Understand that shared reading involves children in a great deal of language repetition, often language that is different from or more complex than the language they can currently use in speech. This experience gives children a chance to practice language, learn the meaning of the words, and use the sentence structures of English. Several repetitions of a new language structure, within a meaningful and enjoyable activity, will enable a child to add the new structure to her repertoire. The lap books in the *Orange* and *Green* systems and poetry in *LLI* are very beneficial to children.
- Check understanding to see if you need to explain a concept or vocabulary word that would be familiar to most English speakers but might not be for English language learners.
- Direct attention to pictures and use understandable oral language when you introduce texts to children. Invite children to point to objects and characters.
- Help learners relate new words to words they already know. During and after reading, check with children to be sure they understand vocabulary and concepts. Allow time within the lessons for children to bring up any words they do not know.
- Be sure children understand the prompts you are using before you ask them to demonstrate what they have learned. English language learners might need support for their understanding of the concepts, such as, *first, last, beginning,* and *ending*. For example, they need to understand the concept of "beginning," if they are to respond to a question like, "What letter would you expect to see at the beginning of. . .?"

- For a home/school connection, encourage children to read aloud to a parent or sibling at home, even if that parent or sibling is not yet fluent in English. If children have siblings at school, request that a sibling support the younger child at home by listening to him read.

SUPPORTING WRITING

- Value and encourage children's drawing. Through drawing, they can represent thinking and connect their ideas to the writing.
- Have children repeat several times the sentence they are going to write so that they will be able to remember it. If the sentence is difficult for children to remember, you may need to reduce the complexity.
- Guide children to produce some repetitive texts that use the same sentence structure and phrases over and over again, so that children can internalize them.
- Once a text has been successfully produced in interactive writing, dictation, or independent writing and children can easily read it, you can use the text as a resource for talking about language—locating specific words, noticing beginning and ending sounds, noticing rhymes, and so on.
- Make time to have children reread their writing and poetry books (called *My Writing Book, My Poetry Book*).
- Demonstrate how to say words slowly, providing more individual help and demonstration, if needed.
- Surround children's independent writing with a great deal of oral language. Talk with children and help them express their ideas in oral language before they write.
- Learn something about the sound system of the children's first language. That knowledge will give you valuable insights into the way they "invent" or "approximate" their first spellings. For example, notice whether they are using letter/sound associations from the first language or whether they are actually thinking of a word in the first language and trying to spell it.
- Help the children use standard pronunciation and spelling of words. Work toward helping children develop knowledge of the visual features of words.

- Notice how English pronunciation improves as children experience reading and talking.
- Be sure children understand the meaning of the words in the Verbal Path for Letter Formation (see page 86 in this Guide) you are using for the writing/recognition of letters. If they do not understand, demonstrate the motions and have them follow.

SUPPORTING PHONICS AND WORD STUDY

- Providing the "hands-on" activities in *LLI* lessons will be very helpful to your English language learners. It will give them a chance to manipulate magnetic letters, move pictures around, and work with word and letter cards. Repeat activities that you find most beneficial for your learners.
- Build quick recognition of the set of picture cards provided in the *LLI* Online Resources. These will form a core vocabulary that children in the group share.
- Support children in naming the pictures on each card, on the Alphabet Linking Chart, and in *My ABC Book*.
- Be sure the print for all charts is clear and consistent so that children who are working in a new langauge (and sometimes a new set of characters) do not also have to deal with varying forms of letters.
- Make sure your English language learners are not sitting where it is hard for them to see the charts. (For poems, for example, sitting at the far side of a chart means that their view is distorted.)
- When needed, use a real object to help children learn a concept.
- Be sure to enunciate your own words clearly and accept children's approximations. If they are feeling their own mouths as they say (or approximate) the sounds, they will be able to make the connections. Sounds and letters are abstract concepts and the relationships are arbitrary. Building understanding of letter-sound correspondence will be especially complex for children whose sound systems do not exactly match that of English. They may have trouble saying the sounds that are related to letters and letter clusters.

- Accept alternative pronunciations of words with the hard-to-say sounds and present the written form to help learners distinguish between them. Sounds that are like each other, have similar tongue positions, and are easily confused, such as *s* and *z*, *r* and *l*, *sh* and *ch*, *f* and *v*, can be quite difficult for English language learners to differentiate. They often have difficulty with inflected endings (*s*, *ed*) because they have not yet achieved control of the language structure.
- Speak clearly and slowly when working with children on distinguishing phonemes and hearing sounds in words, but do not distort the word so much that it is unrecognizable. Distortion may confuse English language learners in that it may sound like another word that they do not know.
- When discussing concepts such as *beginning, ending, first,* and *last*, be sure children understand these concepts.

▶ The *LLI* Systems

Six systems are available in *LLI*:
- *Orange System:* levels A through E (110 lessons)
- *Green System:* levels A through K (130 lessons)
- *Blue System:* levels C through N (120 lessons)
- *Red System:* levels L through Q (192 lessons)
- *Gold System:* levels O through T (192 lessons)
- *Purple System:* levels R through W (204 lessons)

Lessons across the six systems progress from level A (beginning reading in kindergarten) through level W, which represents competencies at the middle and secondary school level. Each level within the systems provides:
- A combination of reading, writing, and phonics/word study.
- Emphasis on teaching for comprehension strategies.
- Explicit attention to genre and to the features of nonfiction and fiction texts.
- Special attention to disciplinary reading, literature inquiry, and writing about reading.
- Specific work on sounds, letters, and words in activities designed to help students notice the details of written language and learn how words "work."
- Close reading to deepen and expand comprehension.
- Explicit teaching of effective and efficient strategies for expanding vocabulary.
- Explicit teaching for fluent and phrased reading.
- Use of writing about reading for the purpose of communicating and learning how to express ideas for a particular purpose and audience using a variety of writing strategies.

There are specific *Lesson Guides* for each *LLI System*, and the systems are coordinated with the grade levels at which they will most likely be used; however, educators may make other decisions as they work to match the program to the needs of particular readers. The systems overlap in levels, but books and lessons for each system are unique, with no overlap of titles or lessons. You may choose to extend the number of lessons at a level on the F&P Text Level Gradient™ by using a set of lessons and titles from another system. For example, after teaching at level E in the *LLI Green System*, you may decide that students need a few additional lessons at that level. You can use level E books and lessons from the *LLI Orange* or *Blue Systems* to meet your students' needs. You may also decide to spend fewer days at a level when you have observable evidence that the students control almost all the competencies specified at the level. These competencies are listed in the excerpt from *The Literacy Continuum* that appears at the end of each level in the *Lesson Guide*.

The *LLI* books have been produced specifically for the intervention system. Written by children's authors, illustrated by high-quality artists, and designed by professionals, they have been created to provide engaging, age-appropriate material while at the same time offering increasingly sophisticated learning opportunities so that students can build a strong reading process over time.

Orange System (Levels A–E)

The books and lessons in the *LLI Orange System* begin with level A and continue through level E. They provide a significant amount of easy reading for children who are having difficulty becoming oriented to print and learning the function of letters and sounds. The books were written with the interest levels of five- and six-year-olds in mind. The *LLI Orange System* is specifically designed to address the interests and needs of kindergarteners who are identified as having difficulties after the first few months of kindergarten. The lessons are also helpful for chilren who are learning English, as they provide easy reading and plenty of opportunities to talk about texts.

Green System (Levels A–K)

The books and lessons in the *LLI Green System* begin with level A and continue through level K. The books were written with the interest levels of first-graders (ages 6–7) in mind. The lessons are specifically designed to address the interests and needs of first grade children who are identified as reading below the expected grade level. In schools that use Reading Recovery®, it is recommended that the lowest-achieving students receive Reading Recovery instruction, and the next tier of students receive *LLI* instruction. *LLI* can also be used for ELL students and special education students for whom the lessons meet the educational program specifications.

Blue System (Levels C–N)

The books and lessons in the *LLI Blue System* begin with level C and continue through level N. The books were written with the interest level of second graders (ages 7–8) in mind. The lessons are designed to address the interests and needs of second graders who are reading below grade level, or older students who are reading below level N. *LLI* has also been used effectively with ELL students and special education students for whom the lessons meet the educational program specifications.

Red System (Levels L–Q)

The books and lessons in the *LLI Red System* begin with level L and continue through level Q. The lessons provide students with opportunities to read a variety of genres. Students engage in intensive work in comprehension, vocabulary, fluency, phonics, word study, and writing about reading. The *LLI Red System* is specifically designed to address the interests and needs of third graders (ages 8–9) but may be used with older students who are reading below level Q. *LLI* can also be used with ELL students and special education students for whom the lessons meet the educational program specifications.

Gold System (Levels O–T)

The books and lessons in the *LLI Gold System* begin with level O and continue through level T. The books were written and illustrated to be appealing to fourth graders (ages 9–10). The lessons are specifically designed to address the interests and needs of fourth graders who are reading below grade level, older students reading below level T, and for ELL students and special education students for whom the lessons meet the educational program specifications.

Purple System (Levels R–W)

The books and lessons in the *LLI Purple System* begin with level R and continue through level W. The books were written and illustrated to be appealing to preadolescents (ages 10–12). The lessons are specifically designed to address the interests and needs of fifth graders who are reading below grade level, older students reading below level W, and for ELL students and special education students for whom the lessons meet the educational program specifications.

▶ LLI System Components

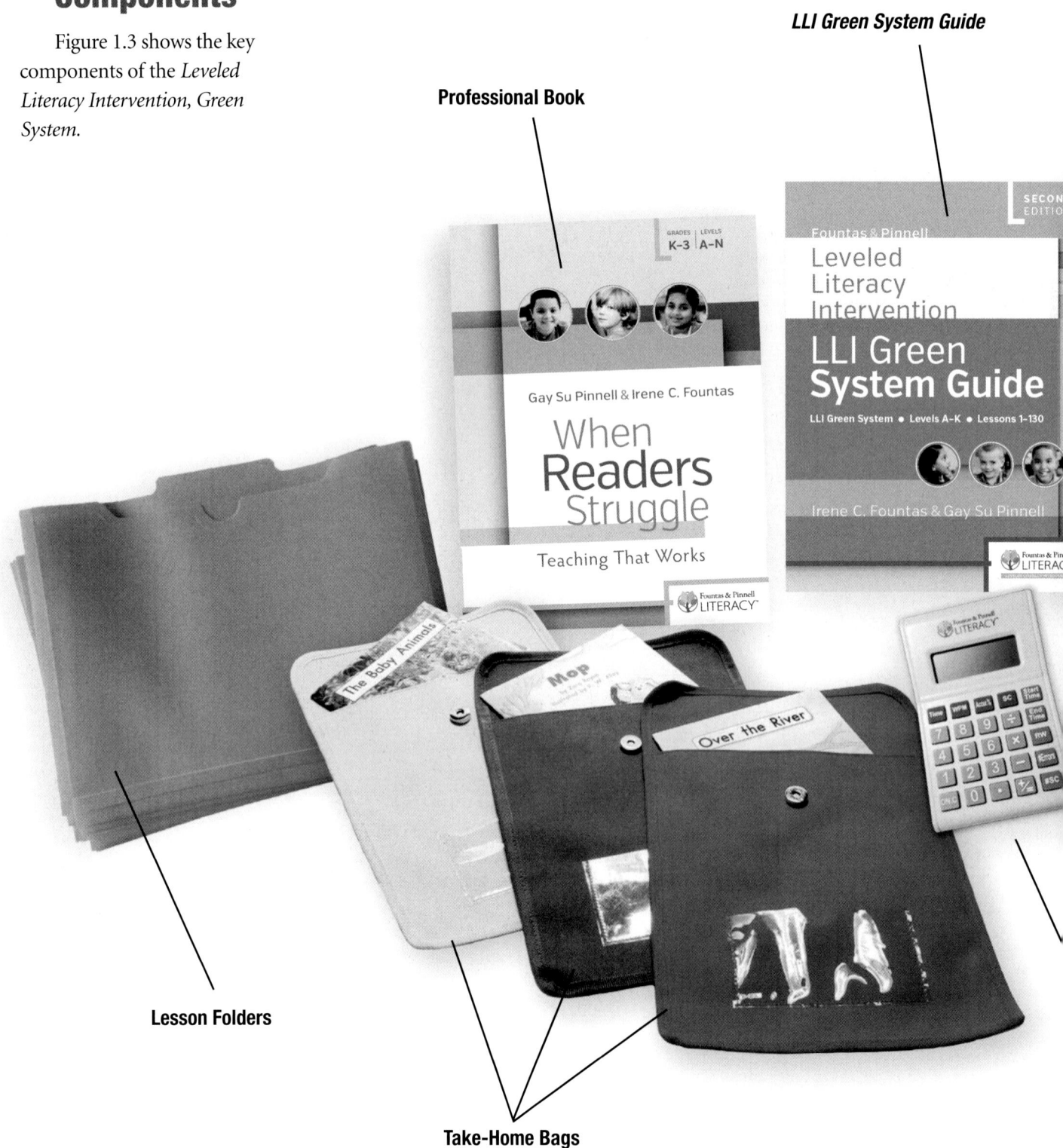

Figure 1.3 shows the key components of the *Leveled Literacy Intervention, Green System*.

Professional Book

LLI Green System Guide

Lesson Folders

Take-Home Bags

FIGURE 1.4 *LLI* Components

LLI Green Lesson Guides

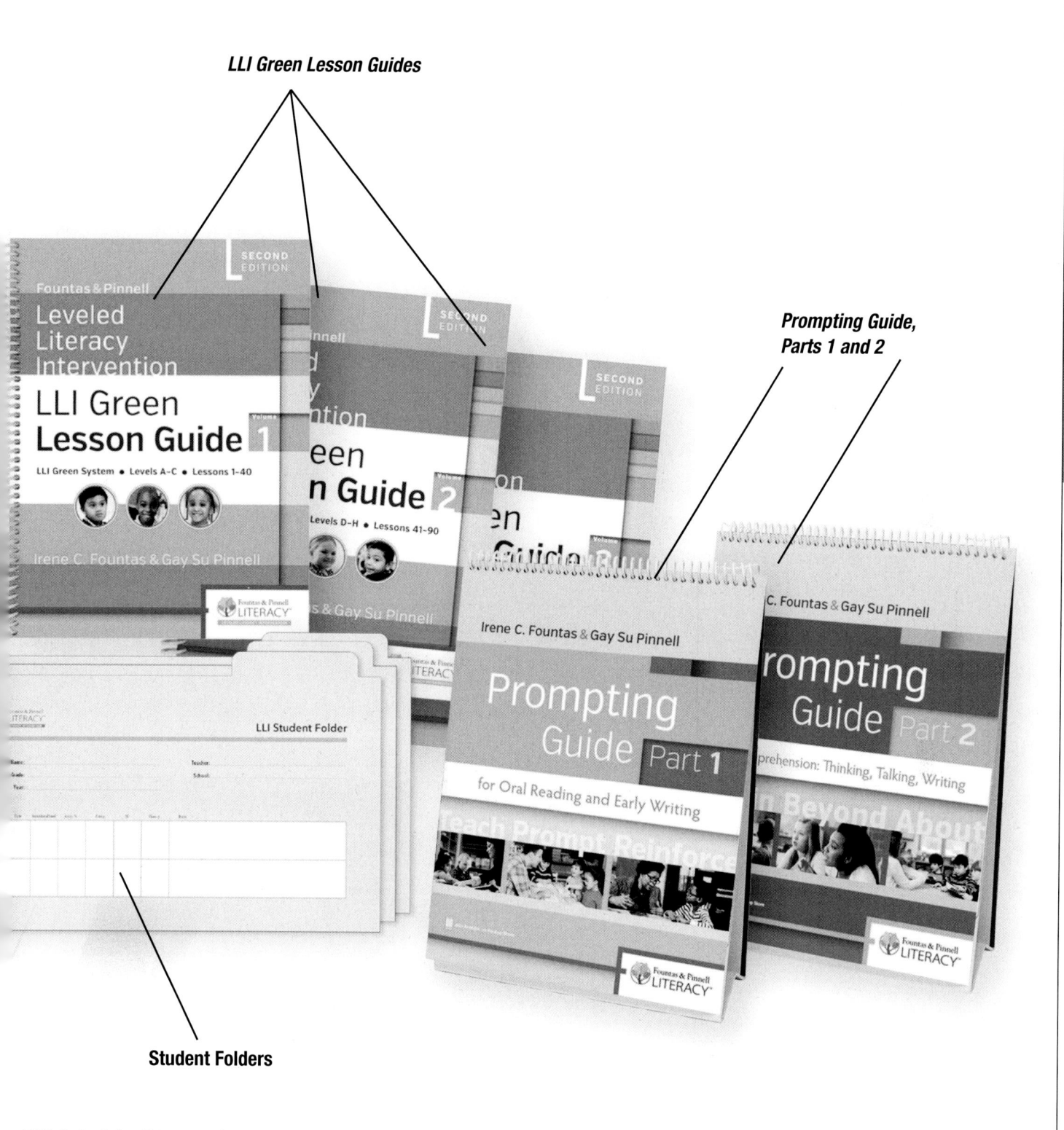

Prompting Guide, Parts 1 and 2

Student Folders

F&P Calculator/Stopwatch

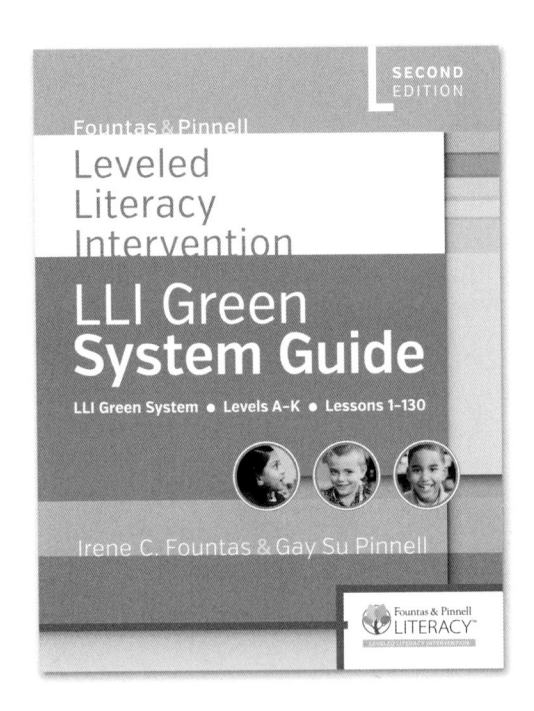

SYSTEM GUIDE

This *System Guide* provides a comprehensive overview of the *LLI Green System,* including important information about each of the components, the lessons, and how to implement the *Green System.*

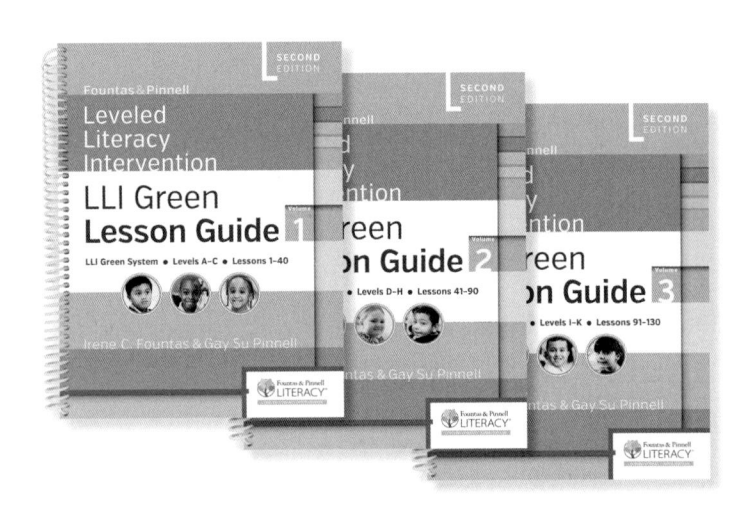

LESSON GUIDE

The teacher's *Leveled Literacy Intervention Lesson Guide* for the *Green System* includes 130 thirty-minute lessons for teaching children in small groups.

At the end of each set of lessons at a level, you will find an excerpt from *The Fountas and Pinnell Literacy Continuum,* containing the important behaviors and understandings to notice, teach, and support at that level.

Small Book

- Genre
- Lesson Number

BOOKS

In the *LLI Green System,* learning takes place with the foundational support of 130 leveled books and lessons. The first ten lessons are called Getting Started lessons and include oversized lap books to facilitate shared reading. The remaining 120 books are smaller, 16-page leveled books, all with full-color illustrations.

Getting Started lap books and small books

The *LLI Green System* includes ten Getting Started lap books and four individual (reduced size) copies of each title: a teacher copy and three copies for the children in the group. On the back cover of each book, you will find the genre, level, book/lesson number, and number of running words. Additional copies or replacement copies can be ordered from Heinemann. The complete list of titles can be found in Appendix A, page 116. The books can be placed in the *LLI* plastic folders provided, and then in hanging folders.

Small books

WRITING BOOKS

Consumable writing books, called *My Writing Book,* in various colors for groups. On the cover you will find room for the child's photograph or illustration. The writing books are filled as children engage in writing in *LLI* lessons. When all pages of a book are completed, the child takes it home and begins a new one. Completed pages are excellent for reading practice. Additional books can be ordered from Heinemann.

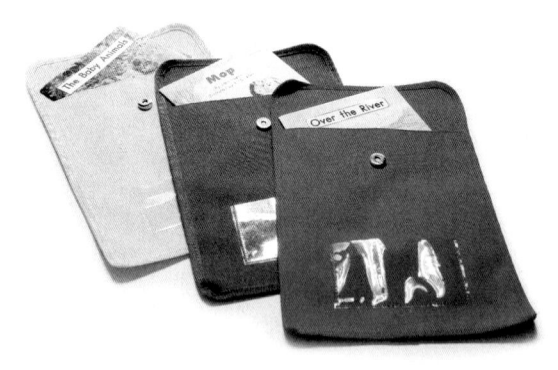

TAKE-HOME BAGS

These brightly colored bags provide a plastic pocket in which you can place a card with the child's name. Children take home items such as word bags, sentence strips, take-home books, fold sheets, parent letters, and other materials for classroom and home connection activities in these bags. They learn the importance of daily responsibilities, and the colorful bag helps them keep track of materials and remember their assigned tasks. They bring back the bag each day. Replacement bags are available from Heinemann.

TAKE-HOME BOOKS

Take-home books are black-and-white versions of the lesson books, with a place on the back cover for children to write their names. Children can keep the take-home books for rereading and to build their own home library of books. Replacement take-home books are inexpensive and can be ordered from Heinemann.

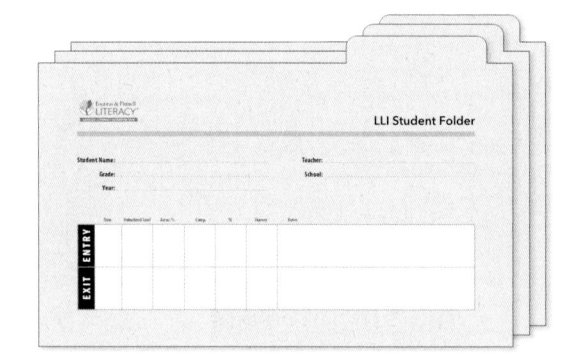

STUDENT FOLDERS

Student folders are provided to keep reading records and other data for each child. The folders can be passed on each year as part of children's records. The inside of the folder includes a graph for tracking a child's entry level, progress throughout *LLI*, and exit-level information.

LESSON FOLDERS

The system includes sturdy, plastic lesson folders to store books and printable lesson resources.

STUDENT WHITEBOARDS

Your purchase of the *LLI Green System* includes a set of eight whiteboards for individual use. One side of each whiteboard is blank, and the other side contains pre-printed sound/letter boxes for use with the lessons. There are three rows of boxes for working with words of three, four, or five letters. As students work with the boxes, you'll want to encourage fast erasing between words, using a small eraser, an old sock, or a soft cloth.

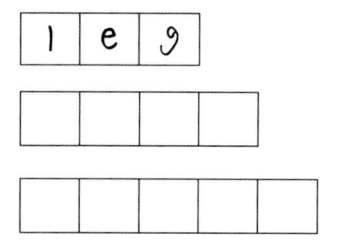

PROMPTING GUIDE, PART 1 FOR ORAL READING AND EARLY WRITING, K–8

Prompting Guide, Part 1 is a tool you will use in each lesson. It provides a quick reference for specific language you can use to teach for, prompt for, or reinforce effective reading and writing behaviors. The Guide is organized in categories and color coded so that you can turn quickly to the area needed and refer to it as you teach. (The *Prompting Guide* is also available in Spanish and for purchase as an app from Apple iTunes.)

PROMPTING GUIDE, PART 2 FOR COMPREHENSION: THINKING, TALKING, AND WRITING, K–8

Prompting Guide, Part 2 is a tool that provides specific language for supporting children's thinking, talking, and writing about reading. Prompts for book discussions and reading conferences are included. As in Part 1, the guide is organized in categories and color-coded so you can turn quickly to the area needed and refer to it as you teach. (The *Prompting Guide* is also available in Spanish and for purchase as an app from Apple iTunes.)

WHEN READERS STRUGGLE: TEACHING THAT WORKS, A–N

When Readers Struggle: Teaching That Works, A–N is a rich guide that supports effective teaching in the lessons. Each lesson refers you to chapters that will be helpful in developing your professional expertise in working with classroom children who find literacy learning difficult.

LLI READY RESOURCES

Your purchase of the *Fountas & Pinnell Leveled Literacy Intervention Green System* includes a box of Ready Resources—preprinted, preassembled items from the General Resources section of the Fountas & Pinnell Online Resources. You'll find enough Ready Resources to last a full school year (or four rounds of *LLI* with groups of three children). To replenish your materials, visit www.heinemann.com. The Ready Resources box is sold as a complete set only. Components are not sold separately. However, all of the consumable materials found in the Ready Resources box may also be downloaded and printed from the General Resources section of the Fountas & Pinnell Online Resources site.

Your *LLI* Ready Resources box includes ready-to-use sets of the following items:

- ❑ Alphabet Linking Chart for Teacher (1 enlarged color, 10 black and white and blank)
- ❑ Alphabet Linking Chart for Students (40 black and white and blank versions)
- ❑ Alphabet Linking Chart Picture Sets (10 for teacher and 40 for students)
- ❑ Consonant Clusters and Digraphs Charts for Teacher (enlarged color)
- ❑ Consonant Clusters and Digraphs Charts for Students (40 black and white, one of each chart)
- ❑ *My ABC Book* (40 copies)
- ❑ *My Poetry Book* (40 copies)
- ❑ *My Writing Book* (40 copies)
- ❑ *My Vowel Book* (40 copies)
- ❑ Laminated Reference Charts (1 of each: The Verbal Path, Ways to Use Magnetic Letters, Letters Made in Similar Ways, F & P Text Level Gradient™)
- ❑ Letter Cards (4 sets, upper- and lowercase)
- ❑ Letter Minibooks (40 copies of each set)
- ❑ Picture Cards (4 sets, black and white)
- ❑ Word Cards (4 sets, or organized by lesson)

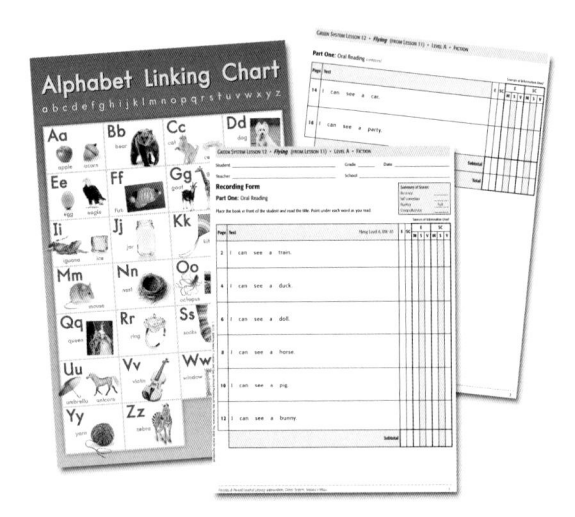

ONLINE RESOURCES

The Fountas & Pinnell Online Resources website (resources.fountasandpinnell.com) is a repository of printable lesson resources, record-keeping forms, and videos that are referenced in the "You Will Need" and "Professional Development Links" sections of the *LLI* lessons, as well as throughout this *System Guide*. Many of these resources can also be found in classroom-ready form in the Ready Resources. See the inside front cover of this guide for access information.

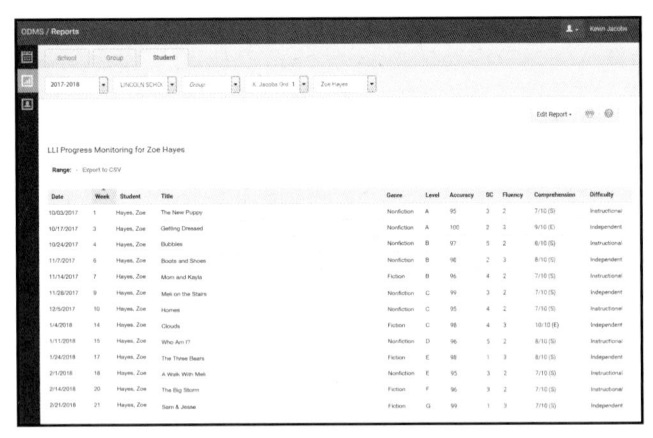

ODMS graph showing child's progress

FOUNTAS & PINNELL ONLINE DATA MANAGEMENT SYSTEM (ODMS) FOR *LLI*

The Fountas & Pinnell Online Data Management System (ODMS) is a web-based, password-protected tool that provides robust support for teachers and administrators in collecting and analyzing student achievement data and monitoring progress over time. (See above.) A one-year individual teacher subscription (for an unlimited number of students) including administrator access is provided with the purchase of an *LLI* system. Teachers and administrators can access data and print reports for groups or individual students. See the inside front cover of this guide for access information.

PROFESSIONAL DEVELOPMENT AND TUTORIAL VIDEOS

The Professional Development Videos feature an overview of the system, model lessons, and instructional routines. The Tutorial Videos provide instruction and practice in coding, scoring, analyzing, and interpreting reading records to inform instruction. This video collection is located within the Fountas & Pinnell Online Resources website. See the inside front cover of this guide for access information.

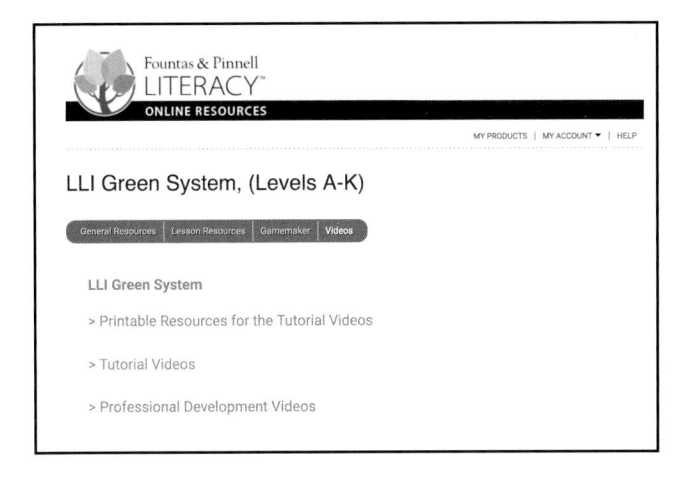

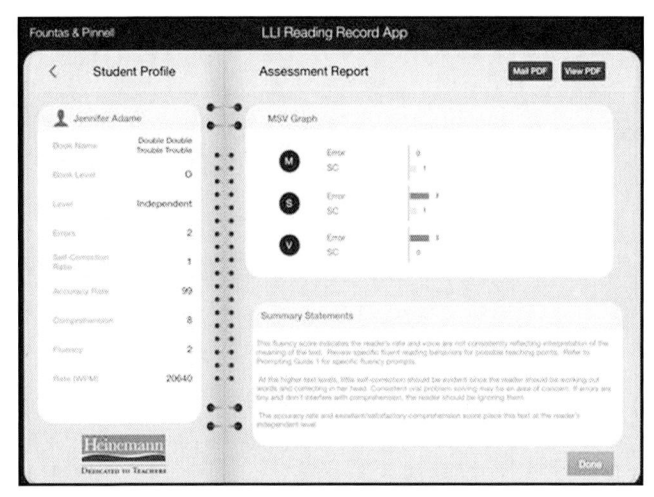

Fountas & Pinnell LLI Reading Record App for ipads

F&P CALCULATOR/STOPWATCH

The F&P Calculator/Stopwatch performs highly specific functions related to taking reading records. With the push of a button, you will be able to see children's reading rate, percentage of accuracy, and self-correction ratio. The F&P Calculator/Stopwatch can be used by any teacher who uses running records to assess children. The calculator is included in the *LLI Green System* to make your work more time efficient. Extra calculators may be ordered from Heinemann.

OPTIONAL PURCHASES FOR *LLI SYSTEM*

Fountas & Pinnell LLI Reading Record App for iPads

The *Fountas & Pinnell LLI Reading Record App* is available through the Apple iTunes store, by searching for "Fountas and Pinnell." The app:

- ❑ Provides all reading record forms electronically
- ❑ Saves individual reading records as PDFs
- ❑ Times the conference
- ❑ Calculates oral reading accuracy, self-correction, fluency, and comprehension
- ❑ Syncs data to the *Online Data Management System (ODMS)*

Fountas & Pinnell Select Collections and Genre Sets

Fountas & Pinnell Select Collections and *Genre Sets* are made up of books from the popular PM Readers, collections that have been hand-selected, leveled, and organized by Irene Fountas and Gay Su Pinnell. Each collection offers high-quality, high-interest books in a range of genres and topics. Each *Select Collections* or *Genre Sets* includes books, a Resource Guide, book lists with levels, press-on level labels, and a sturdy storage container.

section 2

Implementing the *LLI Green System*

▶ Initial Assessment of Children

When implementing the *LLI Green System*, your first goal is to identify the lowest-achieving children in grade one and find the instructional reading level for each of them. It's important at this point to confer with the classroom teacher who has worked with the children for the first few months of school and has had the opportunity to notice the strengths and needs of the children.

▶ Finding Children's Instructional Reading Levels

For entry to *LLI*, it will be necessary to assess the child's instructional and independent reading levels. Systematic assessment is very helpful because the more precise you are in your assessment, the more effective you will be in your teaching. Many of the children who need support will begin at level A or B and will benefit from the Getting Started lessons at the beginning of the *LLI Green System*. Others may begin at later levels, for example, C or D.

Using the *Fountas & Pinnell Benchmark Assessment System 1*

If possible, we recommend that you use the *Fountas & Pinnell Benchmark Assessment System 1* to determine the instructional level of your children because the levels will correlate precisely to *LLI* levels. (If the classroom teacher can give you the recent reading records from the *Fountas & Pinnell Benchmark Assessment System 1*, you will not need to readminister it.) This way, you will be able to identify each child's specific reading level according to the levels used in this intervention. The *Fountas & Pinnell Benchmark Assessment System 1* will also provide critical information on the child's reading strengths and needs in processing strategies, comprehension, and fluency and will link them directly to instruction. In addition, you will be able to select specific assessments from the section called Optional Assessments for diagnostic purposes. For example, at the first-grade level, you may want to use any of the following optional assesments:

❑ Letter Identification—Children say the letters of the alphabet by recognizing the shapes of uppercase and lowercase letters.

- ❑ Early Literacy Behaviors—Children demonstrate that they know and can use the following conventions related to print: finding specific words within a text, matching words they hear with words they read.
- ❑ Reading High-Frequency Words (50)—Children read fifty high-frequency words while the observer notes correct responses and attempts.
- ❑ Phonological Awareness—Initial Sounds—Children identify pictures with the same initial sound as a spoken word.
- ❑ Phonological Awareness—Blending—Children hear and say the individual sounds in a word and then blend the sounds to say the word.
- ❑ Writing Picture Names—Children say words slowly and write the sounds they hear in response to a picture.

Many of the assessments are quick and some, like Phonological Awareness: Initial Sounds, and Writing Picture Names, may be administered in a small group. All of the assessments will provide a wealth of information to inform instruction.

Using Other Benchmark Assessment Systems

If you do not have access to the *Fountas & Pinnell Benchmark Assessment System*, you can use any other benchmark assessments you have in your school or district. Many publishers, including basal publishers, provide correlation charts to connect their assessment systems with the Fountas & Pinnell levels.

Alternative Assessments

If you do not have access to a benchmark assessment, you can use the information from any assessments in the district (e.g., Letter Identification, Phoneme Awareness) and select the below-grade-level performers. Once you have identified these children, you may want to use a quick informal assessment of reading level using leveled books as described in the next section. If you are using a basal system, the chart in Figure 2.1 may be helpful in selecting children who are reading below level. You may find the Instructional-Grade-Level Equivalence Chart (Figure 2.1) helpful, although the Fountas & Pinnell Assessment levels are the most reliable and closely match this intervention.

Assessment Using Leveled Books

A quick and informal way to select children for *LLI* is to have an individual child read aloud one or two books at a particular level. If you have some leveled books in your school, select from that collection. Notice the child's ability to point under each word at levels A and B. Assess the percentage of words read accurately and note specific errors (substitutions, omissions, insertions). The instructional level is the level at which the child reads with 90–94 percent accuracy (A–K) and satisfactory comprehension or 95–97 percent accuracy (L–Z) and satisfactory comprehension. You may want to use the F&P Calculator/Stopwatch to quickly determine an accuracy rate. You would not select for the *LLI Green System* children reading above Level K.

You will have an assessment of accuracy and also insights into the kind of information the child is using when errors are made (for example, words that look like other words or words that are inaccurate but make sense). Errors can sometimes illustrate a child's strengths and give you insights into how to help him or her.

Following the oral reading, involve the child in a conversation that will help you know what he or she understood from the text. You can ask several questions, but the assessment should not feel like an interrogation.

If the level of the text is too difficult, move down the levels until you find something the child can read at instructional level with good understanding. If the level seems easy, move up the levels until you find books that are too hard. Start your instruction with the level a child can read with 90–94 percent accuracy and satisfactory comprehension. Your introduction and teaching will support the child in taking on books at this level.

For children who cannot read books as high as level B, assess letter knowledge using a set of letters from the Online Resources and ask them to write their names and any other words or letters they know. This will give you an idea of the extent to which they are aware of print.

You might want to read a level A book to a child twice and then ask him or her to point and "read" it to

Instructional Grade-Level Equivalence Chart					
Grade	Fountas & Pinnell Level	Basal Level	Reading Recovery® Level	Rigby* PM Level	DRA2* Level™
Kindergarten	A	Readiness	1	1	A, 1, 2
Kindergarten	B		2	2	A, 1, 2
Kindergarten	C	PP1	3–4	3–4	3
Kindergarten	D	PP2	5–6	5–6	4
Grade 1	E	PP3	7–8	7–8	6–8
Grade 1	F	Primer	9–10	9–10	10
Grade 1	G	Grade 1	11–12	11–12	12
Grade 1	H	Grade 1	13–14	13–14	14
Grade 1	I	Grade 1	15–16	15–16	16
Grade 1	J	Grade 1	17–18	17–18	18
Grade 2	K	Grade 2	19–20	19–20	20
Grade 2	L	Grade 2		21	24
Grade 2	M	Grade 2		22	28
Grade 3	N	Grade 3		23	30
Grade 3	O	Grade 3		24	34
Grade 3	P	Grade 3		25	38
Grade 4	Q	Grade 4		26	
Grade 4	R	Grade 4		27	
Grade 4	S	Grade 4		28	40
Grade 5	T	Grade 5		29	40
Grade 5	U	Grade 5		30	50
Grade 5	V	Grade 5			
Grade 6	W	Grade 6			
Grade 6	X	Grade 6			60
Grade 6	Y	Grade 6			
Grades 7–12	Z	Grades 7–12			70, 80

FIGURE 2.1 Instructional Grade-Level Equivalence Chart

*The Rigby and DRA2 levels are based on different criteria than Fountas & Pinnell levels so those correlations are less reliable. The Fountas & Pinnell levels and the Reading Recovery levels are the most reliable and closely matched to this intervention.

you. You will learn the extent to which the child can remember language patterns (cued by pictures) and the degree to which he can track print. Children at this level would start the intervention lessons at level A.

▶ Selecting Children for the Intervention

If children are reading below the level indicated for their grade at a specific time of the school year, you may want to select them for *LLI*.

To help you do that, we have designed a general Instructional Level Expectations Chart (Figure 2.2). Use this chart to keep goals in mind for each grade level, but be flexible based on the goals and expectations of your school/district.

In your school, you may have many children who do not meet expectations for grade-level reading—many more than can be served in the intervention. In this case, begin with the children who need the most help and serve as many children as you can. On the other hand, your school or district may have higher-level expectations than are indicated in the chart so some children may need intervention to meet your school/district-specific goals. If students cannot fully participate and learn from the level of instruction in the classroom, they can benefit from *LLI*. Adjust the levels accordingly.

Forming *LLI* Groups

Any form of grouping requires some compromise. Ideally, you would teach each reader individually so you could meet individual needs and provide very specific instruction to help that particular reader move forward. We recommend

Fountas & Pinnell
INSTRUCTIONAL LEVEL EXPECTATIONS FOR READING

	Beginning of Year (Aug.–Sept.)	1st Interval of Year (Nov.–Dec.)	2nd Interval of Year (Feb.–Mar.)	End of Year (May–June)
Grade K		C	D	E
		B	C	D
		A	B	C
				Below C
Grade 1	E	G	I	K
	D	F	H	J
	C	E	G	I
	Below C	Below E	Below G	Below I
Grade 2	K	L	M	N
	J	K	L	M
	I	J	K	L
	Below I	Below J	Below K	Below L
Grade 3	N	O	P	Q
	M	N	O	P
	L	M	N	O
	Below L	Below M	Below N	Below O
Grade 4	Q	R	S	T
	P	Q	R	S
	O	P	Q	R
	Below O	Below P	Below Q	Below R
Grade 5	T	U	V	W
	S	T	U	V
	R	S	T	U
	Below R	Below S	Below T	Below U
Grade 6	W	X	Y	Z
	V	W	X	Y
	U	V	W	X
	Below U	Below V	Below W	Below X
Grades 7–8	Z	Z	Z	Z
	Y	Y	Z	Z
	X	X	Y	Y
	Below X	Below X	Below Y	Below Y

KEY
- Exceeds Expectations
- Meets Expectations
- Approaches Expectations: Needs Short-Term Intervention
- Does Not Meet Expectations: Needs Intensive Intervention

The Instructional Level Expectations for Reading chart is intended to provide general guidelines for grade level goals, which should be adjusted based on school/district requirements and professional teacher judgment.

© Fountas, Irene C. & Pinnell, Gay Su and Heinemann, Portsmouth NH, 2012.

FIGURE 2.2 Instructional Level Expectations Chart

intensive individual tutoring (e.g., Reading Recovery®) for readers who are struggling the most in grade 1, with additional children who also need extra help being served in intervention groups.

Once you determine the instructional levels of the children, you will want to create small groups of readers who are similar enough that you can begin lessons at a particular level. In the *LLI Green System*, we strongly recommend that you work with three children at a time for an average of 14–18 weeks. We recommend a group of three so that you can:

- ❑ Observe closely and provide strong individual support.
- ❑ Keep all children in the group highly engaged throughout the 30-minute lesson.
- ❑ Use precise language to prompt for effective reading strategies while listening in to individual readers.
- ❑ Observe closely and interact with children as they write to support the development of writing strategies.
- ❑ Maintain efficiency in time management.

Children do not always fall neatly into just the right number of groups. After all, they are individuals who cannot be defined by "reading level." You will probably have to do some problem-solving when you begin to group children. Your goal is to group the children so that the level of instruction will be appropriate for all of them. Our recommendation is to start the group at a text level that allows every child to begin with success. Here are some suggestions:

- ❑ Make some "one level" compromises. Three children whose instructional levels are B, B, and C, for example, may be able to read together and benefit from the intervention lessons starting at level B.
- ❑ If you are working alongside a teacher in a classroom, make arrangements for a child from the neighboring classroom to join the group you are teaching.
- ❑ Take children at the same level from different classrooms (but be sure that it doesn't take too much time to assemble them in the space you are teaching).

Your priority should be to group children efficiently and effectively so that you can teach them at the appropriate level. (See Frequently Asked Questions, page 107.)

Regrouping Children

Any time you work with a group of children, you will notice that they develop differently from each other. You may want to provide extra challenge to a particular child by expecting more writing or placing a basket of extra books for her to read in the center of the table. Of course, if the child makes enough progress to reach grade-level competencies before the rest of the group, you may want to exit the child from the group.

You may move a child from one group to another at any time. Sometimes, after a few weeks, teachers look at their data on all the children and reform their groups. In *LLI*, it is not usually a problem if a child experiences a few lessons for the second time or skips a few books and lessons, depending on his strengths and needs.

▶ Management of *LLI* Groups

Scheduling *LLI* Groups

The *LLI* system is designed to provide intensive, short-term support. Children need daily lessons so that what they learned yesterday can be reinforced and built on today. It is important that the daily lessons are a supplement to, not a substitute for, classroom small-group reading instruction. The supplementary teaching will allow the children to make faster progress and catch up with their peers.

If you provide lessons fewer than five times per week, your children will not make optimal progress. Our research shows the importance of daily lessons in helping children make accelerated progress so they can catch up with their peers. Good, consistent small-group teaching in the classroom is a key factor in supporting ongoing learning. *Additional* intensive small-group instruction is the key to intervention that will bring children to grade level. Readers who struggle need to participate in both classroom reading instruction and *LLI* to close the achievement gap.

For each 30-minute teaching slot in your schedule, you will be able to work with one group. As children reach grade-level performance in an average period of 14 weeks, you will be able to enter another group in the teaching slot. If you have three 30-minute teaching slots per day, you will be able to work with at least six groups in the school year. If you have four teaching slots in the day, you will be able to work with eight groups in the school year. If you have six teaching slots, you will be able to teach twelve groups per year. This means that you can serve from eighteen to thirty-six children in a school year.

If you are using *LLI* throughout your primary grades (K–2), you may begin the teaching year working with first-grade children using the *LLI Green System* or with grade 2 children using the *LLI Blue System* and, as groups exit, you can initiate kindergarten groups, if your schedule allows, using the *Green System*.

Figure 2.3 below shows four teaching slots across the year. This teacher worked half a day with children who needed extra literacy support. This chart shows that the teacher began with two grade 1 groups and two grade 2 groups. As the grade 1 children reached grade level, the teacher initiated three kindergarten groups and another grade 1 group in the four teaching slots. As the kindergarten and grade 1 children reached grade level goals, the teacher initiated two more kindergarten groups and a new grade 1 group.

Each group had three children. The twenty-four children in the first four slots achieved grade-level performance. The nine additional children made significant progress, with six of them reaching grade level. A total of thirty children were served and reached grade level. Three more children made progress but did not yet reach grade level.

Entering the System

Use your assessments to determine a starting point for the system (see pages 21–23). This means that you may start with the intervention at the beginning of any level. It is important to start at a level where you are confident the children will find success. So if you are wavering, decide to start on the lower level. You can always decide not to spend all ten days at a level.

Coordinating *LLI* Lessons with Classroom Instruction

Once the children have entered the *LLI System*, your partnership with the classroom teacher will be critical in helping each child make fast progress and catch up with peers. The following suggestions may be helpful, but you will have many more ideas. Talk together about the importance and benefits of daily *LLI* lessons and frequent small-group instruction in the classroom.

❑ Invite the classroom teacher to observe an *LLI* lesson.

❑ Share the Lesson Record or other record-keeping charts, such as the Letter-Word Record or Reading Graph (all found in the Online Resources), on a regular basis so you both have the same information on the child's progress.

❑ Ask for any information the classroom teacher may have that will inform your teaching (e.g., writing folder, reading list).

❑ Send Classroom Connection suggestions with the child so the teacher can observe the child's reading and writing. Discuss the whole idea of classroom connections with the child's teacher at the beginning of this program. It will help to show some examples of the activities and to talk about how you will explain the task so the children can be independent.

❑ Share the child's writing book, *My Writing Book*, frequently and discuss with the classroom teacher the writing that shows evidence of learning.

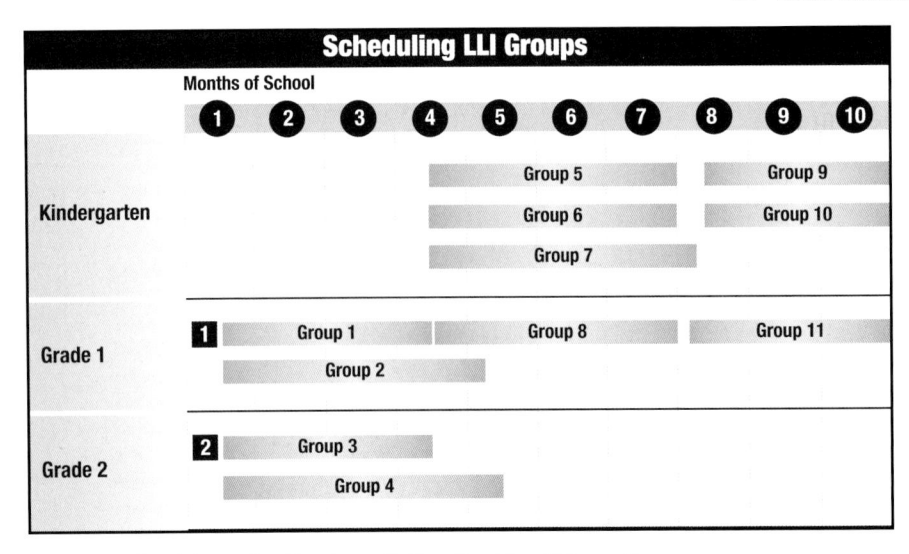

FIGURE 2.3 One Intervention Teacher with Four Teaching Slots per Day

☐ Show the classroom teacher the parent letter (in English, Spanish, French, Hmong, and Haitian-Creole), take-home books, fold sheets, and other materials so they can be aware of what is expected at home. Though you cannot count on home practice for the child's success in the intervention, any extra practice will be a bonus.

Amount of Time in the System

The amount of time a child spends in *LLI* will depend on his entry level and distance from grade-level performance. In the kindergarten years, you will not likely need to keep the children in the intervention more than about 8–10 weeks to bring them to instructional level D. In grade 1, you may need to keep them for 10–14 weeks, depending in the level they enter the program.

You may decide to keep the children a few weeks longer to assure strong grade-level performance or take them slightly beyond, as they will work in the classroom with less support. Just be mindful that this will keep out other children needing the intervention and will shorten their time in it.

Exiting the System

When the children are reading well at the end of a series of lessons that are at least on grade level, you can use your final reading record as an indicator of the children's competencies. Ideally, you will have the *Fountas & Pinnell Benchmark Assessment System* so you can re-administer the leveled assessments to confirm your observational notes, along with each child's classroom performance and your final reading record. You can use Figure 2.4, below, to identify grade-level goals or competencies. Adjust the levels to fit your school or district expectations.

Grade-Level Goals			
Grade	Beginning	Midyear	End
K		C	D
1	D	H	J
2	J	L	M

FIGURE 2.4 Grade-Level Goals

▶ Getting Organized for Teaching

A Space for Teaching

LLI lessons can be taught just about anywhere that you can accommodate yourself and the group of three children. You can use a section of the classroom or a space outside the classroom. The materials are not bulky, and at any one time, it takes only a folder of materials to teach a group of children. You will need a small space in which children can sit facing you so they will not be distracted (for example, in a corner of the classroom or in a small room).

Selecting a Table

The table you choose should not only allow children to sit facing you, it should also allow them to see clearly when you write on a chart or hold up the whiteboard. A horseshoe table or a rectangular table will work well because you'll be able to look directly at children all the time. Notice the height of the table and have the legs adjusted if needed. The table should come just above the children's waists so they can hold the book and look down at it. It is not a good idea to place children on either side of you at a rectangular table because it will be very hard for them to see the visual displays.

Planning and Organizing for *LLI* Lessons

The intervention lessons are designed to require a minimum of planning time for teachers, but you will need to review and think about the week's lessons and print out the corresponding materials from the Online Resources site. If you choose not to use some materials, you can decide not to print them. The first section of your *Lesson Guide*, called Getting Organized for Teaching, will be helpful in this process because it shows what you will print from the Online Resources site and what other supplies you will need prior to starting the teaching.

Some suggestions for planning are listed below:

- ❏ Review the *Lesson Guide* for the appropriate lessons. Notice the "You Will Need" list at the top of the first lesson page. The first materials listed are supplied in the program. Next are the items that you can print out from the Online Resources site. The General Resources—items that you may want to print out once at the beginning of the intervention and use for multiple lessons—have a check mark.
- ❏ Print from the Online Resources site and organize the other materials, such as Recording Forms, words, pictures, sentence strips, markers, word magnets, magnetic letters, and *My Writing Books*, so you can access them efficiently during the lesson. Note that many of these materials are provided in your Ready Resources or in *Fountas & Pinnell Teaching Supplies*, which can be ordered separately.
- ❏ Have all the materials for a group in a plastic tub or basket (e.g., *My Writing Books*, new books for the lesson, word bags, *My ABC Books*).
- ❏ Read the lessons and note any lesson variations needed.
- ❏ Have books organized to use with the group.
- ❏ Have your *Prompting Guide, Part 1* and *Prompting Guide, Part 2* ready to use. You may want to quickly review a section of the guide that you know you will need to use.
- ❏ Note the writing children will be doing, and put the lesson number on the writing book pages.
- ❏ Take note of transitions and think about how to save time.
- ❏ Have record-keeping forms, such as the Recording Form and the Lesson Record, ready on a clipboard with the children's names on them, as needed.
- ❏ Have your calculator ready to use.

- ❏ Consider placing the magnetic letters or words for the lesson in separate sealable bags or small plastic containers so they are ready for use. Some teachers use small metal trays (stove burner covers), cookie sheets, or tackle boxes to presort the letters. You can also place letters or word magnets on a small magnetic whiteboard that you can just hand to each child. Four small whiteboards, printed on one side with Elkonin boxes, are included in your Ready Resources.
- ❏ Consider keeping a rolling cart next to your table to place markers, your whiteboard, and so on.
- ❏ If you move from classroom to classroom, consider a special container to organize your materials or a rolling cart.

MATERIALS AND SUPPLIES FROM YOUR SCHOOL

Here are some basic supplies you'll need to gather from your school (or by ordering the *Fountas & Pinnell Teaching Supplies* described on page 17 of this Guide):

- ❏ A whiteboard and dry-erase marker for group phonics and writing
- ❏ Thin, dark-colored markers for the children to use to write in their *My Writing Books*
- ❏ Chart paper for phonics and writing
- ❏ Card stock for printing games and some charts
- ❏ Dice for playing word games
- ❏ One-inch sentence strips cut from card stock
- ❏ One-inch white correction tape to cover errors in children's writing books or interactive writing
- ❏ Magnetic letters for making words

- ❏ Pocket chart for word work (tabletop or regular)
- ❏ Masking cards and a plastic flag
- ❏ Highlighter marker, which is a yellow or other light-colored marker used to show a letter or word that you or a child mark
- ❏ Large and small pointer
- ❏ Highlighter strips
- ❏ Highlighter tape, which is a type of removable colored tape to place over letters, words, or phrases
- ❏ Erasable pens for word magnets
- ❏ Envelopes for sending words/pictures home
- ❏ Sticky notes

GROUP MATERIALS

Managing small-group work will be much easier if you keep all lesson materials for a group together in one hanging folder or accordion folder. Depending on the lesson, you will need:

- ❏ The plastic folders for the particular lesson in which you can place the new books and the take-home books
- ❏ The plastic folder for the previous day's lesson, in which you have placed the books that children will reread
- ❏ The *Lesson Guide*
- ❏ Words, pictures, magnetic letters, and games you have pre-prepared (in clear, sealable bags)
- ❏ A folder for the group with Lesson Records and completed Recording Forms for children as well as Recording Forms for the week
- ❏ *My Writing Book* for each child
- ❏ *My Poetry Book* for each child
- ❏ *My ABC Book* for each child
- ❏ Alphabet Linking Chart (teacher versions)
- ❏ Alphabet Linking Chart (student versions) for each child
- ❏ Consonant Clusters and Digraphs Charts (teacher versions)
- ❏ Consonant Clusters and Digraphs Charts (student versions) for each child.
- ❏ Table charts

section 3

LLI Green System Lesson Overview

▶ Lesson Guide Organization

There are a total of 130 lessons in the *LLI Green System*. The lessons are divided among two volumes of the Lesson Guide. Two types of lessons are included:

- ❑ 10 Getting Started Lessons
- ❑ 120 Standard Lessons

Volume 1 of the Lesson Guide contains lessons for Levels A–C, including Getting Started, and Volume 2 contains lessons for levels D–E (see Figure 3.1). At the end of each level, you will find the *Fountas & Pinnell Continuum of Literacy Learning* for that level.

The lessons are designed to be taught in a 30-minute time slot, five days per week, for the intensity that will result in optimal progress.

▶ The Lesson Frameworks

In this section, we provide a brief overview of the lesson frameworks, all of which provide structure to support smooth, well-paced lessons that will become very comfortable for you. The students will also benefit from the predictability of the lesson structures as they learn familiar lesson procedures.

There are three different lesson frameworks. The first ten lessons in the *LLI Green System* are called Getting Started. All ten Getting Started lessons use the same framework and engage children in five instructional activities: (1) rereading, (2) phonics/word work, (3) reading a new book with several levels of support, (4) writing about reading, and (5) letter/word work.

Within the standard lessons, there are two types of lesson frameworks: one for the odd-numbered lessons and one for the even-numbered lessons. In both frameworks, the first and sixth pages provide important information for preparation, planning, understanding of the new text and supporting English language learners, connections to the classroom and home, as well as professional development. The second through fifth pages are for your use as you teach the 30-minute lesson.

LLI Green System Lesson Guide Organization

Volume	Lesson #s	Lesson Type
	Getting Organized for Teaching	
1	1–10	Getting Started
	11–40	Standard (Odd-Even)
2	41–60	Standard (Odd-Even)
	61–80	Standard (Odd-Even)
3	81–100	Standard (Odd-Even)
	101–130	Standard (Odd-Even)

FIGURE 3.1 *LLI Green System Lesson Guide* Organization

▶ Overview of Getting Started Lessons

Materials
Here you will find a list of materials you'll need to teach the lesson. Many of the materials can be found in the *Ready Resources* included with this system or printed out from the Online Resources. General resources used in mulitple lessons have a check mark.

Goals
These are the specific teaching goals for the lesson. They will help you think about how the lesson activities support the development of the reading and writing processes.

How the Book Works
Helps you think about the overall structure of the text—the way the writer has organized and presented the story or information. Consider this as you introduce the text.

Text Analysis
Each new book is analyzed to show the specific demands of each text characteristic on the reader.

Lesson Information
The lesson number and level, the system, new book title, and genre.

GETTING STARTED

You Will Need
- *Ant Can't*, Level C
- *Too Much Stuff*, Level B
- *Sam and Papa*, Level B
- Alphabet Linking Chart, enlarged version
- Alphabet Linking Chart from Lesson 6
- unused alphabet pictures from Lesson 6
- magnetic letters
- word bags
- Take-Home Book *Too Much Stuff*

Visit resources.fountasandpinnell.com to download technological resources to support this lesson, including:
- Word Analysis Chart 7
- Teacher Pictures: *cat, turtle, banana, dog, goat, bird, balloon, carrot, spider, ball, toothbrush, tricycle, butterfly, elephant, umbrella* ✓
- Masking Cards ✓
- Student Words: *you, yes* ✓
- Fold Sheet 7
- Parent Letter

LESSON **7** · SYSTEM **Green**
NEW BOOK ***Ant Can't***
GENRE **Fiction**

NEW BOOK
Ant Can't, Level C,
Lap Book and small books

REREADING
Too Much Stuff, Level B,
Lap Book and small books

Sam and Papa, Level B,
small books

Goals

READING
- Read with voice-print match across multiple lines of text.
- Read with crisp pointing under each word.
- Notice rhyming words in a text.
- Understand and talk about comparisons between animals and what they can do.
- Understand how the ant and the spider are alike.

PHONICS/WORD WORK
- Identify the number of syllables in a word.
- Use the Alphabet Linking Chart as a tool for learning about letters.
- Understand that there is a relationship between a letter and a sound.
- Notice distinctive features of letters.
- Recognize several high-frequency words by looking closely at them (*you, yes*).

WRITING ABOUT READING
- Say words slowly, identify some easy-to-hear sounds, and write the letters.
- Compose two or three sentences.

Analysis of New Book Characteristics   *Ant Can't*, Level C

HOW THE BOOK WORKS This fiction book has print on alternating pages with pictures that span across two pages. Each page of print uses simple repeated sentence structures with dialogue, and the writer uses bold print on the last page for emphasis. Ant meets other animals that ask if she can do what they do, and she can't. Ant finally finds something she can do.

GENRE/FORM
- Fiction
- Simple animal fantasy

TEXT STRUCTURE
- Narrative carried by dialogue
- Question and answer on each spread
- Eight brief episodes in which different animals ask a question of an ant
- Each page showing the ant saying, *"No, I can't,"* until the ending

CONTENT
- Familiar animals
- What animals can do

THEMES AND IDEAS
- Each individual has different special skills
- How animals are alike and different

LANGUAGE AND LITERARY FEATURES
- Amusing characters
- Searching for the answer
- Rhyming language
- Satisfying ending

SENTENCE COMPLEXITY
- One four- and two six-word sentences on every left page, except the last page, which has a nine-word sentence
- Use of dialogue (two speakers on each page spread)
- Past tense
- Question structure

VOCABULARY
- Names of animals and actions (bird/fly, bee/buzz, frog/hop, cow/moo, fish/swim, pig/oink, dog/bark, spider/crawl)
- Content words (*ant, met*)

WORDS
- High-frequency words (*a, can, you, said, the, no, I, up, yes*)
- One- and two-syllable words
- See Word Analysis Chart 7 for specific words in each category

ILLUSTRATIONS
- Colorful, humorous drawings across every page spread
- Close match between pictures and text

BOOK AND PRINT FEATURES
- Large font
- Ample space between words
- Five lines on each page of print, except for the last page, which has six lines
- Periods, commas, question marks, quotation marks, exclamation point
- Word in bold on last page to indicate emphasis
- Spaces to indicate paragraphing

Part 1: Rereading and Assessment
Approximately 5 minutes
The first part of the lesson involves rereading the text(s) from the previous day.

Part 2: Phonics/Word Work
Approximately 5 minutes
The second part of the lesson focuses on control of letter and sound knowledge.

Principle
Here you see a concise statement of the phonics principle that anchors this part of the lesson. All principles come directly from *The Literacy Continuum*.

Instructional Routines
You'll use one of five different instructional routines to teach the Phonics/Word Work section of the lesson. The routines vary according to which principle anchors the lesson.

Example
An example of a chart you will use with students, or the work they will do related to the principle.

Rereading
Suggested Language

PROMPTING GUIDE, PART 1
Refer to page 5 as needed

REREADING
- *Too Much Stuff*, Level B, Lap Book and small books
- *Sam and Papa*, Level B, small books

- Use shared reading to reread the small version of *Too Much Stuff* with the children. (Use the lap book if children did not read the small version yesterday.) Then, reread other books as children choose them and time allows. *Point and read the small version of* Too Much Stuff *with me*.
- Invite children to reread *Sam and Papa* independently, using the small books. Read the book with children first if needed.
- As time allows, have children choose other small books to reread independently.
- Reinforce reading left-to-right, with accurate voice-print match, and crisp pointing.
- Have the children locate one or two high-frequency words on select pages.

Phonics/Word Work
Syllables

Principle You can hear, say, or clap the parts in a word. Words can have one or more parts.

Say and Sort
- Show the children the following pictures: *cat, turtle, banana*. Model saying each word while clapping the syllables. *What do you notice about these words?* [Children respond.] Help them to hear that *cat* has one syllable, *turtle* has two syllables, and *banana* has three syllables. Place the pictures across the top of the pocket chart.
- One by one, show the children the following pictures: *dog, bird, goat, balloon, carrot, spider, ball, toothbrush, butterfly, tricycle, elephant, umbrella*. Have the children take turns saying each word and clapping the number of syllables. Then, have them place the picture under the picture on the chart with the same number of syllables.
- Remove the pictures from the chart and have the children sort them again.
- Summarize the lesson by restating the principle.

Extending Letter Knowledge
- If time allows, display the enlarged version of the Alphabet Linking Chart and explain that the chart will help them to think about letters and sounds.
- Give the children the Alphabet Linking Charts they worked on in Lesson 6. Introduce as many new letters as time allows. Have the children color or add the corresponding pictures. Then, read the chart together.
- Save the charts for use in subsequent lessons. If you are having the children build the chart, save the unused alphabet pictures for them to use in subsequent lessons.

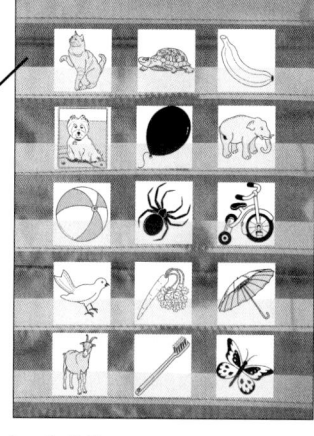

Part 3: Reading a New Book
Approximately 8 minutes
The third part of the lesson provides instructions and teaching language for reading and discussing the new book.

Here you introduce the new lap book, encouraging children to use information from the pictures, as well as their own experiences, to talk about the text.

Specific suggestions are included to scaffold the children's use of the meaning, language, and visual information in print as you read the lap book with them.

Using the lap book and small versions of the same text, children read the book with you.

After several shared readings, children can read without teacher or group support.

Reading a New Book
Suggested Language

NEW BOOK
Ant Can't, Level C, Lap Book and small books

Read To
- As you introduce the children to the lap book, encourage them to notice and use information in pictures, and invite conversation around the text. Build on their comments to expand the amount of language used.
- *The name of this story is* Ant Can't. *What do you notice about these words?* [Children respond.] *They rhyme.*
- Show the children the front cover of the book. *This is Ant, and these are some of the friends she met. Who are some of her friends?* [Children respond.]
- Turn to pages 2 and 3. *What do you notice?* [Children respond.] *Ant met a bird. And the bird said, Ant, "Can you fly?" What do you think Ant said?* [Children respond.] *Ant said, "No, I can't."* Point and read page 2. *Do you notice the question mark?* [Children respond.] *That tells you the bird is asking a question.* Point out the quotation marks (talking marks) around what bird said and what Ant said.
- Repeat the process on each page spread, inviting the children to think about what the friends and Ant will say each time.
- At the end, have the children predict what Spider will ask. Then, point and read. *The word* yes *is in dark letters, and that means you should read it a little louder—make it sound important.*
- Invite the children to talk about the story.

PROMPTING GUIDE, PART 2
Refer to pages 18 and 19 as needed

Read With
- Reread the text with the children as you point crisply under each word.
- Turn to a few different pages and have the children say a particular high-frequency word (*can, you, said, the, no*). *What letter do you expect to see first?* [Children respond.]
- Then, have the children find a word by pointing under it. Notice how quickly and easily they can find the word.
- As you read with the children, you may find opportunities to help them notice the sound at the beginning of the name of the animal and its first letter. Show them they can see the animal in the picture and check it with the word.

PROMPTING GUIDE, PART 1
Refer to page 5 as needed

Read By
- Give the children the small book version of the book.
- *Point under each word and read with me.*

Part 4: Writing About Reading

Approximately 7 minutes

In this section of Getting Started, you engage the children in composing sentences to write about the new book using interactive writing.

Writing About Reading

Suggested Language

- MY WRITING BOOK
- PROMPTING GUIDE, PART 1

Refer to pages 21, 23, 25, and 27 as needed

> Ant met a bee.
> "Can you buzz?" said the bee.
> "No I can't," said the ant.

Interactive Writing

- *Let's talk about all the friends that Ant met.* Engage the children in a conversation.
- Using interactive writing, compose two or three sentences about Ant and her friends. For example:

   Ant met a bee.
   "Can you buzz?" said the bee.
   "No, I can't," said the ant.

- Engage the children in constructing some of the words that are almost known or not yet known (e.g., the high-frequency words *no, I, the, can*).
- You may want to select a few words with easy-to-hear consonants for the children to say slowly and write the letter for the first sound (e.g., *met, bee*).
- Place the quotation marks (talking marks) around what the insects said, explaining that the marks show talking.
- Reread the text and have a child make a quick sketch.
- If time allows, have the children locate a few words in the text.

Part 5: Letter/Word Work

Approximately 5 minutes

Another principle from *The Literacy Continuum* brings focus to some quick letter/word work.

Letter/Word Work

Principle Each letter is different.

- Show the magnetic letters *h*, *m*, *n*, and *u*. What do you notice about these letters? [Children respond.] Accept any observation and help them notice that these letters all have tunnels.
- Give each child the magnetic letters *a*, *b*, *d*, *g*, *h*, *m*, *n*, *p*, *q*, and *u*. Have them sort the letters into two groups: letters with circles and letters with tunnels.

Working With High-Frequency Words

- Make *you* on the whiteboard. Read the word and use it in a sentence. You may want to have them show you the word in the new book, *Ant Can't*.
- Give the children the magnetic letters to make *you*, and have them make the word several times, each time checking it by running a finger under the word as they say it.
- Repeat the process with the word *yes*.
- Give the children the words *you* and *yes* to add to their word bags.

Classroom Connection
Suggestions are provided for extending learning in the classroom.

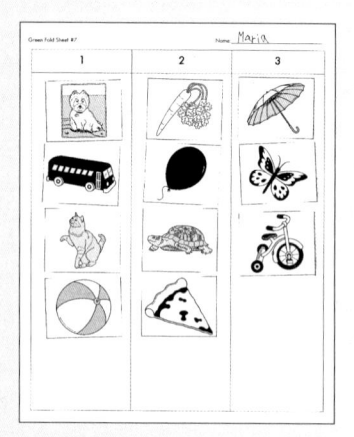

Home/School Connection
Materials like take-home books and parent letters are included for children to gain experience and extend their learning at home.

- Give the children Fold Sheet 7.
- Have the children take the fold sheet back to the classroom to cut apart the pictures and sort them under the numbers, according to the number of syllables the word has. Give the children envelopes to store their pictures.
- Give the children Take-Home Book *Too Much Stuff* to reread in the classroom.

- Have the children take home Fold Sheet 7 and the pictures to sort again. Have them glue the pictures to the fold sheet and share it with family members.
- Have the children read and discuss Take-Home Book *Too Much Stuff* with family members.

Assessing Reading and Writing Behaviors
A list of reading and writing behaviors to notice as you observe students. These behaviors link directly back to the Goals expressed on the first page of the lesson.

Supporting English Language Learners
Important considerations for supporting English language learners in this particular lesson.

Professional Development Links
Suggestions for accessing other professional resources connected to the concepts and teaching in this lesson.

Assessing Reading and Writing Behaviors

Observe to find evidence that readers can:

- read with voice-print match across multiple lines of text.
- use voice-print match and first letters to self-monitor reading.
- recognize rhyming words in a text.
- talk about and contrast how different animals move.
- discuss how the ant and the spider are alike.
- identify the number of syllables in a word.
- use the Alphabet Linking Chart as a tool for learning about letters.
- identify the relationship between a letter and a sound.
- identify the distinctive features of letters.
- learn high-frequency words (*you, yes*).
- say words slowly, identify easy-to-hear sounds, and write the letters.
- compose two or three sentences.

Supporting English Language Learners

To support English language learners, you can:

- **say** and demonstrate what you mean by *You can hear and say the syllables in a word.*
- **support** children in understanding rhyme.
- **have** children look closely at the pictures, say the names of animals, and say the labels for movement and sound.
- **use** the language of the text in a conversational way, and have children repeat the language several times to help them remember the syntax.
- **demonstrate** and monitor for understanding of quotation marks and a question mark.
- **support** children in discussing how the animals move, how the ant is different from some animals, and how it is the same as the spider.
- **monitor** for understanding of the difference between *can* and *can't.*
- **model** saying words slowly and listening for the first sound. Be sure children say the words slowly.
- **be sure** children understand their class/homework, and remind them that they can read to someone even if the listener doesn't speak English.

Professional Development Links

Professional Development and Tutorial Videos, LLI Green System
View "Getting Started" to notice how the teacher supports the children's letter and word learning.

When Readers Struggle: Teaching That Works, Levels A–N
Chapter 6, "Text Matters: A Ladder to Success" (pages 97–98).
Use this chart to understand how to help struggling readers learn about text factors.

Guided Reading: Responsive Teaching Across the Grades, Second Edition
Chapter 6, "Planning for Effective Guided Reading Lessons" (pages 125–126).

Leveled Literacy Intervention System Guide, LLI Green System
Refer to individual sections as needed.

Lessons 11–110 are six-page Standard Lessons. There are two different Standard Lesson frameworks, one for odd-numbered lessons and one for even-numbered lessons.

▶ Overview of Odd-Numbered Lessons

Lesson Information
The lesson number and level, the system, new book title, and genre.

Materials
Here you will find a list of materials you'll need to teach the lesson. Many of the materials can be found in your *Ready Resources* or printed out from the Online Resources. General resources used in mulitple lessons have a check mark.

Goals
These are the specific teaching goals for the lesson. They help you think about how the lesson activities are supporting the development of the reading and writing processes.

How the Book Works
Helps you think about the overall structure of the text—the way the writer has organized and presented the story or information. Consider this as you introduce the text.

Text Analysis
Each new book is analyzed to show the specific demands of each text characteristic on the reader.

You Will Need

- *Mom and Kayla*, Level B
- *The Farmers*, Level A
- *Bubbles*, Level B
- phonogram chart from Lesson 21
- *My Writing Book*
- magnetic letters
- word bags
- Take-Home Book *The Farmers*

Visit resources.fountasandpinnell.com to download technological resources to support this lesson, including:
- Word Analysis Chart 25
- Student Words: *Mom, has* ✓
- Fold Sheet 25
- Parent Letter
- Directions for Snap! ✓

LESSON **25** LEVEL **B**
SYSTEM **Green**
NEW BOOK ***Mom and Kayla***
GENRE **Fiction**

NEW BOOK
Mom and Kayla, Level B

REREADING
The Farmers, Level A
Bubbles, Level B

Goals

READING
- Read with voice-print match across two lines of print.
- Use meaning, language structure, and visual information to self-monitor, self-correct, and solve words.
- Use background information to understand information from the text.
- Actively search for information in pictures and in print.
- Begin to understand compare and contrast.
- Notice similarities between two characters.

PHONICS/WORD WORK
- Recognize and use a phonogram with a VC pattern (-*at*).
- Read high-frequency words quickly.
- Learn high-frequency words (*Mom, has*).

Analysis of New Book Characteristics *Mom and Kayla*, Level B

HOW THE BOOK WORKS This fiction book has alternating pages of print and pictures until the last page. It has two lines of print per page with simple repeated sentence structures. A daughter has smaller facsimiles of her mom's firefighter equipment.

GENRE/FORM
- Fiction
- Realistic fiction

TEXT STRUCTURE
- Narrative
- Eight episodes showing different kinds of apparel and other items related to firefighting

CONTENT
- Firefighting apparel and other items related to firefighting
- Familiar names for clothing

THEMES AND IDEAS
- Mother and daughter relationship
- Contrast of big and little

LANGUAGE AND LITERARY FEATURES
- Simple language pattern that is close to oral language

SENTENCE COMPLEXITY
- Two sentences on every left page with three to five words
- Present tense
- Change in pattern on the last page
- Use of *too*, set off by commas, to mean "also"

VOCABULARY
- Names of clothing and other items (hat, jacket, pants, boots, dog, hose, truck)

WORDS
- High-frequency words (has, a, too, big, little, looks, like)
- One- and two-syllable words
- See Word Analysis Chart 25 for specific words in each category

ILLUSTRATIONS
- Close match between pictures and text
- Drawings on every right page
- Two small pictures beside each line of print on last page

BOOK AND PRINT FEATURES
- Large font
- Ample space between words
- Two lines on each page of print
- Periods, commas, and exclamation point

Part 1: Rereading
Approximately 5 minutes
The first part of the lesson involves rereading the text(s) from the previous day.

Part 2: Phonics/Word Work
Approximately 5 minutes
The second part of the lesson focuses on control of letter and sound knowledge.

Principle
Here you see a concise statement of the phonics principle that anchors this part of the lesson. All principles come directly from *The Literacy Continuum*.

Example
An example of a chart you will use with students, or the work they will do related to the principle.

Rereading

Suggested Language

PROMPTING GUIDE, PART 1
Refer to page 9 as needed

REREADING
- *The Farmers*, Level A
- *Bubbles*, Level B

- Invite the children to reread *Bubbles* and *The Farmers*.
- Following the reading record as the children reread the books, prompt for self-monitoring using meaning and visual information as needed. For example: *Try that again and think of what would make sense* or *Try that again and think of what would look right*.

Phonics/ Word Work

Phonograms With a VC Pattern (-*at*)

Principle You can look at a part (pattern) to read a word. You can make new words by putting a letter or a letter cluster before the part (pattern).

can	sit	ham	fin	cat
man	hit	Sam	tin	bat
fan	fit	jam	pin	rat
ran	pit	ram	spin	sat
plan	kit	clam	grin	flat

See and Say
- Using the five-column chart you created in Lesson 21, have the children read the words in the first four columns. Then, write the word *cat* at the top of the last column and have the children read it with you.
- Write the words *bat, rat, sat,* and *flat* beneath *cat*, saying each word as you write it. Use any word the children may not understand in a sentence.
- *What do you notice about these words?* [Children respond.] Help them see and hear the -*at* pattern in each word. Point out that sometimes there are two letters before the pattern.
- Underline the -*at* pattern in each word and have the children read the list.
- Using the five-column chart the children created in *My Writing Book*, have them write two or three -*at* words in the last column. Have them underline the -*at* pattern and read the words to a partner.
- Now, give the children the magnetic letters *a, b, c, f, l, r, s,* and *t*. Have them make and read two or three words with the -*at* pattern.
- Have the children read the words in all five columns of the group chart with you.
- Summarize the lesson by restating the principle.

150

Part 3: Reading a New Book
Approximately 15 minutes
Suggestions for supporting students' proficient reading of a new instructional-level text.

Introducing the Text
Suggested language for introducing the new instructional-level text.

Reading a New Book
Suggested Language

NEW BOOK
Mom and Kayla, Level B

PROMPTING GUIDE, PART 1
Refer to page 9 as needed

PROMPTING GUIDE, PART 2
Refer to pages as needed

Introducing the Text

- Introduce the book by showing the cover and talking about firefighters and the things they do. *What things do you see?* [Children respond.] *Firefighters usually have a bag with lots of things in it like this hat and these boots.*
- *Turn to pages 2 and 3, and you can see Mom and Kayla. Clap* Kayla. [Children respond.] *What do they have?* [Children respond.] *Mom has a hat, and Kayla has a hat, too.*
- *Say* has. *What letter comes first in the word* has? [Children respond.] *Find* has *and run your pointer finger under it and say* has. [Children respond.]
- *Turn to pages 4 and 5. What else do Mom and Kayla have?* [Children respond.] *They each have a jacket. On every page you will see something that Mom has, and you will see that Kayla has the same thing. Do you notice how they put on the same things every time?* [Children respond.]
- *Now, turn to page 13. What do you notice?* [Children respond.] *They are both wearing the same things. What do they look like?* [Children respond.] *What do they have in their hands?* [Children respond.] *Mom's hose looks big. What about Kayla's hose?* [Children respond.]
- *Say* little *and clap it with me.* [Children respond.] *What letter would you see first in* little? [Children respond.]
- *Turn back to the beginning and read about the other things that Mom and Kayla have and see how Mom and Kayla look.*

Reading the Text

- See *Prompting Guide, Part 1* for language such as *Were you right?* to prompt for consistent self-monitoring, if needed.
- If children are noticing errors, prompt using more than one information source to self-correct. For example: *Does that make sense and look right?*

Discussing and Revisiting the Text

- Invite the children to share their thinking about what they learned from the text.
- *What did you learn about Kayla and Mom?* [Children respond.]
- *How are they alike?* [Children respond.]
- *How are they different?* [Children respond.]
- *Mom is a real firefighter, but what do you think about Kayla?* [Children respond.]
- *Why do you think Kayla likes to dress like Mom?* [Children respond.]
- *Why do firefighters need to wear special clothes?* [Children respond.]

continues on next page

Reading the Text
Suggestions for sampling oral reading and selecting prompts from the *Fountas & Pinnell Prompting Guide, Part 1*.

Discussing and Revisiting the Text
Suggestions for inviting students to share their thinking about the text they read.

Key Understandings

Statements of key understandings from the text. Use these tips to guide the discussion and to observe for evidence of comprehension.

Messages

A statement conveying the main or "big" ideas of the text.

Teaching Points

Suggested teaching points and a reminder to select other points from the *Fountas & Pinnell Prompting Guide, Parts 1 and 2*.

Part 5: Letter/Word Work

Approximately 5 minutes
Another principle from *The Literacy Continuum* brings focus to some quick letter/word work.

Reading a New Book

Suggested Language *(continued from previous page)*

Discussing the Text *(continued from previous page)*

- Continue the discussion, guiding children toward the key understandings and the main message of the text. Some key understandings children may express:

Thinking *Within* the Text	Thinking *Beyond* the Text	Thinking *About* the Text
▪ Mom and Kayla dress up as firefighters. They put the same clothes on. ▪ Mom has big boots. Kayla has little boots. ▪ Mom has a big hose, and Kayla has a little hose. ▪ Mom and Kayla look alike.	▪ Firefighters fight fires and wear special clothing. These clothes protect them from fire. ▪ Kayla's mom is a firefighter. ▪ The pictures show that Kayla's things are little compared to Mom's big things. ▪ Kayla is proud of her Mom and wants to be just like her.	▪ The writer uses words and pictures to show how Kayla and Mom are alike and different. ▪ The writer helps us see how Kayla and Mom feel about each other. ▪ The writer shows us what firefighters wear to fight fires. ▪ This story is fiction.

MESSAGES When you love someone, you sometimes want to be like that person.

PROMPTING GUIDE, PART 1
Refer to page 15 as needed

Teaching Points

- Based on your observations, use *Prompting Guide, Part 1* to select a teaching point that will be most helpful to the readers.
- Revisit a page or two to demonstrate or reinforce effective problem solving.

Letter/Word Work

Principle You need to learn words you see many times because they help you read and write.

- Make *Mom* with magnetic letters on a whiteboard. Read the word and use it in a sentence. You may want to have them locate *Mom* in the new book *Mom and Kayla*. What do you notice about the word that will help you to remember it? [Children respond.]
- Give the children the magnetic letters to make *Mom*, and have them make the word several times, each time checking it with a finger as they say it.
- Repeat the process with the word *has*.
- Give them the words *Mom* and *has* to add to their word bags. Then, have the children work with all the high-frequency words in their word bags and play Snap!
- Be sure the players are seated side by side so they can look at the words right-side up.
- Place the words facedown in two stacks.
- Have the children work in pairs with their own stacks while simultaneously turning over the words one at a time and reading them quietly. When two players lay out the same word, the player who says "Snap!" first gets the word. The player with the most words at the end wins.

Classroom Connection

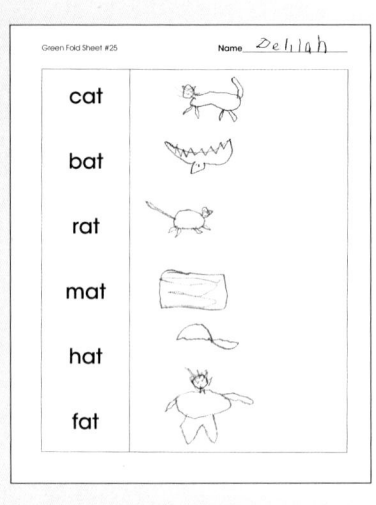

Suggestions are provided for extending learning in the classroom.

Home/School Connection

Materials like take-home books and parent letters are included for children to practice and extend their learning at home.

- Give the children Fold Sheet 25.
- Have children take the fold sheet back to the classroom to read the words and illustrate each one.
- Give children the Take-Home Book *The Farmers* to reread in the classroom.

- Have the children take home Fold Sheet 25 to share with family members.
- Have children read and discuss Take-Home Book *The Farmers* with family members.

Assessing Reading and Writing Behaviors

A list of reading and writing behaviors to notice as you observe students. These behaviors link directly back to the Goals expressed on the first page of the lesson.

Supporting English Language Learners

Important considerations for supporting English language learners in this particular lesson.

Professional Development Links

Suggestions for accessing other professional resources connected to the concepts and teaching in this lesson.

Assessing Reading and Writing Behaviors

Observe to find evidence that readers can:

- read with voice-print match across two lines of print.
- use meaning, language structure, and visual information to self-monitor, self-correct, and solve words.
- discuss background information and understand information taken from the text.
- actively search for and use information from pictures and print.
- understand and discuss how two characters are alike and different (compare and contrast).
- use connections between words to make words and check them left-to-right.
- recognize and use a phonogram pattern (-*at*).
- read high-frequency words quickly.
- learn new high-frequency words (*Mom, has*).

Supporting English Language Learners

To support English language learners, you can:

- **monitor** for understanding of *Try that again and think of what would make sense* and *Try that again and think of what would look right*.
- **check** to be sure children can recognize and name all the words used in Phonics and Letter/Word Work.
- **monitor** children's understanding that firefighters have special clothing and equipment. Use the pictures to provide help to children in naming the items.
- **use** the language of the text in a conversational way, and have children repeat the language several times to help them remember the syntax.
- **check** for understanding of the verb *has*, as well as the words *big, little,* and *too*.
- **use** pictures to help the children in discussing the book.
- **expand** children's language in a conversational manner. If the child says, *Kayla and Mom have the same pants*, you can respond with, *Yes, Kayla and Mom have the same pants.*
- **remind** children to read to someone at home. They can discuss the story in their home language after reading.

Professional Development Links

Professional Development and Tutorial Videos, LLI Green System
View the sample (odd-numbered) *LLI* lesson to analyze word work and think about how the children are developing flexibility.

When Readers Struggle: Teaching That Works, Levels A–N
Chapter 11, "Learning to Solve Words" (pages 232–236).
Use these pages to understand how children develop word-solving strategies.

Teaching for Comprehending and Fluency: Thinking, Talking, and Writing About Reading, K–8
Chapter 4 (pages 45–48). Use this chapter to explore the building of early reading systems including teaching for strategic actions for solving words, self-monitoring and self-correcting, searching for and using information, and summarizing.

Leveled Literacy Intervention System Guide, LLI Green System
Refer to individual sections as needed.

154

▶ Overview of Even-Numbered Lessons

Lesson Information
The lesson number, level, and system, new book title, and genre of the new book are stated here.

Materials
A list of materials for the lesson. Most can be found in the *Ready Resources* provided with the Green System, or printed from the Online Resources. A check mark indicates general materials that can be used in multiple lessons.

Goals
The specific teaching goals for the lesson, organized in three categories: Reading, Word Work, and Writing About Reading.

How the Book Works
Helps you think about the overall structure of the text—the way the writer has organized and presented the story or information.

Text Analysis
Each new book is analyzed to show the specific demands of each text characteristic on the reader.

LESSON 40 — LEVEL C

You Will Need
- *Look!* Level A
- *Clouds*, Level C
- *The Picnic*, Level A
- phonogram chart from Lesson 38
- *My Writing Book*
- magnetic letters
- word bags
- Take-Home Book *Clouds*

Visit **resources.fountasandpinnell.com** to download technological resources to support this lesson, including:
- Word Analysis Chart 40
- Fold Sheet 40
- Recording Form for *Clouds* (or visit Apple iTunes to download the *Fountas & Pinnell LLI Reading Record App*)
- Parent Letter

SYSTEM **Green**
NEW BOOK ***Look!***
GENRE **Fiction**

NEW BOOK
Look! Level A

REREADING
Clouds, Level C
The Picnic, Level A

Goals

READING
- Use meaning, language structure, and visual information to self-monitor, self-correct, and solve new words.
- Understand how the ideas in a book are related to one another.

PHONICS/WORD WORK
- Recognize and use a phonogram with a VC pattern (-*ap*).
- Change the first letter in a word to make a new word.
- Read high-frequency words quickly and easily.

WRITING ABOUT READING
- Compose two or three sentences about a topic.
- Write several high-frequency words quickly.
- Write sentences that begin with a capital letter and end with punctuation.
- Say a word slowly to notice the sounds and then write the letters in sequence.

Analysis of New Book Characteristics   *Look!* Level A

HOW THE BOOK WORKS This book is fiction and has alternating pages of print and pictures until the last page. It has one line on each page of print, repeating a simple sentence structure. The pictures and print reveal various parts of a hidden animal until it is completely revealed on the final page.

GENRE/FORM
- Fiction
- Simple animal fantasy

TEXT STRUCTURE
- Part-to-whole (seeing one part of a giraffe at a time)

CONTENT
- Concept of a giraffe
- Words for body parts of a giraffe

THEMES AND IDEAS
- Hiding
- Putting the parts together

LANGUAGE AND LITERARY FEATURES
- Language pattern that is close to oral language

SENTENCE COMPLEXITY
- One four-word simple sentence on every left-hand page until the last page, which has three words
- Present tense

VOCABULARY
- Parts of the body (feet, legs, tail, neck, eyes, nose, ears)

WORDS
- High-frequency words (look, at, my, me)
- One-syllable words
- See Word Analysis Chart 40 for specific words in each category

ILLUSTRATIONS
- Drawings on every right-hand page
- Close match between pictures and text
- Parts of body adding up to the whole giraffe

BOOK AND PRINT FEATURES
- Large font
- Ample space between words
- One line on each page of print
- Periods and exclamation point

Part 1: Rereading and Assessment

Approximately 5 minutes

The first part of the lesson contains suggestions for guiding students to reread yesterday's new book(s) and for assessing one reader's accuracy.

Rereading and Assessment

Suggested Language

PROMPTING GUIDE, PART 1
Refer to page 13 as needed

REREADING
- *Clouds*, Level C
- *The Picnic*, Level A

- Listen to one child read *Clouds* as you code the reading behaviors on the Recording Form or in the *Fountas & Pinnell LLI Reading Record App*, have a brief comprehension conversation, and make a teaching point that you think will be most helpful to the reader. Score and analyze the reading record following the lesson.
- Have the other children reread *The Picnic* and then *Clouds*.
- As the children reread books, prompt for self-monitoring as needed. For example: *Why did you stop?* and *Find the part that is not quite right* or *Where is the tricky part?*

Phonics/Word Work

Phonograms With a VC Pattern (*-ap*)

Principle You can look at a word part (pattern) to read a word. You can make new words by putting a letter or a letter cluster before the part (pattern).

dad	sip	cap
had	hip	sap
bad	lip	tap
mad	tip	rap
glad	trip	clap

See and Say

- Display the five-column chart you created in Lesson 38 and have the children read the words in the first two columns. Then, write the word *cap* at the top of the third column and have the children read it aloud with you.
- Now, write *sap, tap, rap,* and *clap* beneath *cap*, saying each word aloud as you write it. Use any word the children may not understand in a sentence.
- *What do you notice about these words?* [Children respond.] Help them to see and hear the *-ap* pattern in each word. *Can you think of any other -ap words?* [Children respond.] Add the children's words to the chart.
- Underline the *-ap* pattern in each word and have the children read the third column.
- Open My Writing Book to the chart you created. Write two or three *-ap words* in the third column. [Children respond.] Have them underline the *-ap* pattern and read the words to a partner.
- Now, give the children the magnetic letters *a, c, l, p, r, s,* and *t*. Have them make and read two or three words with the *-ap* pattern.
- Summarize the lesson by restating the principle.
- Save the chart for use in subsequent lessons.

244

Part 2: Phonics/Word Work

Approximately 5 minutes

The second part of the lesson focuses on control of letter and sound knowledge and is anchored by a phonics principle from *The Literacy Continuum*.

Principle

Here you see a concise statement of the phonics principle that anchors this part of the lesson. All principles come directly from *The Literacy Continuum*.

Example

An example of a chart you will use with students or the work they will do related to the principle.

Part 3: Writing About Reading
Approximately 15 minutes
Suggestions for using one of three forms of writing (interactive, independent, or dictated) to write about yesterday's new book.

Student Sample
Examples of children's writing are provided.

Writing About Reading
Suggested Language

- MY WRITING BOOK
- PROMPTING GUIDE, PART 1
Refer to pages 21, 27, and 31 as needed

Independent Writing

- If time allows, you may want to begin by having each child read recent pages from *My Writing Book*. Occasionally, ask the child to locate a word in a sentence that was read.
- *You read about all the shapes that Kate and Tony see in the clouds. Write about some of the shapes that Kate and Tony tell each other about.* Sentences may include:
    Look at the cloud.
    It looks like a bird.
    It looks like a hat.
- Prompt children to write the high-frequency words quickly (e.g., *it, look, at, the, like*). Also, prompt them to write a capital letter at the beginning and to use end punctuation.
- Use words such as *hat* as opportunities for children to say words slowly, listen for the three sounds, and write each letter.
- Have children reread and illustrate their sentences.

Part 4: Reading a New Book
Approximately 5 minutes
The fourth part of the lesson introduces a new book levels below the book introduced in the odd-numbered lesson.

Introducing the Text
Specific suggestions to scaffold the child's use of the meaning, language, and visual information in print.

Reading a New Book
Suggested Language

NEW BOOK
Look! Level A

PROMPTING GUIDE, PART 1
Refer to page 14 as needed

PROMPTING GUIDE, PART 2
Refer to pages as needed

Introducing the Text
- Introduce the book by talking about the children's experiences playing hide-and-seek. *In this book, an animal is hiding behind a tree. On each page, the animal shows one part of its body until you can see the whole animal come out from behind the tree at the end of the book.*
- Turn to pages 2 and 3. *What does the animal say to look at?* [Children respond.] *It says, "Look at my feet."*
- Now, turn to pages 4 and 5. *What does the animal say to look at?* [Children respond.] *The animal says, "Look at my legs." What letter would come first in* at? [Children respond.] *The letter is* a. *Find* at. *Put your pointer finger under it and say it.* [Children respond.]

Reading the Text
- Children should be able to read the text independently.
- If needed, prompt for self-correction. For example: *Something wasn't quite right* or *Try that again.*

Discussing and Revisiting the Text
- Invite the children to share their thinking about the text.
- *Where is the animal hiding?* [Children respond.]
- *What clues does the animal give to help you figure out what it is?* [Children respond.]
- *When did you figure out what kind of animal it is? What clue gave it away?* [Children respond.]
- Continue the discussion, guiding children toward the key understandings and the main message of the text. Some key understandings children may express:

Thinking *Within* the Text	Thinking *Beyond* the Text	Thinking *About* the Text
• An animal is hiding behind a tree. • The animal shows different parts of its body. • At the end of the story, the animal stands in front of the tree and shows us that it is a giraffe.	• The giraffe wants us to guess what kind of animal it is. We know this because the giraffe only shows one body part at a time. • A giraffe is unique because of its spots, its colors, and especially its long neck. • We can piece together clues, one by one, to solve a mystery or answer a question. Words and illustrations help readers to think about how the clues connect to each other.	• The illustrator gives clues in each picture. She shows the different shapes, colors, and patterns of each body part. This helps us guess what kind of animal is hiding. • The book title tells us to look carefully at all the clues drawn in the illustrations.

MESSAGE If you piece together clues one by one, you can solve a mystery or answer a question.

PROMPTING GUIDE, PART 1
Refer to page 14 as needed

Teaching Points
- Based on your observations, use *Prompting Guide, Part 1* to select a teaching point that will be most helpful to the readers.
- You may also want to reinforce children's self-correction behaviors. For example: *You knew that wasn't right.*

246

Reading the Text
Suggestions for sampling oral reading and selecting prompts from the *Fountas & Pinnell Prompting Guide, Part 1.*

Discussing and Revisiting the Text
Suggestions for inviting children to share their thinking about the text they read.

Key Understandings
Statements of key understandings from the text. Use these tips to guide the discussion and to observe for evidence of comprehension.

Messages
A statement conveying the main or "big" ideas of the text.

Teaching Points
Based on your observations, select key teaching points to benefit readers. Use *Prompting Guide, Part 1* to teach for, prompt for, or reinforce effective reading behaviors.

Part 5: Optional Letter Word Work
(if time allows)
The final part of the lesson includes suggestions for optional letter/word work if time allows.

Classroom Connection
Suggestions are provided for extending learning in the classroom.

Home/School Connection
Materials like take-home books, fold sheets, and parent letters are included for children to practice and extend their learning at home.

Optional Letter/Word Work

Principles You can say a word slowly. You can hear each sound in a word. You can change the first letter in a word to make a new word.

- Give children the magnetic letters *b, d, i, g, p,* and *w* and have them arrange the letters across the top of the whiteboard.
- Have them construct the word *big* by saying the word slowly to hear three sounds in sequence. After they have constructed the word, have them check the sound sequence with their pointer finger.
- *Now, change the first letter to make a new word, pig. Be sure and check it with your pointer finger.* [Children respond.]
- Repeat the process with *dig* and *wig*.

Working With High-Frequency Words
- Have children lay out the words from their word bags on the table. They may have different words, because some may have taken home words they found very easy. Have children take turns reading a word to the group and putting it back into the word bag. If the other children have that word they may put it away, too. Play until at least one child has no words left on the table.

Classroom Connection

Home/School Connection

- Give children Fold Sheet 40 to take back to the classroom.
- Have the children draw clouds that might look like something else. Then, have them write a sentence about each cloud.
- Give children Take-Home Book *Clouds* to reread in the classroom.

- Have the children take home Fold Sheet 40 to share with family members.
- Have children read Take-Home Book *Clouds* to family members.

Assessing Reading and Writing Behaviors
A list of reading and writing behaviors to notice as you observe students. These behaviors link directly back to the Goals expressed on the first page of the lesson.

Assessing Reading and Writing Behaviors

Observe to find evidence that readers can:
- use meaning, language structure, and visual information to self-monitor, self-correct, and solve words.
- understand how the ideas in a book are related to one another.
- recognize and use a phonogram with a VC pattern (-*ap*).
- change the first letter in a word to make new words.
- read high-frequency words quickly and easily.
- compose sentences about a topic.
- quickly write several high-frequency words.
- write sentences that begin with a capital letter and end with punctuation.
- say a word slowly to notice the sounds and then write the letters in sequence.

Supporting English Language Learners

To support English language learners, you can:
- **monitor** for understanding of all prompts, including *Why did you stop?*
- **check** to be sure children can recognize and understand all the words used in Phonics and Letter/Word Work.
- **go over** the words for the giraffe's body parts.
- **use** pictures to discuss the book.
- **expand** children's language in a conversational way.
- **encourage** children to repeat each composed sentence several times before they begin writing.
- **monitor** children for articulating some words slowly before beginning to write.

Professional Development Links

Professional Development and Tutorial Videos, *LLI Green System*
Time each part of a few of your lessons. Then view the sample *LLI* lessons to help you think about your pacing and ways to save time.

When Readers Struggle: Teaching That Works, Levels A–N
Chapter 8, "The Phonological Base for Learning to Read and Write" (pages 195–196). Use these pages to examine supportive teacher language during writing.

Guided Reading: Responsive Teaching Across the Grades, Second Edition
Chapter 16, "Teaching for Monitoring, Searching, and Self-Correction Behaviors." Use this chapter to explore self-monitoring and self-correcting behaviors.

Leveled Literacy Intervention System Guide, LLI Green System
Refer to individual sections as needed.

Supporting English Language Learners
Important considerations for supporting English language learners in this particular lesson.

Professional Development Links
Suggestions for accessing other professional resources connected to the concepts and teaching in this lesson.

▶ Overview of *The Literacy Continuum*

At the end of each level in the Lesson Guide, you will find the corresponding pages from the Guided Reading section of *The Fountas & Pinnell Literacy Continuum: A Tool for Assessment, Planning, and Teaching* for that level. You'll want to refer to these pages as you plan for and teach the lessons at each level.

Level Designation
Every page in the Continuum is identified by level.

Section 1: Characteristics of Readers
A brief description of what you may find to be generally true of readers at the particular level.

Thinking *Within* the Text
Evidence that readers are thinking within the text includes solving words, monitoring self-correcting, and adjusting their reading and understanding of the text.

LEVEL **D** — **Behaviors** and **Understandings** to **Notice**, **Teach**, and **Support**

Readers at Level D:

At level D, readers process and understand simple fiction and fantasy stories and easy informational texts. They can track print with their eyes over two to six lines per page without pointing, and they can process texts with more varied and more complex language patterns. They notice and use a range of punctuation and read dialogue, reflecting the meaning through phrasing, intonation, and appropriate word stress. Readers can solve many easy, regular two-syllable words—usually words with inflectional endings such as *-ing* and simple compound words. Pointing may occasionally be used at difficulty, but readers drop the finger when they are confident and are reading easily. The core of known high-frequency words is expanding. Readers consistently monitor their reading, cross-check one source of information with another, and often use multiple sources of information. Readers use text and pictures to construct the meaning of stories and nonfiction texts. They infer meaning from pictures and connect the meaning of texts to their own experiences. At level D, readers process and understand simple and some split dialogue.

Thinking Within the Text

SEARCHING FOR AND USING INFORMATION
- Read left to right across three to six lines of print
- Match word by word over three to six lines of print, with all sentences beginning on the left
- Coordinate eyes and pointing to search for and use visual information in print
- Use return sweep to read several lines of print after the first line
- Reread to search for and use information from language structure or meaning
- Search for and use information from pictures that match the print closely, have few distracting details, and clearly support meaning
- Use clear separation of illustrations and print to search for and use information
- Use consistent layout of illustrations and print to search for and use information
- Use language patterns close to oral language to search for and use information
- ●●Recognize more than one repeating language pattern in a text and use to search for information
- Use simple sentence structures (subject and predicate with some embedded phrases and clauses) to search for and use information
- Sustain searching for information over a short text (usually sixteen pages with two to six lines of print on each page and fewer than 150 words)
- ●●Search for and use information that appears in beginning and ending phrases
- Notice and use punctuation marks (period, comma, question mark, exclamation mark, and quotation marks in most texts)
- Notice and use capital and lowercase letters
- Search for and understand information in simple dialogue (sometimes in speech bubbles), dialogue with pronouns (often assigned by *said*), and split dialogue
- ●●Search for information in a text that has no repeating language patterns
- ●●Use the chronological order of a simple story to search for and use information
- Use details in the illustrations to search for and use information
- Use labels on photographs to search for and use information
- Use background understanding of familiar, easy content to search for and use information: e.g., family and home, play, pets, animals, school, food, community, friends, daily activities, the human body, weather, seasons, transportation, toys
- Understand that the pictures closely and explicitly support the content and use them to search for and use information

MONITORING AND SELF-CORRECTING
- Show evidence of close attention to print
- Use voice-print match to self-monitor and self-correct over three to six lines of print
- Reread the sentence to problem-solve, self-correct, or confirm
- Use language structure to self-monitor and self-correct
- Use visual features of words to self-monitor and self-correct
- Use recognition of high-frequency words to self-monitor and self-correct
- Reread the sentence to problem-solve, self-correct, or confirm
- Consistently cross-check one kind of information against another to monitor and self-correct reading (i.e., cross-checking meaning with visual information)
- Cross-check using more than one source (visual information and pictures)
- ●●Use two or more sources of information (meaning, language structure, visual information) to self-monitor and self-correct
- ●●Drop finger pointing when confident in reading a text but occasionally bring it back to monitor or confirm when encountering difficulty
- Use pictures as a resource to self-monitor and self-correct
- Use understanding of how the book works to self-monitor and self-correct
- Use understanding of characters to self-monitor and self-correct
- ●●Use understanding of dialogue to self-monitor and self-correct
- Use content knowledge of a simple topic to self-monitor and self-correct
- ●●Use knowledge from pictures to self-monitor and self-correct

SOLVING WORDS
▶ Reading Words
- Recognize words in clear, plain font that are on a white or very light background
- Recognize more than twenty-five high-frequency words quickly and easily
- Recognize one-, two-, and some three-syllable words fully supported by the pictures
- Read some simple regular plurals formed with the endings -s or -es that are fully supported by pictures and language structure

continues

A double bullet indicates a new behavior that you expect to see evidence of at this level.

313

Thinking *Beyond* the Text

When readers think beyond the text, they make predictions and connections to previous knowledge and their own lives. They also make connections between and among texts.

LEVEL D — Behaviors and Understandings to Notice, Teach, and Support

Thinking Within the Text *(continued)*

- Read words that are repeated within the same text: e.g., *am, like, we, this, look, said, here, my, she, come*
- Read verbs with inflectional endings (e.g., *-s, -ing, -ed*) fully supported by pictures and language structure
- Read words with very easy, predictable, and decodable letter-sound relationships
- Read words with easy spelling patterns with the support of pictures and language (VC, CVC, CVCe)
- Say a word and predict its first letter
- Locate easy high-frequency words in a text: e.g., *and, to, up, said, with*
- Notice visual features of a word and use them to locate or read the word
- Read some words containing apostrophes (simple contractions and possessives)
- Read simple words that assign dialogue: e.g., *said, asked*
- •• Read simple connectives

▶ **Vocabulary**

- Understand the meaning of some words that are new but easy to understand in the context of the text and with picture support
- Expand understanding of the meaning of words by connection with the pictures and/or understanding the context: e.g., *zoo, farm, circus*
- Read and understand a few simple words that stand for sounds (onomatopoetic words)
- Understand vocabulary words that are in common oral vocabulary for early readers (Tier 1)
- Understand the meaning of simple regular plurals formed with the endings *-s* or *-es*
- Understand a few simple adjectives describing people, places, or things
- •• Understand simple contractions using an apostrophe and letters from the word *not*
- •• Understand words with an apostrophe indicating possession

- •• Understand some words that require the use of multiple sources of information (background knowledge, pictures, visual information)
- Understand words that indicate characters: e.g., easy-to-read names, family members, community members such as teachers
- Understand words that show the action of the plot: e.g., verbs such as *is, go, run, ran, like, ride, can*
- Understand words such as *I, me,* and *we* that may indicate the narrator of a text
- Understand the meaning of simple words that assign dialogue: e.g., *said, asked*
- •• Read and understand the meaning of simple connectives
- Recognize and understand labels for familiar objects, animals, people, the human body, weather, daily activities, simple processes such as cooking or growing plants
- •• Use details in illustrations to understand new vocabulary

MAINTAINING FLUENCY

- Sustain momentum through an entire short text
- Read mostly without pointing but with correct voice-print match
- Notice periods, quotation marks, commas, exclamation marks, and question marks, and begin to reflect them with the voice through intonation and pausing
- Read with phrasing
- Demonstrate stress on words in a way that shows attention to meaning
- Stress words that are in bold
- Reread to notice the language or meaning
- Show recognition of dialogue with some phrasing even when in varying structures: e.g., *said Mom* and *Mom said*
- •• Recognize and use ellipses in some texts to show that a sentence finishes on the next page

ADJUSTING

- Slow down to problem-solve words and resume reading with momentum
- Recognize that a text is fiction and tells a story with a beginning, middle, several episodes, and end
- Understand that a nonfiction book gives facts
- Notice labels on photographs and use them to understand the words in the text
- •• Adjust reading to notice information in photographs
- •• Adjust to accommodate some variety in layout of illustrations and print

SUMMARIZING

- Remember important information while reading to understand the meaning of the text
- Talk about the important information after reading
- Remember the order of events in a simple story and talk about them after reading
- •• Summarize the problem in a simple story and talk about the solution
- Remember and talk about clear, simple ideas that are easy to identify
- •• Understand when sequence is important (e.g., cooking, planting) and talk about events or steps in order

A double bullet indicates a new behavior that you expect to see evidence of at this level.

Thinking *About* the Text

Thinking analytically about the text as an object helps readers notice and appreciate elements of the author's craft, such as use of language, characterization, organization, and structure.

LEVEL D — Behaviors and Understandings to Notice, Teach, and Support

Thinking Beyond the Text

PREDICTING
- Use varied language structures to anticipate the text
- Make predictions based on information in pictures that closely match the text
- Predict the ending of a story based on reading the beginning and middle
- Make predictions based on knowledge of the events of everyday life: e.g., family, cooking, play, pets, school, food, community, friends
- ••Make predictions based on understanding a simple sequence of events with a problem and outcome
- Make predictions based on personal experiences and knowledge: e.g., family and home, play, pets, animals, school, food, community, friends, daily activities, the human body, weather, seasons, transportation, toys
- ••Make predictions based on a temporal sequence: e.g., plants growing, eggs hatching, weather changing, food cooking

MAKING CONNECTIONS
- Make connections between personal experience and a text
- Make connections among books in a series
- ••Use background knowledge to understand settings: e.g., home, school, park, community
- Identify recurring characters or settings when applicable
- ••Bring background knowledge of traditional literature to recognize common characters and events in a folktale
- ••Use background knowledge to understand settings close to children's experience: e.g., home, school, park, community, and (if applicable) beach and snow
- Make connections between background knowledge of familiar content and the content in the text
- Make connections among texts on the same topic or with the same content
- ••Access background knowledge to understand simple processes: e.g., ice melting, food cooking, building an object

SYNTHESIZING
- Talk about what is known about the topic before reading the text
- ••Talk about the text, showing understanding of events or topic
- ••Talk about the events of a simple plot
- Talk about what is learned about characters and problems in a story
- Talk about any new labels for content that are learned from the text
- ••Identify new knowledge gained when reading a text

INFERRING
- Infer meaning of story or content from pictures that add meaning to the text
- Make inferences about where the story takes place (as shown in pictures) to help understand it
- Talk about characters' feelings based on inference from pictures and text, especially dialogue
- Talk about the pictures, revealing interpretation of a problem or of characters' feelings
- Infer humor that is easy to grasp: e.g., silly characters, funny situations
- ••Infer some obvious character traits from the story and pictures: e.g., kind, brave, funny
- Infer ideas about familiar content: e.g., friendships, family relationships, self, nature, food, health, community
- ••Infer simple processes by noticing the steps: cooking, water freezing, plants growing

Thinking About the Text

ANALYZING
- Understand how the ideas and information in a book are related to each other
- Understand how the events, content, and ideas in a text are related to the title
- Recognize that a text can be imagined (fiction) or it can give information (nonfiction)
- ••Understand that a story can be like real life or can be something that could not be true in real life (fantasy)
- Recognize settings that are familiar: e.g., home, school, neighborhood
- Recognize and follow a chronological sequence of events
- ••Identify a simple story problem and how it is resolved
- ••Recognize and understand variety in narrative structure: e.g., cumulative tale, circular story
- Recognize that there are characters (people or animals in a story)
- ••Recognize characters that are typical of animal fantasy or traditional literature
- ••Notice that illustrations add to important story action
- Use language and pictures to talk about a text (title, beginning, several episodes, ending)
- Recognize that a text can have true information
- Understand that a nonfiction book gives facts or tells how to do something
- Recognize that a process happens in time order
- ••Understand that illustrations and photographs add to the ideas and information in a text
- ••Use some specific language to talk about types of texts: e.g., *family, friends, and school story*
- Use some specific language to talk about literary features: e.g., *beginning, ending, problem, character*
- Use some specific language to talk about book and print features: e.g., *front cover, back cover, page, author, illustrator, illustration, photograph, title, label*

CRITIQUING
- Share opinions about a text
- Share opinions about an illustration or photograph
- ••Have favorite books and say why

A double bullet indicates a new behavior that you expect to see evidence of at this level.

Section 4: Planning for Letter and Word Work

A list of suggestions to help you select word study activities that will enable you to tailor instruction on words to the specific demands of the level of text.

LEVEL **D** — **Behaviors** and **Understandings** to Notice, Teach, and Support

Planning for Letter and Word Work After Guided Reading

Using your recent observations of the readers' ability to take words apart quickly and efficiently while reading text, plan for one to three minutes of active engagement of students' attention to letters, sounds, and words. Prioritize the readers' noticing of print features and active hands-on use of magnetic letters, a whiteboard, word cards, or pencil and paper to promote fluency and flexibility in visual processing.

Examples:

- Recognize a few easy high-frequency words quickly (for example, *as, by, came, get, had, her, his, out*)
- Make or write high-frequency words quickly (*make, this, but, come, him, his*)
- Review making and breaking apart high-frequency words from previous levels
- Recognize and break apart several CVC words easily and quickly (*man, pet, hit, box, cut*)
- Make, break apart, or write several CVC words quickly (*man, pet, hit, box, cut*)
- Hear and divide CVC words into onsets and rimes (*m-an, p-et, h-it, b-ox, c-ut*)
- Add *-s* to a singular noun to make a plural noun and read it (*dog/dogs*)

- Say and clap the syllables in one-, two-, and three-syllable words (from pictures)
- Change the beginning phoneme of a word to make a different one-syllable word (*day, may*)
- Change the ending phoneme of a word to make a different one-syllable word (*men, met*)
- Match pictures with letters by beginning or ending sounds (*farm, flower, frog; book, milk, park*)
- Sort letters quickly by a variety of features—uppercase or lowercase; tall or short; with or without long straight lines, short straight lines, circles, tails
- Read the Alphabet Linking Chart in different ways—singing, by letter names, pictures and words, all vowels, all consonants, letters only, backwards order, every other letter

316   *A double bullet indicates a new behavior that you expect to see evidence of at this level.*

section 4

Teaching in the *LLI* Green System

▶ Key Aspects of Teaching *LLI* Lessons

In *LLI* lessons, instruction centers around four critical areas: reading texts, writing texts, phonics/word work, and oral language learning. Children read numerous books, write stories, learn phonics skills in a systematic way, and expand their oral language, including vocabulary.

Reading Texts in *LLI* Lessons

In grade one, some children are still developing early reading behaviors. They are learning the differences between the print and the pictures and are also learning to:
- ❑ read left to right across a word
- ❑ read left to right across a line of text
- ❑ return to the left after reading a line
- ❑ read the left side of the page before the right
- ❑ understand what a letter is
- ❑ understand what a word is
- ❑ understand that words are made of letters
- ❑ easily identify letters by their distinct features
- ❑ understand that letters in a word are always in the same order
- ❑ understand that there are spaces between words in a text
- ❑ understand that you can get information from pictures
- ❑ match one spoken word with one written word in print
- ❑ self-monitor and self-correct their errors
- ❑ stop at a period
- ❑ raise the voice at a question mark
- ❑ show excitement at an exclamation point
- ❑ use bold print to show emphasis
- ❑ use quotation marks to identify dialogue
- ❑ read a core of high-frequency words
- ❑ use letter/sound relationships
- ❑ use information from pictures
- ❑ use language structure to read
- ❑ use the meaning of the story to read
- ❑ read with phrasing and fluency

As they progress through the typical range of texts for grade one (A–K), children will also learn to:

- use letter-sound relationships to make words and monitor accuracy
- notice mismatches in reading
- use meaning and language to solve new words and check on accuracy and comprehension
- recognize a large core of high-frequency words
- use word parts to solve new words
- check the letter sequence of the word with the meaning
- check the meaning and language with print
- self-correct using meaning, language, and visual information

When you use the lap books and the small books, children have massive opportunities to read texts and develop these early reading behaviors. *Prompting Guide, Part 1* will also help you to teach for, prompt for, and reinforce these behaviors and understandings. It is a key tool for your use while children are reading the text and for selecting teaching points after the reading.

At about level C, children will gradually stop pointing at words and will learn to read with phrasing and fluency (see *When Readers Struggle: Teaching That Works, A–N*, Chapter 16: "Teaching for Fluency in Processing Texts"). In the *LLI* system, you will find books that support fluent reading—books with dialogue, plays for rereading, texts with repetition, texts with natural language, texts on familiar topics, texts with familiar vocabulary, texts with known high-frequency words, texts with words in bold type, and texts that support fluent phrasing.

A large section of the *Prompting Guide, Part 1* includes language that supports fluent reading. Key areas include stress, rate, pausing, phrasing, intonation, and integration. It also provides language for other critical areas of teaching—solving words, searching for and using information, and monitoring and correcting errors. You will want to refer to each of these sections as you determine areas of need during your teaching.

As your children develop effective processing strategies at a given level, they will be given increasingly challenging books at the next level on the *Fountas & Pinnell Text Level Gradient™*. It isn't necessary for all children to read every book at a given level. Based upon observations and assessment, you may decide that some children can move more quickly up the gradient, and you may want to skip some lessons. Be sure you've been taking running records of each child's reading, and consider phonics understandings when making this decision. At grade one your ultimate goal should be to bring children successfully to level K

Writing Texts in *LLI* Lessons

In *LLI*, children will have numerous opportunities to write about their reading. Your goal is to help them develop early writing strategies using three main approaches—interactive writing, dictated writing, and independent writing. Your role in each supports conventional writing of a text that will be reread.

In Interactive Writing, you share the pen and select teaching points to support new learning or reinforce partially controlled behaviors. When children already control a word (or when it is too difficult to attempt) just write it quickly for them. After you construct the text together, children reread it together as a shared reading text.

In Dictated Writing, you read aloud a sentence then repeat it, reading the words slowly. Support children as they write each word. For unknown words, write them on the whiteboard or help children think how to use sound boxes to support sound analysis of words with regular and easy-to-hear sound sequences (Elkonin boxes) or letter boxes (after Level G) to support visual analysis. See Instructional Procedures for

FIGURE 4.6 Small books and *Prompting Guide, Part 1*

A child rereads sentences he has written independently.

LLI, page 63 to help children write high-frequency words quickly, say words slowly, form letters efficiently, and use what they know about words. The children can reread and illustrate their sentences when time allows.

In Independent Writing, you invite children to compose their own sentences. Scaffold the writing as needed in a similar manner as Dictated Writing. Again, if time allows, have children reread and illustrate their sentences.

Remember to also use *Prompting Guide, Part 1* as a tool for supporting early writing behaviors, composing, constructing words, and forming letters.

Phonics and Word Work in *LLI* Lessons: Letters, Sounds, and Words

An effective reader demonstrates strong control of letter-sound relationships and word structure as part of the reading process. We have designed the lessons to provide explicit teaching and numerous opportunities for the application of principles in a sequential and developmentally appropriate way. The making of words, using a variety of materials, provides numerous kinesthetic experiences for strong teaching. In addition, children learn how to recognize and take words apart as they read. The *LLI* student books are also designed to build phonics and word knowledge (see *When Readers Struggle: Teaching That Works, A–N*, Chapter 11, "Learning to Solve Words: Effective and Efficient Phonics").

In the *LLI Green System*, children develop several areas of phonics knowledge, early literacy concepts, phonemic and phonological awareness, letter knowledge, letter-sound relationships, easy spelling patterns, word meanings, and a core of at least 100 high-frequency words, which become a foundation for learning other words. In addition, they learn efficient letter formation. (See Appendix D, Master Plan for Word Work in the *LLI Green System*.)

Oral Language Learning in *LLI* Lessons

An important aspect of teaching in *LLI* lessons is the expansion of oral language, including vocabulary. Children have many opportunities in the lesson to converse with each other and with the teacher. Because the group is small, the amount of opportunity for talk is increased.

The lessons provide explicit demonstrations of how to use language. Engage children in conversation about their experiences and about texts, expanding their knowledge of language structure as they talk. As you introduce new books, give children opportunities to say and hear new words, phrases, and sentences. In the writing segment, engage them in talking about ideas and composing several sentences. In these lessons, oral language surrounds their literacy learning. (See *When Readers Struggle: Teaching That Works, A–N*, Chapter 7, "Language Matters: Talking, Reading, and Writing.")

Teaching with the *LLI* Lessons

In Part 3 of this Guide there are brief overviews of Getting Started Lessons as well as the Odd- and Even-Numbered Lessons. On the following pages, we provide more detailed descriptions of these three lesson frameworks.

Children often use magnetic letters for phonics and word/letter work.

We expect that you will use your knowledge and observations to modify the lesson suggestions as needed. No one lesson plan will fit all readers. Your decision making across the lesson is critical as you respond to the specific strengths and needs of the individual children you teach.

You will find that the lesson structure described here and in the *Lesson Guide* provides for a smooth, well-paced 30-minute lesson and that your children will benefit from the predictability it provides. While the time frame may vary by a minute or two, try not to get bogged down on any one part of the lesson. You may find that a timer is helpful in pacing the lesson. We suggest using a digital timer or the F&P Calculator/Stopwatch to keep track of time. (Note that the Calculator/Stopwatch does not have an alarm.) If too much time is spent on any one part of the lesson, it will not be possible to complete the combination of tasks, all of which are essential. With time and practice, you will find that your teaching of the lessons becomes smoother and more efficient.

The instructional activities within the 30-minute lesson are designed to:

- Support children in reading a new text that has opportunities to extend comprehension, vocabulary, and processing strategies.
- Develop fluency and phrasing through rereading.
- Help children learn about letters, sounds, and words.
- Learn to apply knowledge of phonics to word solving while reading continuous text.
- Extend comprehension through discussion, teacher's instruction, and writing.
- Learn how to write about their reading.
- Display new understandings in classroom work.
- Develop the habit of home reading.

▶ Teaching the Getting Started Lessons

The first ten lessons in the *LLI Green System* are designed to engage children in highly supported reading and writing experiences. They learn how to read simple books and poems, write messages, work with sounds and letters, and engage in conversations about text with a great deal of your support and teaching. Your goals are to help children become active, engaged learners and to begin to build a foundation of early reading and writing behaviors.

All children entering *LLI* will benefit from the Getting Started Lessons, but they will be especially important for children who have not yet learned to look at print in a memorable way—those who aren't able to read level A books. (Some teachers use the term pre-level A.) In those first ten lessons, observe children closely to notice that they are:

- matching voice to print on simple text with crisp finger pointing.
- moving across lines of text left to right.
- able to identify the first letter of a word and beginning to connect it with a word they know, for example, their name.
- getting information from the pictures and the print.
- rapidly learning the names of letters and beginning to connect them with words.
- beginning to build a small bank of high-frequency words to recognize in their reading and use in their writing.

You may also notice some danger signs. You will want to intervene immediately if you notice that children are:

- chanting along with you but not looking at the print.
- writing or guessing random letters with no relationship to sounds.
- trying to memorize text and looking at the pictures to produce it.
- not pointing crisply *under* words while reading.
- having to reread the entire sentence to locate a word (a technique that they may display at the earliest levels but one that should give way to searching for visual information).

Before beginning the Getting Started Lessons with children you may want to read Chapter 10 in *When Readers Struggle: Teaching That Works, A–N* (pages 201–230) for more ideas on how to support these beginning readers and writers.

If, after ten Getting Started Lessons, you observe that a child is still having difficulty looking at and using print, you will need to observe carefully and be ready to jump in and support the child as he or she develops these essential understandings of how print works. The section on Early Reading Behaviors in *Prompting Guide, Part 1* will be an important resource as you teach, prompt, and reinforce these behaviors.

Each Getting Started Lesson includes the following components. Figure 4.1 below shows an approximate pacing for the Getting Started Lessons.

Pacing for Getting Started Lessons (Lessons 1–10)	
Approximate Time: 30 minutes	
5 minutes	Rereading*
5 minutes	Phonics/Word Work
8 minutes	Reading a New Book (Lap Book and small books)
7 minutes	Writing About Reading
5 minutes	Letter/Word Work

*In the first lesson, find any text children have read and can reread, or you can skip the rereading.

FIGURE 4.1 Pacing for Getting Started Lessons

Part 1: Reading (5 minutes)

In the first part of the lesson, children read lap books with you as you point to the words. You may want to have children say and find a few words in the text after reading. Then children point and read the small books softly and independently at level A. For levels B and C texts, children point and read the small books in unison with you to assure voice-print match. The last Getting Started lap book in the *Green System* is level D.

Part 2: Phonics/Word Work (5 minutes)

In the second part of the lesson, you engage children in a variety of experiences in working with sounds and letters. They learn how to recognize their names, listen for sounds, and connect them with letters.

Part 3: Reading a New Book (8 minutes)

In the third part of the lesson, introduce a new lap book by pointing under each word as you read aloud and engage children in conversation about the text. In some books, you have the opportunity to introduce characters from the series books children will read later. Next, invite the children to read *with* you as you point. Finally, children point and read the text softly and independently at level A. At levels B and C, the children point and read the small books in unison with you to assure voice-print match. At level C, however, you want them to start reading without the aid of a finger so that they can begin to read with phrasing and fluency. They can bring the finger back in at points of difficulty, but the eye should begin to take over the process of tracking print.

Part 4: Writing About Reading (7 minutes)

In the fourth part of the lesson, children discuss and write about yesterday's new book. Engage children in composing one or two sentences about the new book they read in the previous lesson. Then, using interactive writing, share the pen with children at selective points. Children write what they are able, for example, beginning letter, known word—and you fill in the rest. You'll want to guide children to use conventional spellings because the writing products become reading material for the children.

Part 5: Letter/Word Work (5 minutes)

In the last part of the lesson, engage children in hands-on work to learn about how print works. Children work with name puzzles; letters, words, and pictures; magnetic letters; Letter Minibooks; and other materials.

▶ Teaching Standard Lessons (Odd-Numbered)

The ten Getting Started Lessons are followed by two types of standard lessons. Beginning with Lesson 11, you'll use the odd-numbered lessons to introduce a new *instructional-level* book. The focus is on reading, discussing meaning, and phonics/word work. Figure 4.2 on the next page shows an approximate pacing for the odd-numbered lessons.

Pacing for Odd-Numbered Lessons	
Approximate Time	
5 minutes	Rereading
5 minutes	Phonics/Word Work
15 minutes	Reading a New Book (Instructional Level)
5 minutes	Letter/Word Work

FIGURE 4.2 Pacing for Odd-Numbered Lessons

Part 1: Rereading Books (5 minutes)

In the first part of the lesson, children reread the new book from the previous lesson softly while you observe their processing. Rereading develops fluency and offers the child a chance to perform smooth processing. During and after reading, you may prompt for strategic actions and briefly discuss the meaning of the text. The emphasis is on engagement and enjoyment and reading the whole book.

Part 2: Phonics/Word Work (5 minutes)

The second part of the lesson provides some very explicit and systematic instruction to help children learn how written language "works." In early lessons you work with children to develop phonemic awareness, which means hearing the individual sounds in words. Hearing and identifying the sounds in words helps children to connect sounds to letters. In this section, we provide specific suggestions for teaching children how to connect sounds and letters. If several activities are suggested, be sure to teach the principle and have the children apply it. Skip the additional suggestions if time is a problem.

Part 3: Reading a New Book (15 minutes)

In the third part of the lesson introduce the new book, which is at the children's *instructional* level. An instructional-level text is one that children can read *with* teacher support. There are four steps in reading the new instructional-level book.

1. INTRODUCING THE TEXT

Engage children in a conversation that supports their proficient processing of a new text at the instructional level, keeping the genre statement in mind when introducing the text. The introduction may include:

- ❑ Providing an overview of the meaning of the whole text.
- ❑ Using in conversation some specific language structures that will help children read the text.
- ❑ Conversationally using specific vocabulary words that are important for the text.
- ❑ Helping children locate known and unknown words (thinking about the sounds and letters).
- ❑ Helping children notice particular features of the words or the print.
- ❑ Pointing out important features (such as text organization, punctuation, organization, and illustrations).

Not all elements described above need to be included in every introduction. Guidance is provided in each lesson, but think about the children's needs and select from and add to the introductory conversation. Children should participate rather than just listen; each time the lesson suggests "Children Respond," you are inviting conversation. You can use *Prompting Guide, Part 2* as a resource to support introductory conversation. Remember that the introduction is not long, so keep attention focused on the text rather than expanding to wider topics. The text is selected at a

The teacher keeps attention focused on the text rather than on wider topics when giving an introduction.

challenging level to offer opportunities for learning. Even with the introduction, children will have problem solving to do.

2. READING THE TEXT

The new book reading includes some explicit teaching for processing strategies. At levels A and B, the children need to point crisply under each word. At level C, you help them start to use their eyes without the aid of the finger so they can begin to read with phrasing and fluency.

While children are reading, interact with each of them briefly. You can listen to one at a time. Ask them to read very softly. Observe and listen as they read; lean in to interact briefly with individuals as needed. We recommend that you have the children read silently beginning at about level H or I, so children in the *LLI Green System* (A to G or H) will be reading orally, but softly so as not to disturb others. You can simply turn from one child to another and listen. If they are reading so softly you cannot hear them, just lightly tap the child you want to hear and he can raise his voice a little.

When you interact with individuals, teach, prompt for, or reinforce effective reading behaviors. (See *Fountas & Pinnell Prompting Guide, Part 1.*)

Be cautious about interrupting the child's processing to correct too many errors. Sometimes it is wiser to wait until the end of the book to make a teaching point. Other times children will find and fix their errors on their own. If it is necessary to intervene, prompt the child to use the source of information that will help him or her solve the problem quickly.

- ❑ *Teaching* involves demonstrating, or modeling, behaviors. It means intervening to show the child what you want him to do. For example, you could say, "Watch while I read the sentence again and get my mouth ready to say the word (by making the sound of the first letter). Now you try." Or, "Watch while I point right under the words. Now you point and read."

- ❑ *Prompting* means using some precise language to get the child to engage in the behavior. Successful prompting depends on the child's understanding of what you mean, so the behavior must be demonstrated first. For example, you might say, "Try that again and get your mouth ready." Or, "What would make sense and look right?" Use the same language in your prompting as you did in your demonstration.

The teacher interacts with an individual child while the others are reading softly.

- ❑ *Reinforcing* behaviors means giving some very quick and concise comments that just let the child know what he or she did that was effective. For example, you might say, "You got your mouth ready for the word." Or, "You noticed that it didn't look right." Again, remember to use the same language you used in your prompting. Notice that we use purely descriptive language designed to communicate precisely what the child did (rather than "good" or "I like the way you…"). Evaluative remarks like "good boy" or "that's what good readers do" do not really help the reader. The best way to encourage children is to enable them to be successful in processing and to comment specifically on what they do.

3. DISCUSSING AND REVISITING THE TEXT

Invite the children to share their thinking about the book. You may have them turn and talk to a partner before sharing their thinking with each other. This gives all children the opportunity to talk. The children's comments are important, and you want the discussion to be a conversation. Help them listen and talk to each other instead of directing their talk to you. Guide the discussion toward the expression of the key understandings. A suggestion is provided for discussion in this section.

Sometimes children recall important information and even infer some of the important ideas in a text but miss the larger, overarching messages. A "Message" statement below the chart helps you support children in thinking about the bigger, important ideas.

4. SELECTING A TEACHING POINT

Finally, based on your observations in this lesson (as well as ongoing knowledge of the children), do some explicit teaching that will be most helpful to readers. Think about what aspect of the processing you want to reinforce or expand. Use *Prompting Guide, Part 1* or *Part 2* to help in selecting points. One suggestion is provided in the lesson. Teaching points are meant to be concise and direct. Usually they require some demonstration as well as action.

Part 4: Letter/Word Work (5 minutes)

In the fourth part of the lesson, involve children in active exploration of letters and words in order to help them learn how words "work." They will break words apart using magnetic letters, sort words, write words, and acquire a core of high-frequency words.

▶ Teaching Standard Lessons (Even-Numbered)

The even-numbered standard lessons—which start with Lesson 12—offer the introduction of a new easy, or *independent*-level, book for the child. The focus is on writing to extend the meaning of books (as well as to achieve a close look at print, letters, and sounds), on phonics and word work, and on fluency. The even-numbered standard lessons vary slightly in their structure from the odd-numbered standard lessons. The instruction is designed to:

- ❑ Extend the children's understanding of the meaning of the new text.
- ❑ Develop children's early writing skills.
- ❑ Help children notice and use features of the text.
- ❑ Develop fluency and processing strategies through rereading yesterday's new book and encountering a new, but easier, book.
- ❑ Continue teaching children about letters, sounds, and words.

Figure 4.5 shows an approximate pacing for the Even-Numbered Lesson.

Pacing for Even-Numbered Lessons	
Approximate Time	
5 minutes	Rereading and Assessment
5 minutes	Phonics/Word Work
15 minutes	Writing About Reading
5 minutes	Reading a New Book (Independent Level)
If time allows	Optional Letter/Word Work

FIGURE 4.5 Pacing for Even-Numbered Lessons

Part 1: Rereading and Assessment (5 minutes)

In the first part of the lesson, children reread softly the new books that were read the day before. The lesson provides tips for observing and interacting briefly with the readers during this time. Reading yesterday's new book for the second time helps children process with greater ease the challenges that they may have encountered the day before. Use this time to take a reading record on one child, using the Recording Form or in the *LLI Reading Record App* for the instructional-level book that was introduced and read the day before. Listen to the child read aloud while you code the reading behavior and have a brief comprehension conversation. Based on your observations, provide brief teaching points to help the reader problem-solve more efficiently.

During rereading, the teacher briefly interacts with and observes individual readers.

Part 2: Phonics/Word Work (5 minutes)

In the second part of the lesson, continue to expand children's awareness of sounds and letters in words. Examine the principle introduced the day before and add examples to expand children's knowledge or introduce a new principle. If there are several activities are suggested, do only what time allows after working with the new principle.

Part 3: Writing About Reading (15 minutes)

The third part of the lesson involves extending understanding of the text through writing. It is designed to develop early writing strategies. All writing is in conventional form, and we strongly suggest using unlined paper. There are three types of writing about reading activities: interactive, dictated, and independent (See Figure 5.11).

With interactive writing, you compose a text with the children and then, acting as a scribe, write it on a chart with their help. (Children may add a letter, word part, or word.) Examples of interactive writing may appear in each lesson, but you should compose your own sentences.

In dictated writing, children write specific sentences that you read out loud to them. Here, children have opportunities to consider a small piece of text in detail and to think about sounds and letters as they construct words with your support.

In independent writing, children compose and write sentences of their own with your support in using conventional form. The focus is on developing early writing strategies (see *When Readers Struggle: Teaching That Works, A–N,* pages 295–299). Depending on your children's needs, you may choose any of the three kinds of writing for any given lesson. For instance, dictated writing might be specified for a particular lesson, but you might decide that it is more useful for children to engage in interactive or independent writing.

Independent writing may take several different forms according to the purposes of the lesson, for example:

- ❑ Sentences about the text that children can illustrate (at home or in the classroom)
- ❑ Innovations on the text (using the same structure with ideas/words that children contribute)
- ❑ Summary statements
- ❑ Interesting information from the text
- ❑ A response or reaction to the text

These written texts later become texts for reading by children, so they must be clear. All of the writing should be scaffolded so it is written conventionally. Show children how to write in lowercase letters and allow uppercase letters only when needed. Help them use good spacing and capitals as appropriate. If needed, use the Verbal Path (see *Prompting Guide, Part 1,* or Online Resources) to guide letter formation. Help children use sound analysis and visual analysis to spell words correctly.

Remember that writing is most beneficial to learners when it is surrounded by conversation. The children's dictated and independent writing can be done in their blank personal writing books, *My Writing Book*. You may want to type the interactive writing pieces in a large font (about the size of the font in level A texts) and have children glue them in their writing books to reread and illustrate. Or, when sentence strips are used in a lesson, you may want children to glue them in *My Writing Book*. The blank books should be used at your direction. They provide a good way to compile a collection of writing that can be reread and sent home at the end of a series of lessons.

In addition, children may write letters and words in their writing books as part of word study. In the process, they develop a network of knowledge about how words work. As part of word study, they may:

- ❑ practice letter formation
- ❑ write high-frequency words
- ❑ categorize words, noticing different features
- ❑ categorize pictures according to sound and/or match them with letters
- ❑ construct words letter by letter or part by part
- ❑ show connections between words
- ❑ use analogy to construct new words

You might decide to reproduce children's interactive, dictated, or independent writing for children to take home and share with family members. Copy the sentence(s) on strips of paper and cut them up into individual words that children can put in order, glue onto a sheet of paper, and illustrate at home.

Part 4: Reading a New Book (5 Minutes)

Just as with the odd-numbered lessons, the reading of the new, independent-level text consists of introducing the text, reading the text, discussing and revisiting the text, and selecting a teaching point. In the even-numbered standard lessons however, because children will read an independent-level text, you may want to provide a shorter introduction (but an introduction nonetheless). As with the odd-numbered standard lessons, engage children in a conversation during the introduction and draw attention to key concepts, information, and words that they need to process text smoothly.

Refer to pages 56 and 61 in this section if you require a fuller explanation of this part of the lesson.

Optional Letter/Word Work

The phonics/word study work in the *LLI* lesson is designed to supplement the classroom phonics program. If your children need it and time allows, you may want to provide the optional letter/word work that appears at the end of the even-numbered standard lessons. Alternatively, you may suggest it to the classroom teacher to use for follow up.

section 5

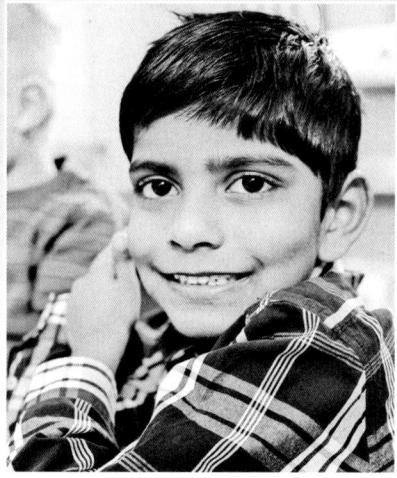

Instructional Procedures and Teaching Materials for *LLI*

In this section, we provide an explanation of several instructional routines and tools that are used throughout *LLI* lessons. It is important to keep in mind that the ways you will support children will change as they gain increased control over reading, writing, word work, and oral language. (See page 77, Relationship Between Teacher Support and Child Control in *LLI*.)

▶ Instructional Procedures in *LLI*

Instructional Procedures for Reading/Comprehension

Throughout the *LLI* lessons, work to support and teach students to construct twelve systems of strategic actions that readers need in order to read with understanding. (See Figure 5.1, Systems of Strategic Actions.) The excerpt from *The Fountas & Pinnell Literacy Continuum*, found at the end of each level in the Lesson Guide, will be a valuable tool for you to use as children move up the text gradient.

INTRODUCING THE TEXT

At the very earliest levels, children are developing an understanding of how books work and how to look at and use print. In early lessons, you provide a high level of support in the form of a rich introduction to each of the books so children are able to read the whole text as independently as possible.

The introduction will include inviting children to talk with you about the pictures, making predictions, connections and inferences. Use *Prompting Guide, Part 2* for suggested prompts to get children thinking and talking. For example:

❑ *How do you think (the character) feels about that?* [Inferring]

❑ *What do you think might happen next?* [Predicting]

A rich introduction must also provide opportunities for children to hear and rehearse the language structures and vocabulary of the book. The language in books is often different from the children's oral language. This is especially true for English language learners. In the article "Talking, Reading, and Writing" (*The Journal of*

FIGURE 5.1 Systems of Strategic Actions

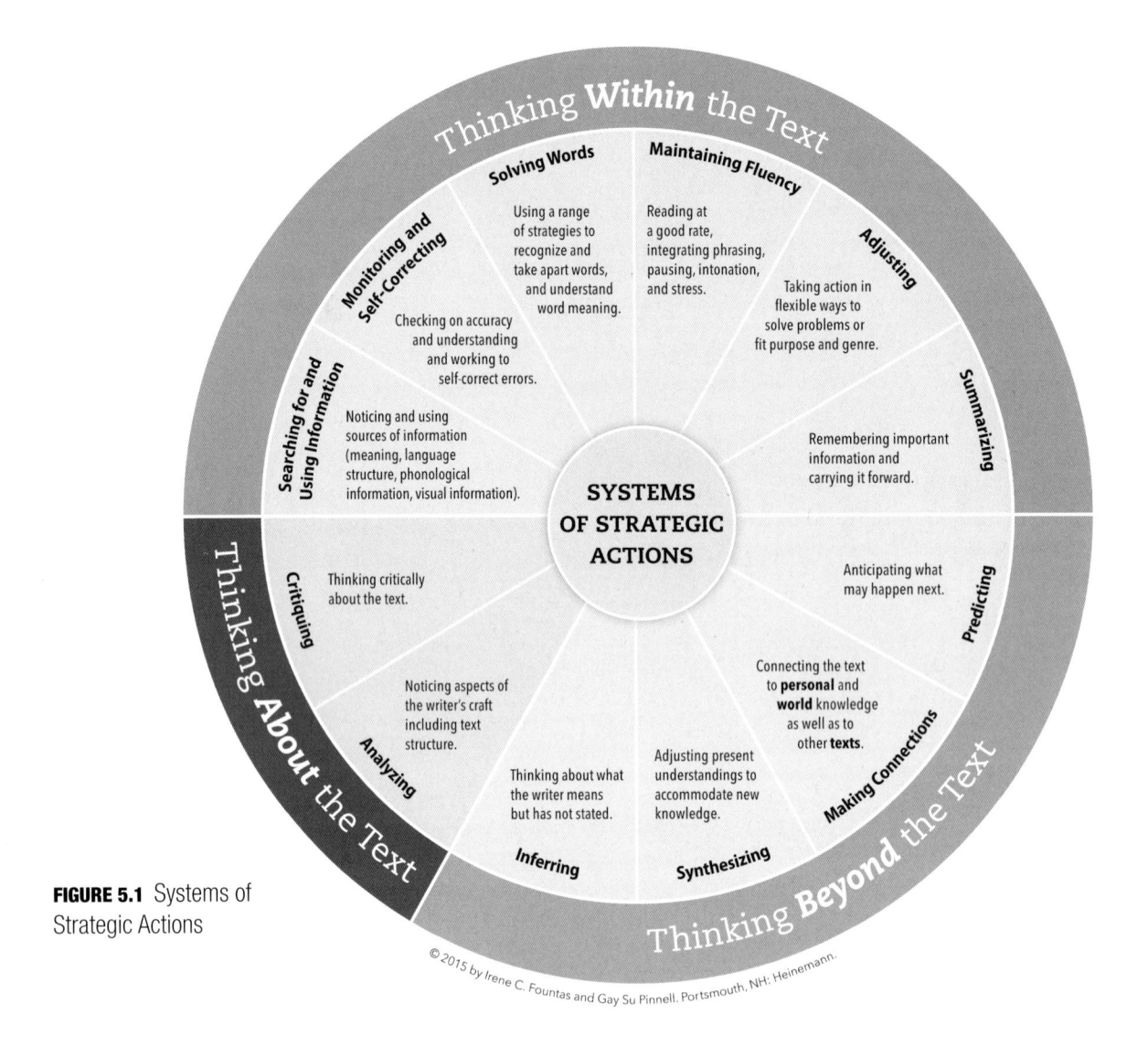

Reading Recovery, Spring 2004*)*, Marie Clay suggests "Teachers should read aloud to students the language that is new to them. Get the new phrase or sentence

- ❑ to the ear (listening)
- ❑ to the mouth (saying)
- ❑ to the eye (reading)
- ❑ to the written product (creating text)."

Your book introduction should also draw children's attention to important words and text features, having them locate punctuation, bold print, familiar words, and new words by anticipating the first letter.

As children become more familiar with how books work and how to use print, they will contribute more to the introduction. Continue to provide the kind of support they need to process texts with excellent comprehension, but leave more information for the children to discover during the reading. This is especially true in the even-numbered lessons because new books are at children's independent level.

READING THE TEXT

As children read the book in a quiet voice, you can sample the oral reading. Your observations will provide helpful information to guide your teaching decisions. The level of support you provide should depend upon what the child already controls, partially controls, and needs to learn to do next. Notice that the language that calls for strategic actions in *Prompting Guide, Part 1* is organized into three categories: Teach, Prompt, and Reinforce. Early modeling and prompting demonstrate and call for explicit actions. When you observe a child taking on those actions independently, use reinforcing language. Each prompt should lead to more control on the part of the reader. Move along this scale of help until the child demonstrates control of a particular strategy.

In each section of the *Prompting Guides* there is a menu of suggested language that ranges from very specific to very general. The following are two examples of prompts that are designed to get children to monitor their mismatches. Your observations will determine what level of support to provide.

- ❑ *Did you notice___?* (point out mismatch) [very supportive]
- ❑ *You made a mistake. Can you find it?* [general]

In early lessons, interact briefly during reading to support children's use of early reading behaviors.

- ❑ *Start here and read this way.* [Reading Left to Right/Return Sweep]
- ❑ *Put your finger under each word.* [Establishing Voice Print Match]
- ❑ *You have too many words. Go back and make it match.* [Monitoring Voice-Print Match]

Once early behaviors have been established, look for evidence of a reader's problem-solving strategies (e.g., searching for and using information, solving words, self-monitoring and self-correcting, and reading fluently). During reading, direct the reader to the source of information that will help him solve the problem. These interactions during reading should be brief and specific so as not to interrupt the flow of the story. For example:

- ❑ *Think about what would make sense?* [Searching for Meaning]
- ❑ *Do you know a word that starts like that?* [Searching for Visual Information]

After the reading, you may want to attend to some other uncorrected errors or reinforce effective problem solving.

- ❑ *Something wasn't quite right. See if you can fix it.* [Self-Correcting]
- ❑ *You made it sound like the character was talking.* [Maintaining Fluency-Intonation]

DISCUSSING AND REVISITING THE TEXT

The discussion after reading is a time to teach children how to think and talk about the books they are reading. In early lessons, teach children how to participate in a book discussion. You will establish routines for:

- ❑ turn-taking
- ❑ listening to one another and building upon others' responses
- ❑ articulating one's thinking clearly, in complete sentences

Model how to get started and invite children to extend their thinking. (This can be accomplished in a few lessons.) As children participate actively in the discussion after reading, you can observe their abilities to summarize, predict, make connections, synthesize, infer, analyze, and critic. Use *Prompting Guide, Part 2* to assist you in selecting language that expands children's thinking. Some examples might be:

- ❑ *What were the most important things the writer had to say?* [Summarizing]
- ❑ *What does this remind you of?* [Making Connections]
- ❑ *Why does the main character say that?* [Inferring]
- ❑ *What do you think might happen?* [Predicting]
- ❑ *Talk about the new information you learned from this book.* [Synthesizing]
- ❑ *What did the writer do to make this story funny?* [Analyzing]
- ❑ *What makes this a good story?* [Critiquing]

Each lesson includes key understandings and a writer's message to help guide the discussions after reading. Your goal is to help children express these understandings in an organized manner, using academic language that is appropriate to their age.

Instructional Procedures for Phonics/Word Work

Young readers need to develop efficient strategic actions for recognizing and solving words as they read. In *LLI* lessons, you will help children gain control of nine areas of word learning so they can begin to develop strong visual processing. (See Figure 5.2, Nine Important Areas of Learning for Phonics and Word Study.)

In *LLI Green*, there are five instructional routines to develop children's knowledge of words and how they work. Most routines engage children in inquiry to generate an important principle. For example, children might be shown a group of words and asked to notice a common feature (e.g., all words end with

Nine Important Areas of Learning for Phonics and Word Study

Early Literacy Concepts (PreK to Grade 1)	Even before they can read, children begin to develop some awareness of how written language works, and they continue to develop concepts about processing print as they read their first books.
Phonological Awareness (PreK to Grade 1)	A key understanding in becoming literate is the ability to hear the individual sounds in words, and rhymes, as well as word parts.
Letter Knowledge (PreK to Grade 1)	Letter knowledge refers to what students need to know about the graphic characters in the English alphabet—how the letters look, how to distinguish one from another, how to detect them within continuous print, how to use them in words, and the names we use to talk about them.
Letter-Sound Relationships	Students continue to learn about the relationships between letters and sounds in English throughout the elementary school years. In addition to the sounds connected to individual letters, they learn the way alternative sounds may be attached to a letter and they learn to look for letter combinations (blends and digraphs) and to see them as units.
Spelling Patterns	Efficient word solvers look for and find patterns in the ways words are constructed. Knowing spelling patterns helps students notice and use larger parts of words, thus making word solving faster and easier. Students begin with simple phonograms (*sat*, *mat*, *cat*) but progress to learning much more complex patterns (*-ign*, *-ight*) and to the recognition of patterns in multisyllable words.
High-Frequency Words	Knowing how to read and write a core of high-frequency words is a valuable resource for students as they build their reading and writing processing systems. We can also call these "high-utility words" because they appear often in print and can sometimes be used to help in solving other words.
Word Meaning and Vocabulary	Students need to know the meaning of the words in the texts they read, and they need a continually expanding vocabulary to use in writing. Expanding vocabulary means developing categories of words: labels, concept words, synonyms, antonyms, homonyms, and so on. It also refers to words that appear in print but are not usually used in speech, to technical words, and to academic vocabulary.
Word Structure	Looking at the structure of words will help students learn how words are related to one another and how they can be changed by adding letters, letter clusters, and larger word parts. Students work with base words and affixes (prefixes and suffixes); they can also learn about word roots (Greek or Latin origins). Principles related to word structure include understanding the meaning and structure of compound words, contractions, plurals, and possessives.
Word-Solving Actions	Word solving is related to all of the categories of learning in this chart, but this category specifically focuses on the effective moves readers and writers make when they use their knowledge of the language system while reading and writing continuous text.

FIGURE 5.2 Nine Important Areas of Learning for Phonics and Word Study

silent *e*). However, in some early lessons inquiry is not included because children have not yet learned enough about letters and words to notice the similarities. The Master Plan for Word Work (see Appendix D, page 129) provides an overview of how the principles change over time as children gain in their knowledge of how words work. Another reference tool you may want to refer to is the detailed phonics continuum, *The Fountas & Pinnell Comprehensive Phonics, Spelling, and Word Study Guide*.

HEAR AND SAY

You will use this instructional routine to help students hear the sounds in words and eventually connect those sounds to letters, a key process in building literacy. In early lessons, Hear and Say is primarily an aural task. As children develop their understandings of how words work, they will be asked to represent the sounds they hear by constructing words with magnetic letters or in writing.

Hear and Say typically employs the following sequence. Although the example given below centers on rhyming words, you also will use Hear and Say throughout the year to support children's work with beginning, middle, and ending phonemes, short vowel sounds, digraphs, onsets and rimes, and how changing a phoneme can make a new word.

1. Say words that are connected by the way they sound. [*man/can, me/he, hot/pot*]
2. Children search for phonological patterns. [end parts that sound the same]
4. Help children articulate the principle. [Some words have end parts that sound the same. They rhyme.]
4. Children work with words to apply the principle. [They say word pairs and tell whether the word pairs have end parts that sound the same (rhyme).]
5. Summarize the learning by restating the principle.

SEE AND SAY

Efficient word solvers look for and find visual patterns in the way words are constructed. Recognizing familiar patterns helps students notice and use larger parts of words, which makes word solving faster and

can	sit	ham	fin	cat
man	hit	Sam	tin	bat
fan	fit	jam	pin	rat
ran	pit	ram	spin	sat
plan	kit	clam	grin	flat

FIGURE 5.3 See and Say: Working with words that have a VC pattern.

easier. The See and Say routine described below helps students examine and identify familiar patterns in words, such as the CVC and CVCe patterns, and learn to make new words by putting a letter or letter cluster before the familiar pattern.

The See and Say routine generally follows this sequence:

1. Show words that have a common spelling pattern. [*can, fan, man, ran*]
2. Children search for visual patterns. [Each word has the phonogram pattern -*an*.]
3. Help children articulate the principle. [You can look at the spelling pattern to read a word. You can use the spelling pattern to write a word. You can make new words by putting a letter or letter cluster before the pattern.]
4. Children work with words to apply the principle. [Children read words with the pattern. Children write words with the pattern.]
5. Summarize the learning by restating the principle.

SAY AND SORT

Sorting helps children look closely at features of letters or words and make connections between them. Using the Say and Sort routine illustrated below, children form categories of pictures, letters, or words that are similar by sound, feature, word pattern, or word part. In the following example, children sort pictures by the number of syllables in the words they represent, but across the lessons they will sort by other features as well, such as first sound or letter, rhymes, or letter clusters

1. Show and say words—or show pictures and say the names of the pictures—that have a common feature [words/pictures: *cat, bus, turtle, carrot; banana, umbrella*]
2. Children search for the common feature. [The words have one, two, or three syllables.]
3. Help children articulate the principle. [Words can have one or more parts. You can hear, say, and clap the parts in a word.]
4. Children work with words or pictures of words to apply the principle. [Children sort the words or pictures according to the number of syllables.]
5. Summarize the learning by restating the principle.

FIGURE 5.4 Say and Sort: Sorting pictures of words according to their initial sounds.

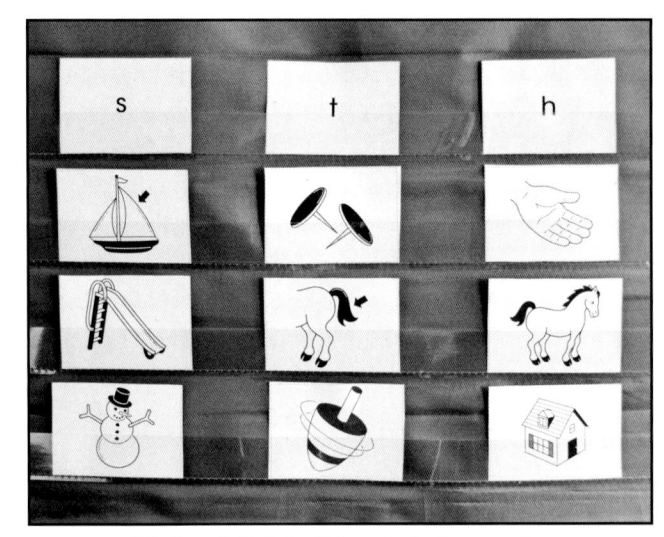

FIGURE 5.5 Find and Match: Helps students learn the connections between letters and sounds.

FIND AND MATCH

You will use the Find and Match instructional routine to help students learn the connections between letters and sounds. The example provided below focuses on ending consonant sounds, but you'll also use Find and Match to support students in matching sounds and letters at the beginning or end of words, locating and connecting rhyming words, matching letters and pictures of words that begin or end with the same sound, or pairing words that start and end with the same sounds.

1. Show words or pictures of words that go together. [*ball, bed; car, cake*]
2. Children search for connections between the words or pictures of words. [the same sound and the same letter at the beginning of words]
3. Help children articulate the principle. [You can match the sound and the letter at the beginning of a word.]
4. Children work with words or pictures of words to apply the principle. [Match words or pictures of words by beginning sounds and letters.]
5. Summarize the learning by restating the principle.

HEAR, SAY, AND WRITE: SOUND AND LETTER BOXES

D. B. Elkonin, a Russian psychologist, developed sound and letter boxes to help children think about the sounds and letters in words. The technique has also been used by Marie Clay and by other researchers and educators. You can use the structure of sound boxes to help children listen for and identify each sound in a word. You will model by drawing the boxes and then will support students in using them.

Early in the *Green System*, you can introduce sound boxes in the absence of letters to help children identify individual sounds. This is particularly helpful when children are not yet able to hear the sounds in sequential order. Draw a box (alternatively, you could use one of the preprinted whiteboards included with the *Green System* or download sound boxes from the

Online Resources) for every sound in the word. The goal is for children to learn how to use the boxes for sounds by saying words slowly and listening for each sound in sequence.

Use the routine below for sound boxes with letters. You'll make one box for every *sound* or *phoneme* (not every letter) in each word.

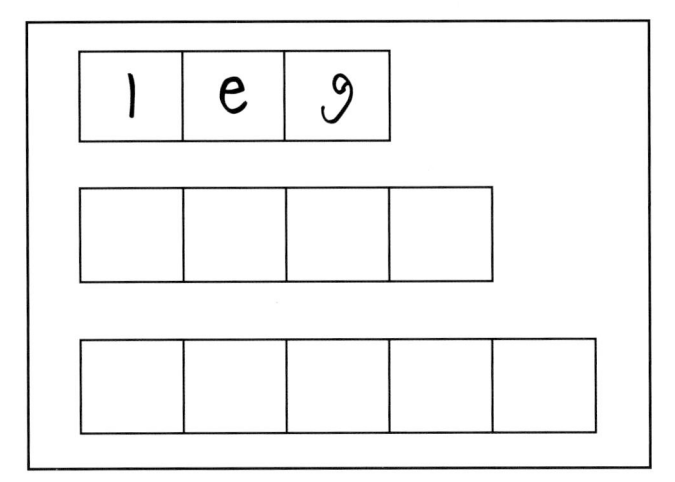

FIGURE 5.6 Sound boxes help children listen for and identify each sound in a word.

1. Model saying a new word slowly (*r-u-n* for *run*), being careful not to distort the individual sounds.
2. Children say the word slowly, listening for each sound in sequence, and running a finger under each box in sequence.
3. Help children articulate the principle. [Letters and sounds can be matched in words.]
4. With your guidance, children write a letter for each sound they hear, one letter per box. In the beginning, you may choose to accept letters that are not in the correct sequence, focusing instead on whether children can connect letters to sounds.
5. Children work with words and boxes to apply the principle. [Children say a word slowly, identify each sound in sequence, and independently write the letter that represents that sound in a box, in sequence.] If children are using the preprinted whiteboards, encourage fast erasing between words using an old sock or soft cloth.
6. Summarize the learning by restating the principle.

At about level G, when children can independently say words slowly, identify all easy-to-hear vowel and consonant sounds, and write the letters that represent those sounds independently and in sequence, you can move on to letter boxes. Here, there is a box for every *letter* in the word, regardless of the number of phonemes. The boxes help children notice the discrepancies between the number of sounds and the number of letters. They can begin to learn about consonant blends (two letters that make one sound; e.g., /ch/) and vowel pairs (as in *eat*) as well as about silent letters.

1. Model saying a word slowly, being careful not to distort the individual sounds.
2. Children say the word with you and run a finger under the boxes, thinking about how the word looks. The goal is for children to say it slowly by themselves.
3. Children write each letter they expect to see in the word.
4. Move from three letter boxes to four or five as children become more proficient.
5. Summarize the learning by restating the principle.

(For more information, see *When Readers Struggle: Teaching That Works A–N*, pages 218–219.)

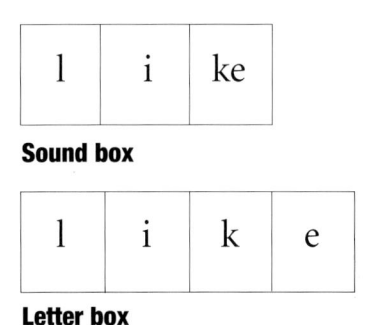

Sound box

Letter box

Instructional Procedures for Working with High-Frequency Words

In *LLI*, children build and work with a collection of high-frequency words, which are introduced during the Letter/Word Work portion of Getting Started lessons and in the odd-numbered standard lessons. The words, which come from the books children have recently read, are available for download from the Online Resources.

Children need to be able to recognize high-frequency words quickly and easily. These words are enormously beneficial to beginning readers, who can use them to:

❑ understand the concept of a word as letters with white space on either side;

- understand the concept of a word in language;
- monitor voice-print match;
- monitor accuracy;
- self-correct;
- notice letter-sound relationships or word parts;
- notice connections between words to solve new words;
- begin to write words correctly; and
- read and write at a good rate.

Children need multiple opportunities to work with a word in order to know it. According to Clay, "Change over time is recognized by a teacher who can judge a word read or written to be: new; only just known; successfully problem-solved; easily produced, but easily thrown; well known (recognized in most contexts); and known in many variant forms" (from *Change Over Time in Children's Literacy Learning*, by Marie Clay, page 123).

Once children are able to recognize high-frequency words, they should be able to use them to solve new words (e.g., *the* to *then*; *is* to *in*; *an* to *and*; *an* to *man*).

FIGURE 5.7 Word Bag: Children develop a collection of high-frequency words throughout their time in *LLI* and store them in plastic bags.

In most of the lessons that feature high-frequency words, you'll use the following routine:

1. Show children the word (using chart paper, magnetic letters, or a whiteboard) and read it while running your pointer finger under it, left to right. Use the word in a sentence.
2. Have children locate the word in the new book they are reading (or rereading).
3. Have children notice and talk about an important feature of the word that may help them learn it (e.g., silent letter, spelling pattern, digraph).
4. Have children make the word with magnetic letters several times, each time reading the word and checking the sound sequence by running their pointer finger under it, left to right.
5. End by asking children to put the word into word bag.

If you find that children are not acquiring words quickly and the word bags are filling up, take inventory on the words that seem to be very difficult. Stop adding words for a while and use a variety of methods to help children learn harder words. For example, children can:

1. Make the word with magnetic letters using a model. Then, make it without a model and use the model to check. Then make it, scramble the letters, and make it again three times. Each time check the word by running a finger under it and/or checking with a model.
2. Write the word quickly in all four corners of a page of *My Writing Book*.
3. Write it, cover it, check it, and write it again.
4. Make the word three ways—write it, make it with magnetic letters, and make it with letters from the online resources.
5. Locate the word several times in a book, attempting to "find it quickly" and "find it again."

Use these methods until you can "retire" the word because children can read it quickly when going through the words in their word bags.

PRACTICING HIGH-FREQUENCY WORDS

You'll also use spare moments to let children practice their growing control of high-frequency words. Here are a few suggestions, and you will undoubtedly come up with more.

1. Have children turn over the words one at a time, read each word, and place it in one of two piles: one for words they know and another for words they are learning. Next, have each child choose a word that he or she is learning, read it, make it with magnetic letters, and, if time allows, write it.

2. Have children lay out their words, faceup, in front of them. Say, "Find a word that starts with the letter *a*." You can use any other word feature, such as a phonogram, consonant cluster, vowel, or ending sound. Children then find the word, read it, and put it away in their word bags.

3. Have children lay out their words, facedown, and then turn over a word and read it, leaving it faceup. If they do not know the word, they turn it facedown again. The children continue (with help, if needed) until all words are faceup.

4 Have two children lay out their words, faceup, in front of them. One child reads through the words from a stack while the other two find those words in their own bags and place them in a pile, one by one. They continue until all the words are in piles.

5. Children each choose a word, make it with magnetic letters, read the word to check it by running a finger under it, and then check it, letter by letter, against the word they chose. If time allows, you can then have children write the word, read it, and check it letter by letter.

6. Children each choose a word and look at it carefully. Then, without looking at the word, they attempt to make it with magnetic letters or to write. Finally, they check the word against the model and make corrections if needed.

7. Children lay out their words, faceup, and find two words that are connected in some way. They take turns showing the two words to the other children and asking them to guess how the words are connected (e.g., same first letter, same number of letters, same ending sound).

WRITING HIGH-FREQUENCY WORDS

It's important for children to learn to write high-frequency words quickly and easily. When you want them to learn a word, have them write it fast several times in their writing books until they can write it without stopping. (See Figure 5.9.)

Working with Words in Text

It is beneficial for children to use their eyes to locate specific words in a text. The real challenge to the beginning reader is not to memorize a word in isolation but to read it within continuous text while keeping the meaning in mind. Locating words will help to develop this ability because it will familiarize children with the visual searching needed to recognize the word by its features. Children can locate *known* or *unknown* words. Locating known words helps them to recognize the word rapidly and without a great deal of effort while reading. Locating unknown words helps them think

FIGURE 5.8 Word Cards: A variety of games and activities provide students regular practice with new words.

FIGURE 5.9 Learning to write high-frequency words quickly is as important as being able to read them.

FIGURE 5.10 Using the pointer finger to locate a high-frequency word.

about and predict the beginning letter and remember other visual details about a word. Some routines for locating a word are:

1. Suggested language when the children know some beginning sounds: "What letter would you expect to see at the beginning of *but?*" [Children respond.] "Find it, run your finger under it, and say it."

2. Suggested language when children are recognizing high-frequency words: "You know the word *the*. Think how it looks." (Show a model on the whiteboard if needed.) "Find *the* on this page and put your finger under it." [Children respond.] "Turn the page and find *the* on the next page and put your finger under it." (Notice how quickly children can locate the word.)

Introducing New Words to Learn

As you help children learn new words, use some of the following teaching suggestions:

❑ Use language that makes it clear you are talking about a *word* (not a letter): "This word is [word]." (Some children confuse letters and words and may be focusing on only a *part*.)

❑ Encourage children to look at the beginning of the word and show them what that means.

❑ Read the word as you run your finger under it, left to right.

❑ Ask children to look closely at the word and say what they notice at the beginning.

❑ Ask children to look at the word and then read it as they run a finger under it, left to right.

❑ Use another word to help children remember a new word: *an, and; the, then.*

❑ Help children notice the first letter and then look across the word left to right to notice more.

❑ Give children magnetic letters in order to build the word left to right.

❑ Using magnetic letters, have children break a word by pulling down the first letter and then the rest of the letters. Then have them put it together again.

Instructional Procedures for Writing About Reading

There is a strong relationship between reading and writing. When young children write about reading in a way that is meaningful to them, they select, organize, and integrate information. When writing a message, the language is slowed down so children can pay closer attention to letters, sounds, words, and punctuation. Through writing, young children can learn a great deal about how print works. Children will have numerous opportunities to compose and construct sentences about their reading in the even-numbered lessons. Your goal is to help them develop early writing strategies. (See *Prompting Guide, Part 1; When Readers Struggle: Teaching That Works, A–N*, Chapter 13, "Extending Reading Power: Writing to Read"; and *The Literacy Continuum*, Writing, Kindergarten Goals.)

In reading, the leveled texts create a gradient of difficulty that helps the teacher determine what needs to be learned next. In writing, it is the teacher's responsibility to create that gradient. There is suggested language in each lesson, but it will be your observations of children during reading, writing, and word work that should determine what children can control independently in writing, what they can do with your support and what that support will look like. For example, you might help children use a blank page from *My Writing Book* (see page 12) to:

❑ practice a newly introduced high-frequency word

❑ hear and record easy-to-hear initial consonants

❑ leave spaces between words

❑ gain control of letter formation, using the Verbal Path

❑ contribute end punctuation

Three Kinds of Writing in *Leveled Literacy Intervention* Lessons		
Interactive Writing	You and the children compose a message together. ❑ Together, write the message in large print on a chart that everyone can see. ❑ Engage in conversation as you compose and write the message together. ❑ Use *Prompting Guide, Part 1* to support early writing strategies and letter formation and to help the children construct a text in conventional form. ❑ Have children take over the writing at particular points that have instructional value. For example, ask a child to contribute the writing of a letter or word, reread the message, or revisit the text for letter or word study. ❑ Provide a typed copy for children to glue in their writing books and illustrate. Or, write the sentences on sentence strips to cut up and have children assemble and glue on paper.	Interactive writing engages children in aspects of the writing process in a highly supported way.
Dictated Writing	Read aloud a sentence, then reread it as children write it in their blank writing books with your support. ❑ For unknown words, engage children in word solving using sound or letter boxes (see Instructional Procedures in *LLI*, page 63) prompting them to use sound or visual analysis, or helping them think of words they know (see *Prompting Guide, Part 1*). Alternatively, write words on a whiteboard for children to check or copy. ❑ Use the Verbal Path (see Verbal Path for Letter Formation, page 86) and *Prompting Guide, Part 1* to support letter formation. ❑ Have children reread their sentences when finished and draw a picture. ❑ Have children highlight words or word parts.	Children learn how to go from oral to written language. They experience word solving within a meaningful sentence. They reread and check their work.
Independent Writing	The children compose a written text independently. ❑ The text may be a list, a message or sentence, labels for pictures, or any other type of writing. ❑ Provide support as needed for children to write in conventional form for the purpose of rereading. ❑ Use the *Prompting Guide, Part 1* to support the construction of the message and to support early writing strategies.	Children develop independent control of early writing strategies. They learn to represent ideas in different ways. They learn to self-monitor (check on themselves) in writing.

FIGURE 5.11 Three Kinds of Writing About Reading in *LLI* Lessons

FIGURE 5.12 The teacher shares the pen during interactive writing.

As children learn more about how words work you might help them:

- ❑ write simple words with easy-to-hear sound sequences, using sound boxes
- ❑ write words by connecting them to known words (*can* and *ran*)
- ❑ work on a simple two-syllable word by clapping syllables and working on each separately
- ❑ use the practice page to try a word and check it before putting the word in their sentence

In *LLI Green* lessons, there are three instructional routines for Writing About Reading—Interactive Writing, Dictated Writing, and Independent Writing (see Figure 5.11 on pp. 73). Each routine is described below.

INTERACTIVE WRITING

In interactive writing, you talk with children about a book and compose a simple response to the reading on a chart. The value of interactive writing is that it engages children in every aspect of the writing about reading process in a highly supportive way.

1. You and the children compose and write the response in one or two sentences.
2. Share your pen with children at selected points and invite them to contribute what they are able, (e.g., high-frequency words, some letters, end punctuation) as you quickly write the rest. When necessary, you can write a well-known word to keep the writing moving quickly.
3. Children reread the sentence several times to determine what word will be needed next and to monitor what has been written for making sense and looking right. Children should illustrate the sentences if time allows.
4. The writing that has been produced becomes a resource for rereading. You might type the writing so children can glue it into *My Writing Book* or you may write one or two sentences on a strip of oak tag (or other stiff paper) for children to cut up, reassemble, and glue into *My Writing Book*.

DICTATED WRITING

In dictated writing, you talk with children about an aspect of the book and then dictate one or two sentences for them to write. The value of dictated writing is that it gives children an opportunity to experience a well-constructed response with a clear focus.

1. Children write the dictated sentences with your support in *My Writing Book*. When dictating, give children the whole sentence first, then repeat it word by word, keeping an eye on how children are writing and steering them toward conventional spellings.
2. Some of the words will be known. For unknown words, help children engage in word solving, using word parts and letter sequences. Draw sound boxes for simple words with predictable letter-sound relationships (see Hear, Say, and Write: Sound and Letter Boxes, page 68–69). For particularly challenging words, write the words on a whiteboard for children to copy.
3. Children read their writing to be sure it makes sense and looks right.
4. Revisit the dictated sentences for a particular teaching point if time allows.

FIGURE 5.13 Children listen as teacher reads a sentence for them to write.

INDEPENDENT WRITING

In Independent Writing, you talk with children about a book as they compose one or two sentences in *My Writing Book*. The value of independent writing is that children begin to develop control over all aspects of composition. Independent Writing is also highly engaging and motivating because the children are working with their own personal ideas and language.

1. Children compose their responses. You may need to help some children shape or extend the language through conversation, modeling interesting vocabulary and conventional language structures.
2. Children write their responses in *My Writing Book* with your support.
3. Some of the words may be known. For unknown words, help children engage in word solving, using word parts and letter sequences. Draw sound boxes for simple words with predictable letter-sound relationships (see Hear, Say, and Write: Sound and Letter Boxes, page 68–69). For particularly challenging words, write the words on a whiteboard for children to copy.
4. Children read their writing to be sure it makes sense and looks right.
5. Children reread their writing to you or the group.
6. Children illustrate their sentences if time allows

Using *The Literacy Continuum* to Guide Instruction

See pages 95–96 for an overview of *The Literacy Continuum* pages that are included at the end of each level in the *Lesson Guide*. The Continuum lists specific behaviors and understandings that are required for students to read successfully at the specific level. The behaviors and understandings are cumulative across the levels. They include important competencies students need to think within, beyond, and about texts. In other words, the reader is taking on a variety of new demands as the texts grow more challenging. The reader also will be applying the same strategic actions but in more sophisticated ways to more complex texts. For example, a student reading at level G and successfully meeting the demands of the text is also able to meet the demands of texts at levels E and F. The understandings include much more than simply reading the words accurately. This section also includes additional suggestions for word work. If your students have good control of the principles in the Phonics/Word Study part of the lessons, you might substitute one of the options. Or, you may want to offer some of the suggestions to the classroom teacher.

All *LLI* lessons are designed to help you accomplish the goals listed in *The Literacy Continuum* for the level. Your goal is to help readers meet the demands of successive levels of text, and in the process, expand their systems of strategic actions. Refer regularly to this section to monitor student progress and guide your teaching.

The following suggestions may help you teach the lessons more effectively:

- ❑ Read each new book carefully with *The Literacy Continuum* goals in mind. Think about what your students can do and then find behaviors and understandings that they control, partially control, or do not yet control.

- ❑ Read the introduction to the text and teaching points for the lesson, keeping in mind the processing needs of your students. Make any adjustments you think are necessary to meet the needs of your particular students.

- ❑ Look at the Phonics/Word Study part of the lesson and the suggestions for word work at that level in *The Literacy Continuum*. Make any adjustments you think are necessary to meet the needs of your particular students.

- ❑ As you near the end of a series of 28 standard lessons, look at *The Literacy Continuum* to see what your students now control and what they

FIGURE 5.14 Through independent writing children begin to develop control over all aspects of composition.

need to learn to successfully process texts easily at this level. If most are in place, move to the next level.

❑ As students grow more proficient and reading becomes easy at the level, look at the behaviors and understandings for the next-higher level. Because the reading process is built by applying the same set of complex strategies to increasingly more difficult texts, you'll find many of the same strategies that you've been teaching for. At each level, you will find new understandings and more complex versions of the same understandings.

▶ Using *Prompting Guide, Part 1* in *LLI* Lessons

The *Fountas & Pinnell Prompting Guide, Part 1* provides precise language for you to use to support children as they read and write.

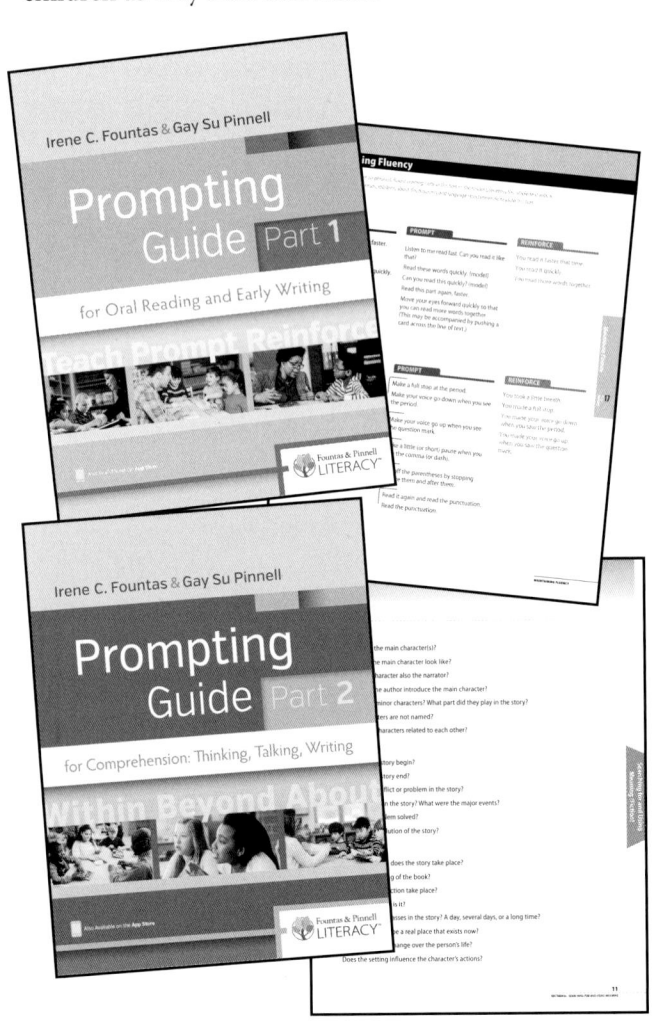

FIGURE 5.15 *Prompting Guides, Part 1* and *Part 2* sample pages

The first section provides language to teach early reading behaviors and support systems of strategic actions as evidenced in oral reading. There are three columns, one with teaching language, a second with language for prompting readers to engage problem-solving actions you have taught, and a third for reinforcing effective behaviors that are newly emerging.

The second section provides language for supporting early writing behaviors; letter formation; and composing and constructing words in interactive, independent, and dictated writing.

▶ Using *Prompting Guide, Part 2* in *LLI* Lessons

The *Fountas & Pinnell Prompting Guide, Part 2* is for teaching readers to focus or expand their thinking. These prompts are designed to deepen understanding when children are discussing and revisiting the text. Use the prompts to engage children in expanding their thinking about the meaning of the text.

Prompting Guides, Part 1 and *Part 2*, are also available in Spanish and as eBooks from Apple iTunes.

▶ Working with Series Books in *LLI* Lessons

One of the unique features of *LLI* is the large collection of series books. Across the *LLI* systems, we have created a variety of series.

Some of the advantages of series books are:

❑ Children become interested in the topics, characters, or plots so that they are motivated to read more.

❑ Children experience the satisfaction of bringing a great deal of background knowledge to reading.

❑ Readers get to know characters so that they are better able to talk about their characteristics and infer their feelings and motivations.

❑ Children have the experience of reading connected text over time.

❑ Readers learn the process of making many connections between texts—typical situations, problems, settings, character traits, style of writing and illustrations.

Appendix B presents the entire range of series books in the *Orange, Green,* and *Blue LLI Systems* because you may be using more than one system in your school. You can always borrow from one system to use in another to develop interest in a series. If you do not have all three systems, take opportunities to connect the series books in the system you do have.

Since *LLI* is designed for flexible use, you may start your groups at any level appropriate to their current abilities. That means children may be reading a fiction series book without having read the other titles in the series. That is not a problem because every text stands alone; however, you may want to create chances for children to read and enjoy the easier books (on lower levels) in a series by adding them to the rereading segment or letting children take them to the classroom for independent reading.

When children have read one or more of the books in a series, it is easy for them to form expectations when they are introduced to a new book in the same series. The following are some suggestions for using series books:

- In the introduction to a text, make explicit connections between books by holding up other books and remind children about the characters and events.
- For nonfiction texts, remind children of the ways information is usually presented in the whole series. In this way, you set expectations for the way information is organized in the genre.
- Substitute previously read books in a series for the Rereading portion of the lesson so the texts are fresh in children's minds. Or, suggest they take the other books back to the classroom for independent reading.
- Take a day to reread all the books in a series and talk about the characters in fiction or the way nonfiction texts are organized. Do some writing about the series. Write about a character or create another story in the series. Use nonfiction series as a model for children to write about something they know.
- When working in one collection, borrow series books from other collections. Have children use them for extra reading in the classroom.
- As children become more advanced, have them try writing their own stories about a character. Or, create a group story using interactive writing.

Series books provide a strong scaffold for reading comprehension. Children have the experience of continuing meaningful reading over a longer period of time and extend their ability to remember important elements of texts.

▶ Relationship Between Teacher Support and Child Control in *LLI*

As a teacher, you will always vary the level of support you provide for children in processing and understanding texts. When children encounter a challenging new text (especially at a new level), for example, high teacher support is required. For less-challenging texts, teacher support may still be needed but at a lower level. As children develop more control of important behaviors and understandings, teaching shifts to give the learner more control of the task. This gradual release of responsibility takes place across the components of the *LLI* lesson.

In the chart in Figure 5.16 (pages 78–79), we have summarized key points for you to think about as you introduce the text and as the children read and discuss it, so you can vary your teaching decisions in relationship to the reader's competencies at each level. You can learn more important information about making effective teaching decisions in *When Readers Struggle: Teaching That Works, Levels A–N*.

▶ Instructional Tools for *LLI*

In this section we describe, in alphabetical order, tools you will use in *LLI* lessons to enrich your instruction and make it more powerful.

Many of the tools descibed here can be found in the *LLI Green Ready Resources*. Others are available for download at resources.fountasandpinnell.com.

You can find more information on these tools in *When Readers Struggle: Teaching That Works, A–N*, Chapter 10, "Learning About Print: Early Reading Behaviors" and Chapter 12, "Using Words: How to Build a Repertoire."

Levels of Teacher Support in *LLI*

Introducing the Text

High Support	Moderate Support	Low Support
The teacher: ❏ provides a rich introduction so children can access the whole text as independently as possible. ❏ talks about the meaning of the whole text, inviting children to talk about the pictures and make predictions, connections, and inferences about what they see. ❏ provides opportunities for children to hear the languages structures and vocabulary. ❏ invites children to rehearse language and vocabulary with her. ❏ draws children's attention to important words and text layout.	*The teacher:* ❏ supports children's ability to hear and use new vocabulary and language structures. ❏ discusses the meaning of the whole text. She may leave some information for children to discover during the reading. ❏ does not attend to every page in the book. ❏ encourages children to contribute to the introduction. They may bring background knowledge to the topic/story or predict what might happen.	*The teacher still:* ❏ draws children's attention to new and challenging vocabulary, language structures, or text features on a few pages of the book. ❏ encourages children, through conversation, to contribute to the introduction and to construct meaning, but leaves more information for children to discover during the reading.

Reading the Text

High Support	Moderate Support	Low Support
The teacher: The teacher samples the oral reading closely to observe children's ability to use early reading behaviors. She interacts briefly to help support strategic actions during the reading. The teaching is direct and specific. For example: ❏ *Start here, and read this way.* [reading left to right/return sweep] ❏ *Put your finger under each word.* [establishing voice-print match] ❏ *You have too many words. Go back and make it match.* [monitor voice-print match]	*The teacher:* The teacher samples the oral reading to observe children's ability to search for and use a variety of sources of information, monitor and self-correct errors, maintain fluency, and adjust reading to solve problems. She interacts during the reading if children need help solving a problem. So as not to interrupt the flow of the story, the prompts quickly encourage children to use what they know. ❏ *Can you think about what would make sense?* [searching for meaning] ❏ *Do you know a word that starts like that?* [searching for visual information]	*The teacher still:* The teacher may sample the oral reading behaviors of one or two children. She does not interrupt the children's processing, and intervenes only when children are muddled and can't move forward. ❏ *Use your finger to break the word.* [word parts] ❏ *Read from the beginning and try it again.* [searching for multiple sources of information] She may choose one or two teaching points after the reading to reinforce effective reading behaviors and expand children's current problem-solving repertoire.

FIGURE 5.16 The level of support you provide diminishes as children become more competent at each level.

Levels of Teacher Support in *LLI*, continued

Reading the Text, *cont.*

High Support	Moderate Support	Low Support
	After the reading, she may attend to other errors or reinforce effective problem solving. ❑ *Something wasn't quite right. See if you can fix it.* [self-correcting] ❑ *You made it sound like the character was talking.* [maintaining fluency-intonation]	❑ *You knew something wasn't quite right, and you knew how to make it right.* [self-monitoring] ❑ *You are nearly right. Can you add the ending to make it look right?* [searching for visual information]

Discussing the Text

High Support	Moderate Support	Low Support
Early on, the teacher invites children to talk about the story. Her goal is to get children talking about the book. She models for them how to summarize the information in the book and prompts children to think beyond and about the text. The teacher helps children express their understandings using language that is clear and precise. ❑ *The writer told mostly about ____. What do you want to remember about this book?* [summarizing] ❑ *This book reminds me of ____. What does it remind you of?* [making connections] ❑ *How do you think ____ feels? Why do you think that?* [inferring]	As children become more familiar with book discussions, the teacher helps them deepen their thinking beyond and about the text. Modeling her thinking is still an important feature of the discussion. ❑ *This book was about ____. Why might learning about ____ be important?* [synthesizing] The teacher asks children asks children for evidence from the text that supports their understanding. ❑ *How did the writer make the [character, plot, setting, topic] interesting to you?* [analyzing]	Children are now very familiar with discussing texts. The teacher may still model her thinking, but she also invites children to build on one another's understandings. She prompts children to think deeply about the important ideas, messages, and inferences using precise academic language. ❑ *What information made you change your predictions?* [predicting] She invites children to analyze and critique texts. ❑ *Why do you think the writer wrote this book?* [analyzing] ❑ *What makes this a good information book?* [critiquing]

FIGURE 5.16 *cont.*

Alphabet Linking Chart

The Alphabet Linking Chart shows letter forms and simple pictures that provide a clear letter-sound link to key words. You'll use this chart in many of the early lessons and as an important classroom resource throughout the year.

The lessons call for these different versions of the Alphabet Linking Chart:

- ❑ a full-color enlarged version
- ❑ a black-and-white enlarged version
- ❑ an enlarged version with letters but no pictures for use with the Alphabet Linking Chart Picture Set
- ❑ a black-and-white student version with letters and pictures
- ❑ a black-and-white student version with letters only for use with the Alphabet Linking Chart Picture Set

When you introduce the Alphabet Linking Chart, we suggest you use the enlarged version that has letters but no pictures. You'll find this version in the *LLI Ready Resources*, or you can download it from the Online Resources and enlarge it yourself. Initially, you will hold up pictures from the Alphabet Linking Chart Picture Set (available online) and ask children to think about the beginning sound in each picture's name and to match that sound to a letter on the chart. With your help, children then glue each picture below its corresponding letter. Each day, children will read only the letters that have pictures below them. Building the chart with children in this way over several days gives them ownership because they have participated in making it.

Alternatively, you might want to introduce the chart using the enlarged black-and-white version. Instead of gluing pictures in the appropriate boxes, you can have children color them in.

Whichever chart you choose to begin with, be sure to have children either glue or color in the same pictures in their individual copies of *My ABC Book*, which you will also find in your *Ready Resources* or in the Online Resources.

After you've introduced the Alphabet Linking Chart, you can have children read it in a variety of ways. They can read:

- ❑ the whole chart in order
- ❑ just the pictures
- ❑ just the letters
- ❑ just the uppercase letters
- ❑ just the lowercase letters
- ❑ the consonants only
- ❑ the vowels only
- ❑ the chart
- ❑ every other letters
- ❑ letters as you point to them randomly

13 Consonant Clusters and Digraphs Charts *one of each for every child*

The Initial Consonant Clusters and Digraphs chart includes pictures whose names begin with two- and three-consonant blends and digraphs. The Final Consonant Clusters and Digraphs chart includes pictures whose names end with two-consonant blends and

FIGURE 5.17 Alphabet Linking Chart

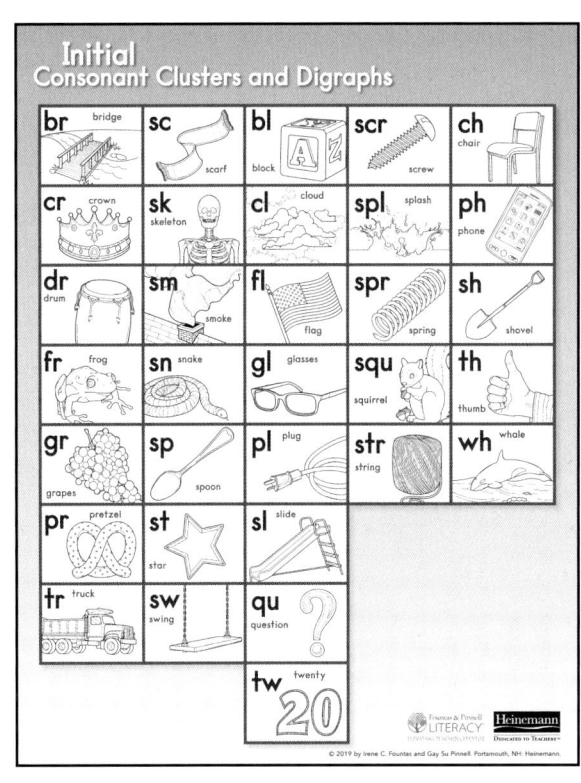

FIGURE 5.18 Initial Consonant Clusters and Digraphs

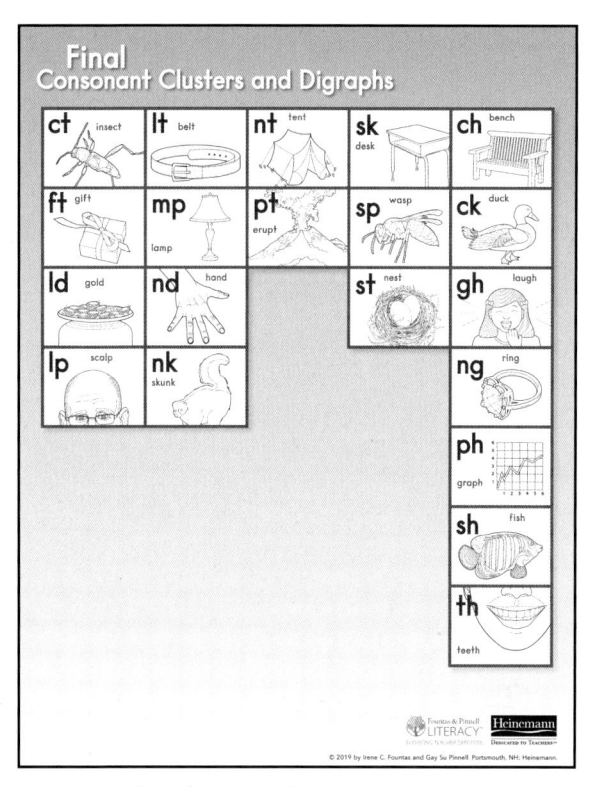

FIGURE 5.19 Final Consonant Clusters and Digraphs

digraphs. You will find a four-color, enlarged version of each chart in the Ready Resources box included with your purchase. They can also be printed from the General Resources section of the Online Resources site.

These charts are designed to help students develop quick recognition and blending of initial and final consonant clusters and digraphs. Use them for quick review or as a reference when needed in reading and writing. For quick recognition, you can have students:

- Read the blends and digraphs on the charts in order, either vertically or horizontally.
- Read randomly as you point to various blends or digraphs.
- Read every other blend or digraph.

Fold Sheets

Fold sheets, referenced in the Classroom Connection and Home/School Connection portions of the lessons, contain suggested activities for classroom and home practice. Fold sheets, which fit nicely in the take-home bags, are available for download in the Online Resources.

Letter and Word Games

Word, letter, and phonics games are a way to help children learn some very basic foundational understanding. Games are fun and interesting and require children to look carefully at words, letters, and parts of words. The *LLI Green System* includes two basic games, Lotto and Follow the Path.

LOTTO

Making the Game Lotto game boards can be printed from Online Resources. Print one game board, preferably on card stock, for each student. The players' boards should all be different from one another.

Playing the Game Give each player a game board. Place the letter, picture, or word cards and plastic chips or other markers in the middle of the table. Players take turns drawing a card and reading it out loud. Other players search their game boards for a corresponding letter, picture, or word and mark the ones that correspond. The first player to cover an entire board wins the game. The game can continue until others fill their cards.

FIGURE 5.20 Lotto game

corresponding number of spaces. If you're using cards, have each child read aloud the number drawn before moving his or her game piece.

Depending on whether you've added letters, words, or pictures to each spot on the game board, you might have students perform a certain action before moving on, such as saying the next letter in the alphabet, reading a word and saying the beginning or ending sound, looking at a picture and clapping the syllables in the word it represents, and so on.

The player who gets to the end of the path first wins the game.

Letter Minibooks

Letter Minibooks are short books focused on individual letters and sounds. They also focus on letter clusters and their relation to sounds. Letter Minibooks help children:

- ❑ develop familiarity with letters and how they look.
- ❑ practice efficient directional movements for making letters.
- ❑ learn letter names.
- ❑ practice saying a series of words beginning with the same sound several times in succession.
- ❑ build knowledge of concrete objects and their beginning letters and sounds.

Each time you introduce a new Letter Minibook you can:

1. Start by saying: "This is a book that is all about the letter [name of letter]. [Name of letter] stands for the sound, [make the sound].

FOLLOW THE PATH

In Follow the Path, players throw a die or draw a number card to move their markers along a curved path. The objective is to be the first to reach the finish line (or the end of the path).

Making the Game Download and print the game board from the Online Resources, and glue or write words, letters, or pictures into each space. Be sure to create an interesting finish box at the end (e.g., the zoo, the moon, an actual finish line).

Playing the Game Each player shakes the die and lets it fall (or selects a number card) and moves the

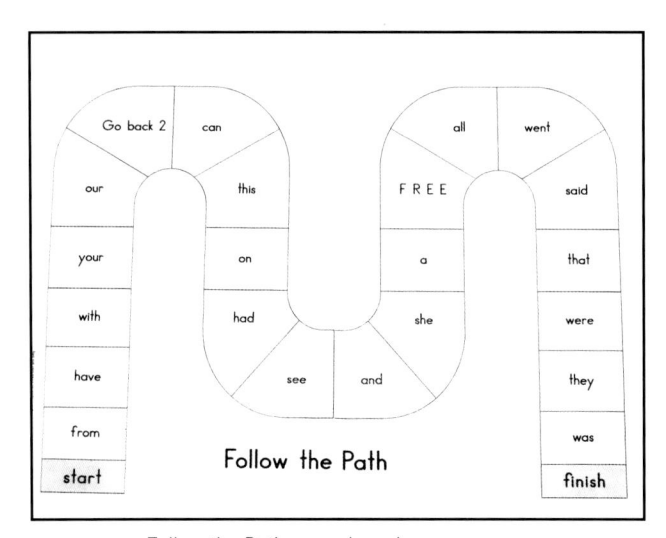

FIGURE 5.21 Follow the Path game board

FIGURE 22 Letter Minibooks

2. Ask children to trace and say the letter on the front cover of the minibook.

3. Demonstrate how to "read" each page of the Letter Minibook by saying the name of the letter and the objects.

4. Invite children to read the letter minibook when they are familiar with it.

Based on your knowledge of the letters and sounds the children know and need to know, you may vary your selection of minibooks to use.

Magnetic Letters

Magnetic letters have many benefits for young readers (see Ways to Sort and Match Letters and Twenty-Five Ways to Use Magnetic Letters in the Online Resources). Brightly colored magnetic letters are concrete, and children can manipulate them easily and notice their distinctive features. Using magnetic letters, children can:

1. Make their names. "Find the letters in your name."

2. Match letters: *a, a; t, t.* "Find letters that look the same."

3. Match uppercase and lowercase letters: *Aa, Bb.* "For each small letter, find the big letter that matches it."

4. Place letters in the order of the alphabet. "Say the alphabet and put the letters in the same order."

5. Separate the vowels from the consonants. "Put vowels on the right side and consonants on the left."

FIGURE 5.23 High-frequency words made with magnetic letters

6. Sort letters in a variety of ways: "Find the letters with long sticks and the letters with short sticks." "Find the letters with tunnels." "Find the letters with circles." "Find the letters with dots." "Find the letters with tails." "Find the letters with a slant."

7. Make a word left to right, read it with a finger (left to right), and then check it letter by letter with a printed word or a word written on a whiteboard.

8. Make a simple word (CVC or CVCe) and then write it on paper with a marker—checking the word letter by letter when finished.

9. Look at the array of letters (either all or a limited number), choose a letter, and say its name (or sound).

10. Lay out an array of letters and play Find a Letter. You say the name of a letter, and children find it and say its name quickly. You may have many of the same letter mixed in so they can "find all the *h*s."

11. Attend to visual features of letters by sorting letters into two circles drawn on paper, one with the letter *h* and the other with the letter *o*. Ask them to say how the other letters are like *h* or *o*.

12. Change the first letter of a simple word (e.g., *cat*) to make a new word.

Reading requires rapid visual discrimination of letter forms embedded in text, so it is important that letter knowledge become quick and easy. It's a good idea for children to begin activities with magnetic letters by arranging the letters you give them across the top (or bottom, if you prefer) of a whiteboard. Then, as they identify letters needed to make or change words, they can pull down each one, saying its name and sound if known. Some *LLI* lessons contain sorting activities but you can supplement these with the activities in "Twenty-Five Ways to Use Magnetic Letters."

My ABC Book

In the *LLI Orange* and *Green Systems,* children use *My ABC Book* to help them develop their knowledge of the whole alphabet, upper- and lowercase letters, features of letters, and letter-sound relationships. (You'll find copies in the *LLI Green Ready Resources,* or you can print these books from Online Resources. Consider enlarging a copy and mounting it on card stock to make a lap book.)

FIGURE 5.24 *My ABC Book*

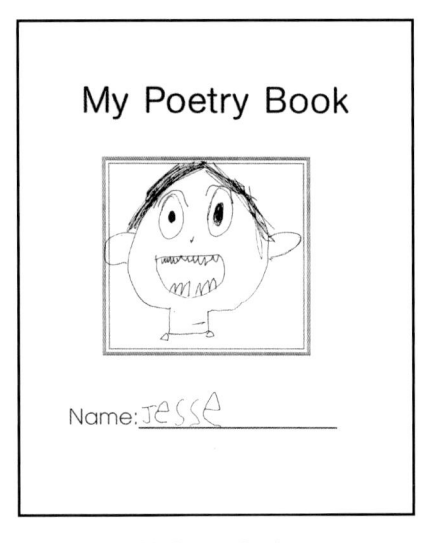

FIGURE 5.25 *My Poetry Book*

My ABC Book has the upper- and lowercase letter on each page, along with a key word and picture. The pages for vowels show pictures for words that have both short and long sounds. *My ABC Book* is built systematically across several lessons. Children can:

- ❑ Read it from beginning to end, saying letters and words under key pictures.
- ❑ Use it in conjunction with the Alphabet Linking Chart.
- ❑ Read only the letters.
- ❑ Read only the words under the key pictures.
- ❑ Search for a particular page and letter.
- ❑ Write a new word on the appropriate page.
- ❑ Draw more pictures of things that begin with the letter on a page.

My Poetry Book

This useful resource contains all of the poems used in lessons for the *Green System*. Poems are introduced gradually as indicated in lessons, so you will want to keep the books with all of the materials for a particular group. Hand them out to children when you want them to reread poems or read a new poem.

You will find multiple copies of *My Poetry Book* in your *LLI Green Ready Resources*. Additionally, you can download and print copies from the Online Resources, and then staple each on one side. In addition to the copies of *My Poetry Book*, your *Ready Resources* box also contains enlarged versions of poems used in the lessons. Children will read from the enlarged versions in a shared way. Or, as you read the poems, children can turn to the right page in *My Poetry Book* to read along. At the the conclusion of *LLI* lessons, children can take the book home to keep and read. Children can use *My Poetry Book* to:

- ❑ reread favorite poems;
- ❑ take back to the classroom to read;
- ❑ draw pictures to go with the poems;
- ❑ highlight words or word parts;
- ❑ notice rhyming words and highlight them; and
- ❑ notice word endings and highlight them.

My Writing Book

Each child in *LLI* gets a copy of a writing book, called *My Writing Book*. Children can personalize their copies by drawing a picture of themselves in the box on the cover. Use the right-hand pages for independent or dictated writing, starting a new page for each activity. Use the left-hand pages for children to practice letters or for sound or letter box work. You may also have children do some word writing in the Phonics/Word Work part of the lesson. The writing book is also used for children to glue and illustrate cut-apart sentences. All writing in the writing book is in conventional spelling to support reading.

You'll find copies of *My Writing Book* in your *Ready Resources* and also in the Online Resources for downloading and printing.

FIGURE 5.26 *My Writing Book*

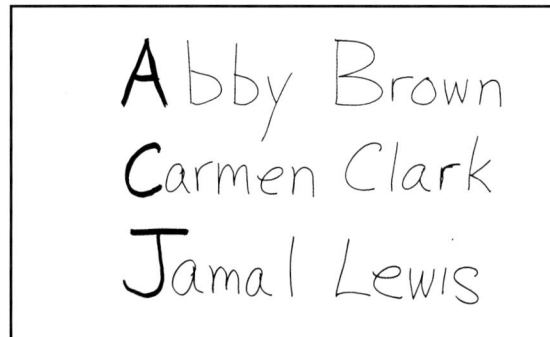

FIGURE 5.27 Name Chart

FIGURE 5.28 Name Folder and Puzzle

Name Chart

The name chart, which you will make yourself on chart paper, is a useful tool for helping children learn about letters, sounds, and words. For each group you teach, you'll use the name chart to list their names, usually in alphabetical order by the first letter. Some teachers write the first letter of each name in red and the rest of the name in black. The print should be clear, and names should not be jammed together. You'll use the name chart as a resource in phonics and letter/word work.

Name Puzzle

Name puzzles will help children begin to learn about letters, using their own names. By putting together their names, children learn how to look at letters and notice their distinguishing features and orientation. They learn that words are made up of letters and that the order of letters is always the same. Here are some suggestions for making and using name puzzles:

1. Have children cut up a set of letters (from Online Resources) and use the letters to form their names. They can store the letters in an envelope glued into their folders. Their folders should have their names already printed on them.

2. Arrange children in a circle and have them place their folders open flat in front of them, so you can check their work.

3. Emphasize that each letter should look the same as the letters written on the folder.

4. Using a chopstick or other small pointer, point to each letter, demonstrating how to check letter by letter and saying the letters as you go.

5. Show children how to mix up the letters so they can form the name again.

6. Be sure all the children have formed their names at least once.

Oral Games

Quick oral games like those described below can be effective tools for helping children learn to listen for and identify individual syllables and phonemes, words in sentences, and onsets and rimes. You'll want to limit the games to a minute or two each.

BLENDING

Have children blend sounds, word parts, or syllables. For example, you say *c-a-t*, and they say *cat*. Children can also learn how to blend the onset with the rime (e.g., *c-at, cat*) or syllables (e.g., *ba/na/na, banana*).

SEGMENTING

Have the children segment sounds in words. For example, you say *cat* or show the picture of a cat and they say *c-a-t*. Children can also learn how to segment *dog* to *d-og* and *cat* to *c-at*.

MANIPULATING PHONEMES

Have children add sounds to the beginning or end of words or change a sound in a word (e.g., *and, band; an, ant; look, took*).

Sentence Strips

You can make sentence strips out of card stock or any kind of sturdy paper. Cut them apart word by word, mix them up, and have children put them together and reread them. They can then glue the words in *My Writing Book* and illustrate them. Or, you can put the cut-up words in envelopes and children can take them back to the classroom or home to glue on paper for more practice.

Lap Books

In shared reading, you point under each word in large-print text as you read it or as children read with you. When children have strong voice-print match, you can put the pointer at the beginning of each line. Alternatively, in Getting Started Lessons children can point to the text in their small books and read with you as you point to the words in the lap book. Bear in mind, however, that children will need to learn to read at their own rate without relying on the support others. After ten Getting Started Lessons, they will be reading independently after a supportive introduction.

Table Charts

For shared reading of poetry and other texts, as well as the Phonics/Word Work part of the *LLI* lesson, you may want to make a chart to work on and/or refer to over several days. You may find it useful to keep these charts handy all the time. They do not need to be as large as you would use for an entire class since you will be working with a small group of three children, but the print should be large enough for the group to see across the table. Here are several alternatives:

- ❑ Make the charts on chart paper that you can fold once and keep in the folder for that group of children. Clip the charts to the top of an easel.
- ❑ Make the charts on oversized card stock and join them with two rings at the top. If you have a tabletop easel, you can use it to prop up the chart or you can hang it from a chart rack or use a standing easel.
- ❑ Purchase a large, unlined sketch pad for each group, or share one by creating multiple sections with tabs. Make your charts right on the pages. Draw columns and write words and glue pictures and word cards in the correct columns. Use tabs to identify phonograms or consonant clusters quickly.

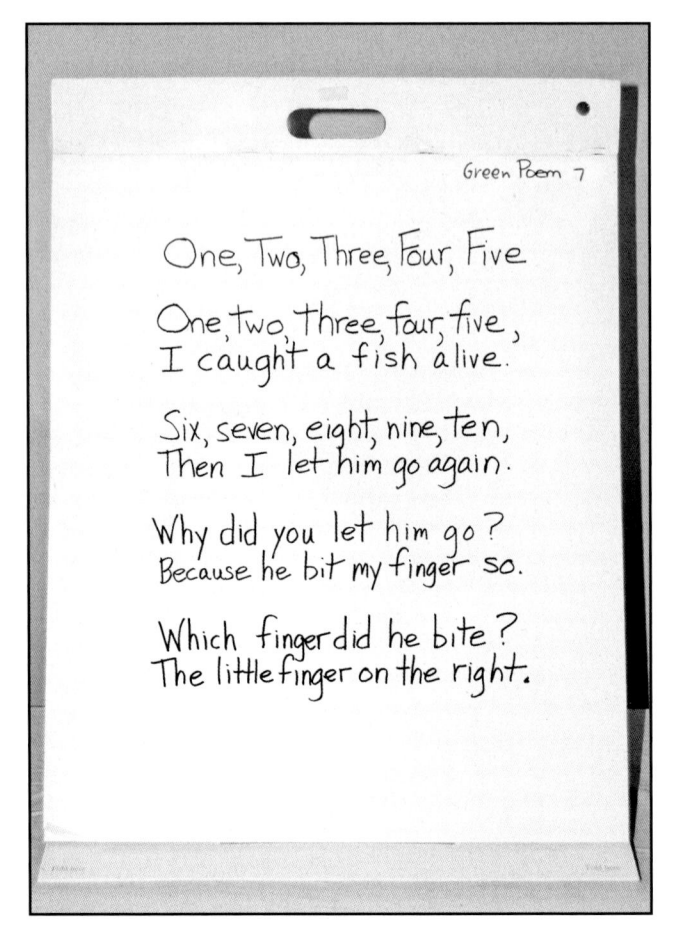

FIGURE 5.29 Table Chart with Poem

Resist the temptation to prepare these charts in advance, unless it is recommended in the lesson. Phonics or word charts are far more powerful if the children participate in their construction and have a feeling of ownership. When you no longer need a chart, you may send it home with one of the children (taking turns) to share with a family member.

Verbal Path for Letter Formation

The Verbal Path is designed to help children get their hands moving the right way to form letters. You can print the Verbal Path directions from the Online Resources. The goal is for the motor routines to become automatic and unconscious without the support of words. Try having children practice a group of letters that are formed similarly before moving to another group (e.g., *a* and *c, d* and *g, o* and *q*).

Verbal Path for the Formation of Letters

Sometimes it helps children to say aloud the directions for "making" a letter. This "verbal path" helps them to understand the directional movement that is essential. In addition, it gives the teacher and child a language to talk through the letter and its features. Here, we suggest language for creating a verbal path to the distinctive features of letters.

Lowercase Letter Formation

Letter	Path	Letter	Path
a	pull back, around, up, and down	n	pull down, up, over, and down
b	pull down, up, around	o	pull back and around
c	pull back and around	p	pull down, up, and around
d	pull back, around, up, and down	q	pull back, around, up, and down
e	pull across, back, and around	r	pull down, up, and over
f	pull back, down, and cross	s	pull back, in, around, and back around
g	pull back, around, up, down, and under	t	pull down and cross
h	pull down, up, over, and down	u	pull down, around, up and down
i	pull down, dot	v	slant down, up
j	pull down, curve around, dot	w	slant down, up, down, up
k	pull down, pull in, pull out	x	slant down, slant down
l	pull down	y	slant in, slant and down
m	pull down, up, over, down and up, over and down	z	across, slant down, across

Uppercase Letter Formation

Letter	Path	Letter	Path
A	slant down, slant down, across	N	pull down, slant down, pull up
B	pull down, up, around and in, back and around	O	pull back and around
C	pull back and around	P	pull down, up, and around
D	pull down, up, around	Q	pull back and around and cross
E	pull down, across, across, and across	R	pull down, up, around, in, and slant down
F	pull down, across, across	S	pull back, in, around, down, and back around
G	pull back, around, across	T	pull down, across
H	pull down, pull down, across	U	pull down, around, up, and down
I	pull down, across, across	V	slant down, slant up
J	pull down, curve around, across	W	slant down up, down up
K	pull down, slant in, slant out	X	slant down, slant down
L	pull down, across	Y	slant in, slant, and down
M	pull down, slant down, slant down, pull down	Z	across, slant down, across

FIGURE 5.30 Verbal Path for Letter Formation

section 6

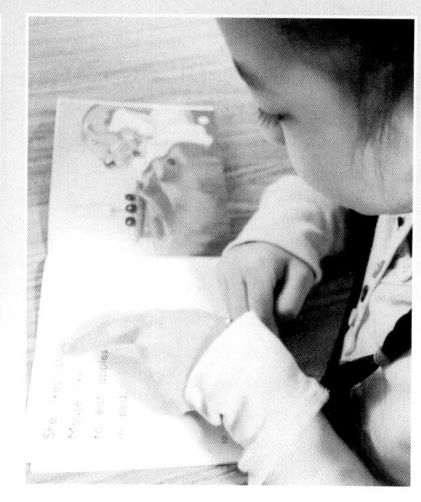

Assessment and Record Keeping in the *LLI System*

▶ Continuous Assessment

Assessment is the act of collecting information or data about the learners you teach. When you conduct the initial assessment of your children at the beginning of the intervention using the *Fountas & Pinnell Benchmark Assessment System* or some other benchmark system, you collect important information about each child's reading level, comprehension, fluency, and processing strategies. This information is critical for beginning instruction at an appropriate level and with appropriate emphases, but children will change rapidly.

Throughout *LLI*, you will collect even more valuable information from your informal observations of children as they read and write during the daily lessons. With a group size of three, you will also take a reading record on each child approximately every six days. This standardized assessment procedure will capture the reading behaviors the reader controls independently. Over time, you can use these reading records to monitor progress. This section of the *System Guide* provides suggestions, examples, and forms for collecting, analyzing, and organizing the formal and informal data that you will need to guide your instruction.

What follows is a brief overview of the systematized process for coding, scoring, and analyzing reading behaviors. The *LLI Green System* Tutorial Video provides in-depth information and as much practice as you need to become skilled in all aspects of using reading records and linking the information to instruction. Use the video to work at your own pace.

The professional book *When Readers Struggle: Teaching That Works, A–N* provides detailed descriptions of reading behaviors as well as numerous examples for analysis. In these resources, you will learn what each type of behavior tells about the "in-the-head" systems the child is likely using or neglecting as she processes a text. This analysis will help you determine the emphasis for your teaching. You will also find much helpful information in *Guided Reading: Responsive Teaching Across the Grades*.

▶ Administering the Reading Record Using the Recording Form

A reading record is a systematic tool used to code, score, and analyze a child's precise reading behaviors. By using a standardized system to gain an objective assessment of the child's reading *without* your teaching support you learn what children can do independently. (See Figure 6.1 for a completed reading record using the Recording Form.)

We have provided a Recording Form for each instructional-level book read in the system. As described in Section 4 of this guide, an assessment is taken in the even-numbered lessons, on the instructional-level book read in the previous lesson. (These forms can be printed from the Online Resources or, if you have purchased the *Fountas & Pinnell LLI Reading Record App*, you can take the reading record on your iPad and sync your data directly to the *LLI Online Data Management System*.) During the assessment, listen to one child read, code

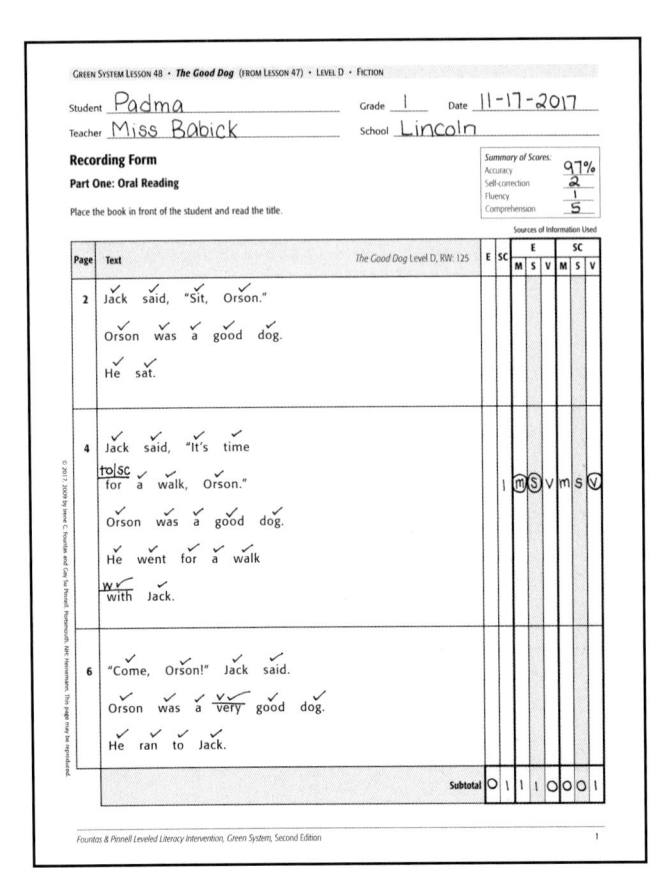

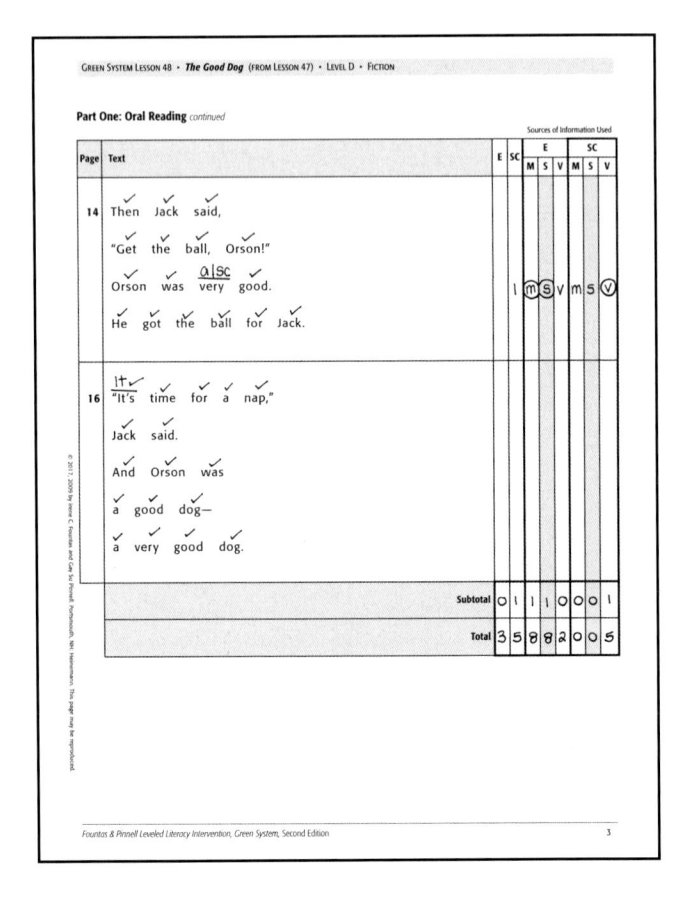

FIGURE 6.1 Completed Reading Record Using the Recording Form

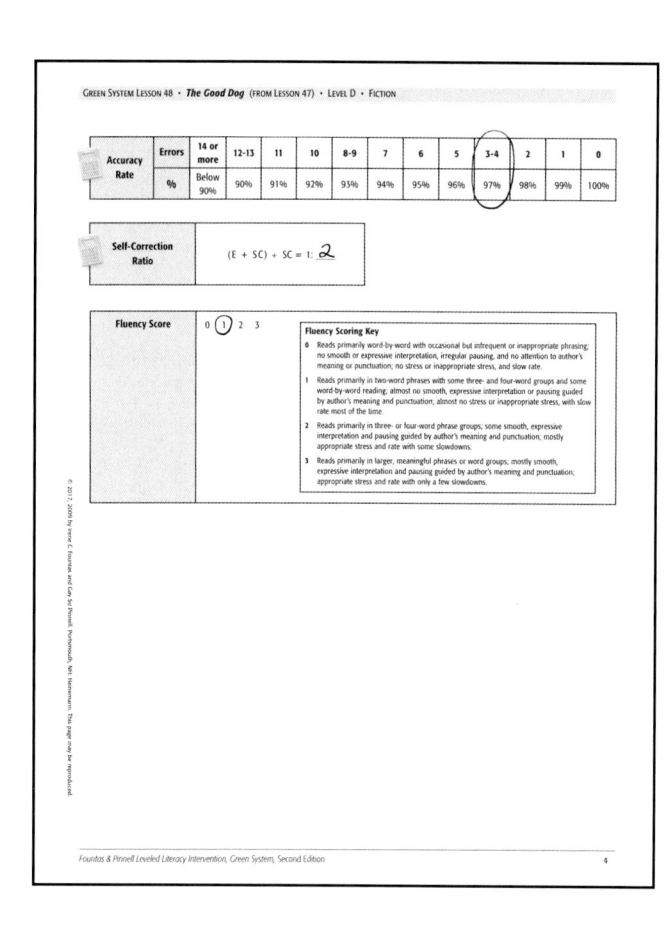

FIGURE 6.1 Cont.

the reading behavior, give a score for fluency, have a brief comprehension conversation, and make a teaching point that you think will be most helpful to the reader. While you do this, the other children in the group are quietly (or, at later levels, silently) rereading previously read books.

Begin by reading the book title and the introduction provided on the Recording Form to the child and ask her to begin reading the book orally. While you are coding the child's reading behavior, observe what she can do without your support. Do not help or interfere in any way, verbally or nonverbally, except to say "You try it" if she appeals for help or give a "told" if she attempts something and/or will not move on. Wait no more than three seconds before you give a "told" so as to prevent the meaning to be lost. A "told" is counted as an error.

▶ Oral Reading

Coding Reading Behaviors on a Recording Form

As a child reads, observe the precise behaviors and mark on the typed text using the coding system shown in Figure 6.2. Be sure to use the standardized coding system so your coding can be read by others and the information is consistent. Refer to the Tutorial Video for extra support.

Starting at level C, as you code the reading record, pay attention to how a child's reading sounds. Make quick notes during the reading. Immediately after a child finishes reading orally, rate his or her fluency by circling the appropriate score on the fluency rubric (see Figure 6.3). Consider the phrasing, intonation, pausing, stress, and reading rate as well as the integration of all dimensions of fluent processing.

Assessing Fluency

We have designed a four-point holistic rubric that you may want to use to keep a record of your students' growth as fluent readers (see Figure 6.3). Listen carefully to how the reading sounds. You can use the rubric any time you sample oral reading from a student and particularly when you take a running record.

As you use the rubric, consider each dimension of fluency as well as the student's overall integration of

Coding and Scoring Errors At-A-Glance

Behavior	What Reader Does	How to Code	Example	How to Score	
Accurate Reading	Reads words correctly	Do not mark or place check (✓) above word	no mark or ✓✓✓ / Get the ball		No error
Substitution	Gives an incorrect response	Write the substituted word above the word	can / could	Substitution, not corrected	1 error
Multiple Substitutions	Makes several attempts at a word	Write each substitution in sequence above the word	will | want / was	Multiple substitutions, not corrected	1 error for each incorrect word in text
			will | want | sc / was	Multiple substitutions, self-corrected (SC)	No error; 1 SC
			will / was want / was	Multiple misreadings of the same word, not corrected	1 error for each incorrect word in text
			Jay / Jesse Jasey / Jesse	Multiple misreadings of names and proper nouns	1 error first time missed; no errors after that
			did not / didn't didn't / did not	Misreading contractions (reads contraction as two words or two words as contraction)	1 error each time
Self-correction	Corrects a previous error	Write the error over the word, followed by SC	can | sc / could		No error; 1 SC
Insertion	Adds a word that is not in the text	Write in the inserted word using a caret	only ∧		1 error per word inserted
Omission	Gives no response to a word	Place a dash (-) above the word	— / and	Skipping a word / Skipping a line	1 error per word / 1 error per word
Repetition	Reads same word again	Write R after the word	✓R / play		No error
Repeated Repetitions	Reads the same word more than once	Write R for first repetition, then write a number for additional repetitions	✓R2 / each		No error
Rereading	Returns to the beginning of sentence or phrase to read again	Write an R with an arrow back to the place where rereading began	↓✓ ✓ ✓ ✓ R		No error
	Rereads and self-corrects	Write an R with an arrow back to the place where rereading began and a SC at point of self-correction	↓✓ ✓ ✓ ants|sc ✓R / bugs		No error; 1 SC
Appeal	Verbally asks for help	Write A above the word	each^A	Follow up with "You try it"	No error
"You Try It"	The child appeals, the teacher responds with "You try it"	Write Y after the word	each^A | Y	"You try it" followed by correct word	No error
				"You try it" followed by omission, incorrect word, or Told	1 error
Told	Child doesn't attempt a word even after "You try it"	Write T after the word or the Y	each^A | Y | T		1 error
Spelling Aloud	Child spells word by saying names of letters	Write the letters in all capital letters	N·E·T / net	Spelling followed by correct word	No error, no SC
				Spelling followed by incorrect word	1 error
Sounding Out	The child makes the sounds associated with the letters in the word	Write the letters in lower case with hyphens between them	p-a-st-✓ / past	"Sounding out" followed by correct word	No error; no SC
			p-a-st / past	"Sounding out" followed by incorrect word or no word	1 error
			a- | sc / bugs	Sounding the first letter incorrectly and then saying the word correctly	No error, 1 SC

Coding system developed by Marie Clay as part of the running record system in *An Observation Survey of Early Literacy Achievement, Revised Second Edition*, 2006, Heinemann.

FIGURE 6.2 Coding and Scoring Errors At-A-Glance

	A Fluency Rubric
0	Reads primarily word by word with occasional but infrequent or inappropriate phrasing; no smooth or expressive interpretation, irregular pausing, and no attention to author's meaning or punctuation; no stress or inappropriate stress, and slow rate.
1	Reads primarily in two-word phrases with some three- and four-word groups and some word-by-word reading; almost no smooth, expressive interpretation or pausing guided by author's meaning and punctuation; almost no stress or inappropriate stress, with slow rate most of the time.
2	Reads primarily in three- or four-word phrase groups; some smooth, expressive interpretation and pausing guided by author's meaning and punctuation; mostly appropriate stress and rate with some slowdowns.
3	Reads primarily in larger, meaningful phrases or word groups; mostly smooth, expressive interpretation and pausing guided by author's meaning and punctuation; appropriate stress and rate with only a few slowdowns.

FIGURE 6.3 Four-Point Holistic Fluency Rubric

them. At each level of text (after about level C), teach for a score of 3. If your assessment reveals student needs, you can be specific in your teaching.

After listening to a student process a text (or after taking a running record) select the number that most closely resembles the description of 0, 1, 2, or 3. Your goal in teaching during the guided reading lesson is always to teach toward a 3.

Calculating Accuracy

When you take a record of reading behavior, you get many different kinds of information. First, you are able to determine the *accuracy*, that is, the percentage of total words that were read correctly. Accuracy is important, and it is a key factor in effective processing. Children may read a text with high accuracy but understand it only superficially. They may read a text with lower accuracy but remember enough details to get the gist. But in general, there is a relationship between accuracy and understanding. Count the number of uncorrected errors. A chart specific to the text appears on each form to help you determine the accuracy rate as a percentage (see Figure 6.4). The F&P Calculator, provided with your *LLI System*, can speed up the process of calculating percentages.

Likewise with the *Fountas & Pinnell LLI Reading Record App.*

Accuracy Rate	Errors	7 or more	6	5	4	3	2	1	0
	%	Below 90%	90%	92%	93%	95%	97%	98%	100%

FIGURE 6.4 Accuracy Chart

Self-Correction Ratio

Self-correction behavior is an indication that the child is monitoring his reading behavior and attempting to search for multiple sources of information to make sense of the text. If a child makes an error and corrects it, you have powerful evidence of what that reader is attending to and using. Think about how often he notices an error and corrects it or attempts to correct it. Notice what information he uses to correct the error. A self-correction ratio is calculated for levels A–K (see Figure 6.5).

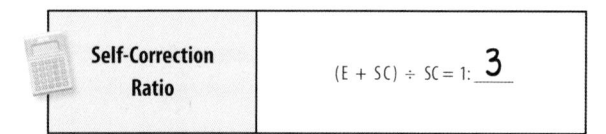

Self-Correction Ratio	(E + SC) ÷ SC = 1: __3__

FIGURE 6.5 Self-Correction Chart

▶ Talking About Reading

The Comprehension Conversation

Once the child has completed the oral reading, have a brief comprehension conversation to gain evidence of understanding. If you have good evidence from yesterday's discussion that this reader can express an understanding, you may want to skip the prompt(s) for it. Before administering the assessment, review the Guidelines for Administering the Comprehension Conversation (see Figure 6.6) to ensure standardization of this measure. In your conversation and evaluation, consider the evidence the child showed from his first reading of the book the day before.

Begin with the general prompt provided on the form to get the child talking about the book. Record the responses as completely as possible and compare them to the key understandings provided. If needed,

Guidelines for Administering the Comprehension Coversation

1. Begin with the general prompt provided on the Recording Form to get the child talking about the book.
2. Record responses as completely as possible on form, and compare to the key understandings provided.
3. If the child says very little or nothing at all, use the prompts provided to encourage conversation and probe for deeper understanding. Remember that the child should be doing most of the talking.
4. If necessary, reword prompts or prompt further by saying "Say more about that," but use this sparingly.
5. Avoid leading children, repeating their answers, or providing answers for them.
6. Provide adequate pauses between prompts to allow child time to respond. It should sound like a conversation, not an interrogation.
7. Allow child to look back in the book if she initiates it. If she starts reading the book to you, prompt with, "Say it in your own words."
8. Score each area, using the rubric provided.

FIGURE 6.6 Guidelines for Administering the Comprehension Conversation

use some of the prompts to probe for deeper understanding. The goal is to have the child do most of the talking. For some children it may be necessary to reword a prompt (e.g., "Say more about that."), but use this only once and do *not* lead children. Often just pausing a few seconds more to listen will also prompt a child to say more. Allow the child to look back in the text if he initiates it. If he starts to read the book again, stop him by saying, "Just tell me in your own words." The conversation will help you determine the child's thinking within, beyond, and about the text.

The comprehension conversation should not sound like an interrogation—more like a conversation between readers who are interested in the book. Be careful not to answer questions or prompts yourself or to ask leading questions. The idea is to gain a realistic picture of a child's ability. Your goal for the child is deep comprehension. The detailed Rubric for Scoring the Comprehension Conversation (see Figure 6.7) will help you determine how deeply children comprehend each book.

Scoring the Comprehension Conversation

If you use the evidence of comprehension from the first reading of the book in the previous lesson in combination with a brief conversation after this reading, you can score the student's thinking in three categories. You may be thinking of some of these questions as you score the comprehension conversation after the reading.

Within the Text

- ❑ Is the reader gaining the literal meaning of the text through solving words, monitoring her own understanding, and accuracy?
- ❑ Can the reader tell what happened or report important facts?
- ❑ Is the reader searching for and using information and remembering information in summary form?
- ❑ Is the reader adjusting her reading to fit the form—and also sustaining fluency?

Beyond the Text

- ❑ Is the reader making predictions?
- ❑ Is the reader making connections with prior knowledge, personal experience, or other texts?

Rubric for Scoring the Comprehension Conversation

3	Student demonstrates proficiency in understanding the text.
2	Student is approaching proficiency in understanding the text.
1	Student demonstrates limited proficiency in understanding the text.
0	Student's comprehension is not proficient.

FIGURE 6.7 Rubric for Scoring the Comprehension Conversation

- ☐ Is there evidence that the reader is inferring what is implied but not stated in the text?
- ☐ Has the reader shown that he is synthesizing information by changing his own thinking?

About the Text

- ☐ Is the reader able to think about the literary elements of the text and recognize the writer's craft?
- ☐ Can the reader think critically about how the text was written?

The Rubric for Scoring the Comprehension Conversation (see Figure 6.7) helps you determine scores for thinking within the text, beyond the text, and about the text. These scores are then tallied to give you a Total Score (see Figure 6.8), which when combined with the student's accuracy score tells you whether the text is Independent, Instructional, or Hard (see Figure 6.9).

A simple summary of the steps in scoring oral reading and a comprehension conversation using the Recording Form can be found in Figure 6.10.

Guide to Total Score for Comprehension Conversation Levels A–K

- **5–6** = Proficient
- **4** = Approaching Proficiency
- **3** = Limited Proficiency
- **0–2** = Not Proficient

FIGURE 6.8 Guide to Total Score for Comprehension Conversation

Summarizing Steps to Scoring Oral Reading and Comprehension Conversation

1. Accuracy: Circle the number of errors on the graph.
2. Self-Corrections: Calculate the SC ratio.
3. Fluency: Circle the fluency rating.
   - 0 = no phrasing or expression
   - 1 = minimal phrasing or expression
   - 2 = some phrasing or expression
   - 3 = mostly phrased and expressive reading
4. Comprehension:
   - Assign points in three categories (Within, Beyond, About the Text), making a decision for each based on these criteria.
     - 0 = not proficient
     - 1 = limited proficiency
     - 2 = approaching proficiency
     - 3 = proficient
   - Circle total comprehension score on the form.
     - 0–2 = not proficient
     - 3 = limited proficiency
     - 4 = approaching proficiency
     - 5–6 = proficient

FIGURE 6.10 Summarizing Steps to Scoring Oral Reading and Comprehension Conversation

Finding Independent, Instructional, and Hard Levels at Levels A–K

Accuracy	Comprehension			
	Proficient 5–6	**Approaching Proficiency** 4	**Limited Proficiency** 3	**Not Proficient** 0–2
95–100%	Independent	Independent	Instructional	Hard
90–94%	Instructional	Instructional	Hard	Hard
Below 90%	Hard	Hard	Hard	Hard

FIGURE 6.9 Finding Independent Instructional and Hard Levels at Levels A–K

▶ Analyzing Oral Reading Behaviors

The following describes ways to analyze the coding of reading behavior. Refer to the *LLI Professional Development and Tutorial Videos* for more support.

Sources of Information Neglected and Used

For each error, write "MSV" in the "E" column (whether self-corrected or not). For each self-correction, write "MSV" (all three letters) in the "SC" column. It is important to think about what led the child to make the error and what she might have neglected. Circle one, two, or three letters for each error or self-correction, without reading beyond the error or self-correction. Don't bother analyzing omissions and substitutions. Think about the following as you analyze each error and self-correction:

- ❑ **Meaning.** Children often make substitutions that indicate they are thinking about the meaning of the text. For example, a child might say *ballet* for *dance*. Ask yourself the question: Did the meaning of the text influence the error? (If so, circle "M" under Sources of Information.)

- ❑ **Structure.** A powerful source of information for a reader is the structure or syntax of language. From our knowledge of oral language, we have implicit knowledge of the way words are put together to form phrases and sentences. It "sounds right" to us. Readers often substitute nouns for nouns or verbs for verbs, indicating an awareness of the syntactic rules of language. For example, a child might say, *We like going* for *We like to ride*. Ask yourself: Does the error fit an acceptable English language structure? (Structure refers to syntax or grammar.) Did structure influence the error? (If so, circle "S" in the column.) Consider your decision taking into account the syntax of the sentence *up to the point of error.*

- ❑ **Visual Information.** Readers often use visual features of print—the letters and words—when they read. They connect these features to phonetic information that exists in their heads. For example, a child might say *park* for *play*. Ask yourself: Did the visual information from the print influence any part of the error (letter, part, word)? (If so, circle "V" in the column.)

Readers often use multiple sources of information as they process texts. For example, if a child substituted *steps* for *stair*, he attended to all three—meaning, language structure, and visual information. In this case, you would circle all three—"M," "S," and "V."

Self-Correction Behavior

A self-correction indicates use of all three sources of information—meaning, language structure, and visual information—because the word(s) are read accurately. At this point you are hypothesizing about *the additional information* a child might have used to correct his error.

If, for example, the child read *ballet* for *dance*, then self-corrected, the error would be coded with an "M", but in the self-correction column, it would be coded "S" and V" because he might have thought about the way the language sounded and might have noticed the *d*. In another example, if the child said *park* for *play* and then self-corrected, code the self-correction column as "M" and "S" because the meaning of the text and the English language structure likely influenced the correction.

The relationship between self-correction rate and progress in reading is not linear. As children progress, observable self-correction decreases and may become nonexistent (not appearing as overt behaviors). We do not desire a 1:1 or 1:2 SC ratio in highly accurate reading. Imagine listening to a reader who is making several errors and self-correcting almost every one; the reading would not sound good, even though the accuracy could be 100 percent. We assume that proficient readers are self-regulating both their oral and silent reading, but we cannot observe it. That is why we switch from reporting a SC ratio to the total number of self-corrections for levels L–Z. If we notice very high accuracy with many self-corrections, we would recommend working with the reader to get smoother processing.

These analyses can help you look quantitatively at a reader's use of different sources of information. Think about what the reader is noticing and what he is neglecting. You can help him attend to the information sources needed as you listen to him read orally or select teaching points after reading. If readers in a group are neglecting to think about what might make sense, you can prompt them to do so. If they are not noticing the word parts that would be helpful, you can draw those parts to their attention. Refer to *Prompting Guide, Part 1* for precise teaching language.

Analyzing Strategic Actions

Now that you have completed your analysis of sources of information used and neglected, look at the behaviors you recorded. Think about the reader as a problem solver. Five areas will be helpful in your thinking:

- ❑ **Early Reading Behaviors.** These are behaviors indicating attention to print features. You want to look for evidence that the child knows how print *works*, for example matching one spoken word with one written word and reading left to right. If he doesn't show evidence that he has these behaviors under control, do some explicit demonstrations.

- ❑ **Searching for and Using Information.** Effective readers *actively* search for the information they need to read with accuracy, fluency, and understanding. They make attempts that, even if not right, show you they are trying out what they know. You can teach readers many ways to search.

- ❑ **Monitoring and Self-Correcting.** Rather than reading along and ignoring errors, you want a child to *notice* when something doesn't fit. The reading may not make sense, or it might not sound or look right. Effective readers are constantly monitoring their own reading accuracy. Signs of monitoring can be rereading or pausing. If a child does not show signs of self-monitoring, you can draw his attention to mismatches and show ways to fix them.

Self-correction is a sign that a child is self-monitoring and working actively to make everything fit—meaning, visual information, and the way the reading sounds. You can prompt for self-correction. Keep in mind that even the most proficient readers will occasionally fail to correct small errors that do not affect comprehension (e.g., *a/the*) because they are placing a priority on reading fluently. Don't interrupt a reader every time he makes an error like this because too much attention to these kinds of errors will slow him down and affect overall processing. Notice if he is making many errors and overtly self-correcting them, which may indicate too much work and a probable loss of comprehension. Remember, you want high accuracy and attention to meaning.

- ❑ **Solving Words.** You want readers to have and use many ways to analyze and solve words. As they learn more, they can recognize more words automatically, but they also need to be able to use word analysis strategies so that they can learn many more words. Readers need a range of strategies for deriving the meaning of words they can decode but do not understand. Take note of how the child is solving unknown words. Is it letter by letter or in larger units? Your teaching should support children in using many different ways to solve words.

- ❑ **Maintaining Fluency.** Effective readers put all sources of information together so that reading sounds fluent and expressive. Think about how a child's reading sounds. If he is not fluent and the text is easy enough, demonstrate fluent reading by showing how to put words together so the reading sounds good.

▶ Using *The Literacy Continuum* to Monitor Progress and Guide Teaching

At the end of each level in the *LLI Lesson Guides*, you will find pages from *The Fountas & Pinnell Literacy Continuum: A Tool for Assessment, Planning, and Teaching* to help monitor progress and guide your teaching. (See Figure 6.11). It lists specific behaviors and understandings that are required for children to read successfully at that level. These behaviors and understandings are accumulative across the levels. They include important competencies children need to think within, beyond, and about texts. In other words, children take on new demands as the texts grow more challenging. For example, a child reading at level F and successfully meeting the demands of a level F text, is also able to meet the demands of a level D or E text. Also included in this section are suggestions for additional word work. If your children have good control of the principles in the Phonics/Word Work section of the lessons, you might want to occasionally substitute one

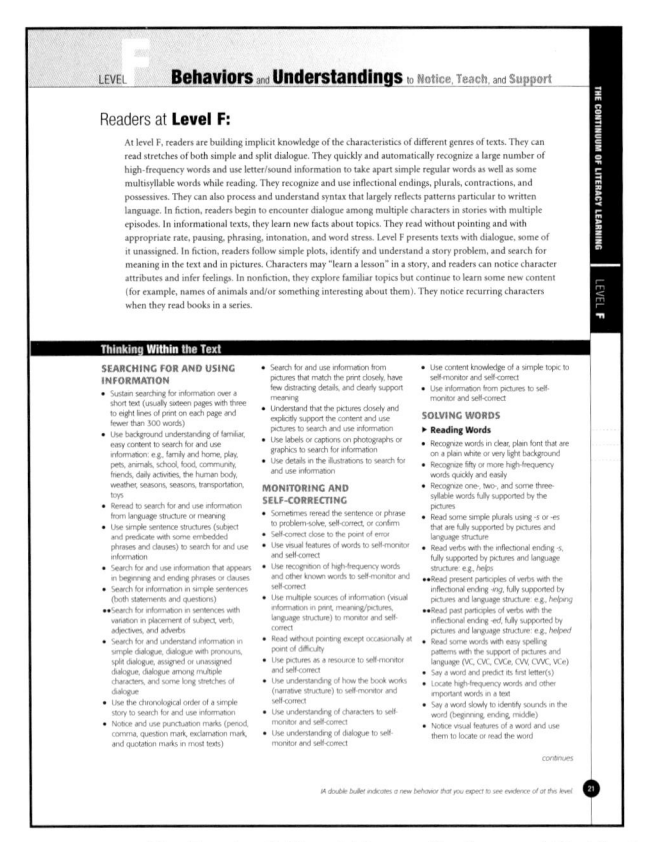

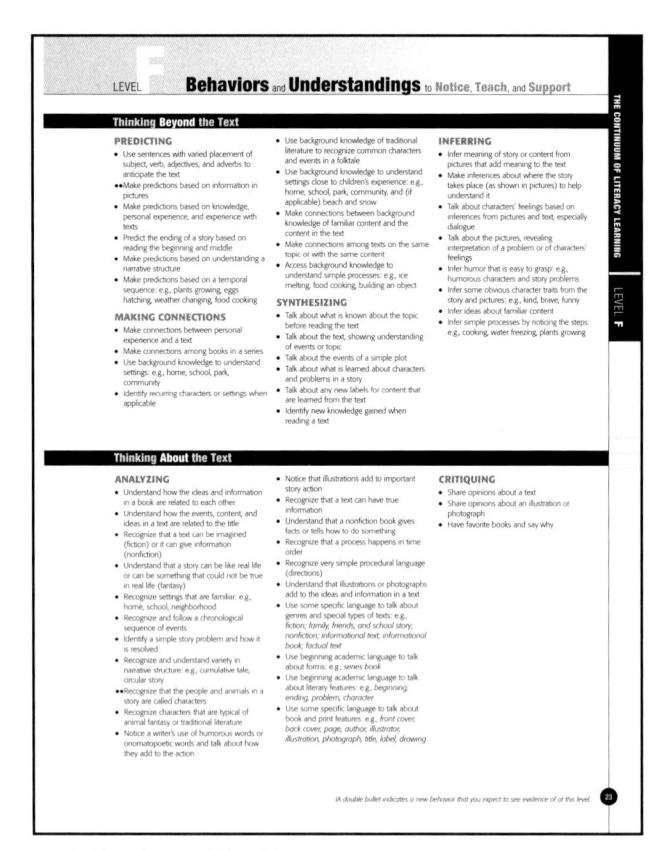

FIGURE 6.11 *The Fountas & Pinnell Literacy Continuum: A Tool for Assessment, Planning, and Teaching*

of these suggestions. Or, you might want to share them with the classroom teacher.

The *LLI* lessons are designed to support the goals listed in *The Literacy Continuum*. Your goal should be to help children meet the demands of successive levels of text and, in the process, expand their systems of strategic actions. The following suggestions may contribute to effective teaching in your lessons:

❑ In advance of the lesson, read the new book with *The Literacy Continuum* goals in mind.

❑ Think about what your children can do, and then find behaviors and understandings that they control, partially control, or do not yet control.

❑ Read the introduction to the text and teaching points for the lesson, keeping in mind the processing needs of the readers. Make any adjustments you think are necessary to meet their needs.

❑ Look at the Phonics/Word Work and at the additional suggestions provide on *The Literacy Continuum* pages, and make any adjustments you feel are necessary for your group.

❑ As you near the end of a level, look at what the readers now control and what they need to know to successfully process texts at this level.

❑ As the readers grow more proficient and reading becomes easy at the level, look ahead to the *The Literacy Continuum* pages for the next higher level. You may find new understandings or more complex versions of the same understandings.

▶ Record-Keeping Forms

To help make your record keeping simple, efficient, and informative, the *LLI* systems include a number of forms you can download from Online Resources. If you are using the *Online Data Management System*, some of the record keeping will take place online so you will not need to print the forms.

Lesson Record Form

The Lesson Record form allows you to make notes about individual students during each part of the *LLI* lesson. There are two versions of this form: with space for a group of three or six students. Notes consist of significant details about what the child is showing evidence of learning how to do or needing to learn how to do. (See *When Reader's Struggle:*

Teaching That Works, A–N, Prompting Guide, Part 1, and the Guide for Observing and Noting Reading Behaviors, Figure 6.12). You can then use your notes to plan what you need to emphasize when you teach the next lesson. To see a complete, filled-in Lesson Record, see Figure 6.13.

Resources

Name: ____________________ Date: ____________________

Key: C=Consistent
P=Partial
N=Not evident

Guide for Observing and Noting Reading Behaviors	C P N	Notes
1. Early Reading Behaviors *Does the reader:* • Move left to right across a line of print? • Return to the left for a new line? • Match voice to print while reading a line or more of print? • Recognize a few easy high-frequency words?		
2. Searching for and Using Information **Meaning** *Does the reader:* • Make meaningful attempts at unknown words? • Use the meaning of the story or text to predict unknown words? • Reread to gather more information to solve a word? • Reread and use the meaning of the sentence? • Reread to search for more details–information, characters, plot? • Reread to gather information to clarify confusions? • Use headings and titles to think about the meaning of a section of text? • Use information in the pictures to help in understanding a text? • Use knowledge of the genre (and its characteristics) to help in understanding a text? • Use knowledge of the genre (and its characteristics) to help in finding information? • Use readers' tools to help in finding information (glossary, index)? **Structure** *Does the reader:* • Use knowledge of oral language to solve unknown words? • Reread to see if a word "sounds right" in a sentence? • Reread to correct using language structure? **Visual Information** *Does the reader:* • Use the visual information to solve words? • Use the sound of the first letter(s) to attempt or solve a word? • Use some, most, or all of the visual information to solve words? • Use sound analysis to solve a word? • Make attempts that are visually similar? • Use knowledge of a high-frequency word to problem solve? • Search for more visual information within a word to solve it? • Use analogy to solve unknown words? • Use syllables to solve words? • Use prefixes and suffixes to take apart and recognize words? • Use inflectional endings to problem solve words? • Recognize words quickly and easily? • Reread and use the sound of the first letter to solve a word? • Problem solve unknown words quickly and efficiently? • Work actively to solve words? • Use multiple sources of information together in attempts at words? • Use all sources of information flexibly to solve words? • Use all sources of information in an orchestrated way?		
3. Solving Words *Does the reader:* • Recognize a core of high-frequency words quickly? • Recognize words quickly and easily? • Use a variety of flexible ways to take words apart? • Use the meaning of the sentences to solve words? • Use the structure of the sentence to solve words? • Use some of the visual information to solve words? • Use known word parts to solve words?		

Fountas & Pinnell Benchmark Assessment System 1

Resources

Key: C=Consistent
P=Partial
N=Not evident

Guide for Observing . . . (cont.)	C P N	Notes
3. Solving Words *(cont.)* *Does the reader:* • Use sound analysis (sounding out)? • Use analogy to solve words? • Make attempts that are visually similar? • Use the sound of the first letter to solve words? • Work actively to solve words? • Use known words or parts to solve unknown words? • Use syllables to problem solve? • Use prefixes and suffixes to take words apart? • Use inflectional endings to take words apart? • Use sentence context to derive the meaning of words? • Use base words and root words to derive the meaning of words? • Make connections among words to understand their meaning?		
4. Self-Monitoring *Does the reader:* • Hesitate at an unknown word? • Stop at an unknown word? • Stop at an unknown word and appeal for help? • Stop after an error? • Notice mismatches? • Notice when an attempt does not look right? • Notice when an attempt does not sound right? • Notice when an attempt does not make sense? • Reread to confirm reading? • Use knowledge of some high-frequency words to check on reading? • Check one source of information with another? • Check an attempt that makes sense with language? • Check an attempt that makes sense with the letters (visual information)? • Use language structure to check on reading? • Request help after making several attempts?		
5. Self-Correcting *Does the reader:* • Reread and try again until accurate? • Stop after an error and make another attempt? • Stop after an error and make multiple attempts until accurate? • Reread to self-correct? • Work actively to solve mismatches? • Self-correct errors?		
6. Maintaining Fluency *Does the reader:* • Read without pointing? • Read word groups (phrases)? • Put words together? • Read smoothly? • Read the punctuation? • Make the voice go down at periods? • Make the voice go up at question marks? • Pause briefly at commas, dashes, and hyphens? • Read dialogue with intonation or expression? • Stress the appropriate words to convey accurate meaning? • Read at a good rate—not too fast and not too slow?		
7. Other Behaviors		

Fountas & Pinnell Benchmark Assessment System 1

FIGURE 6.12 Guide for Observing and Noting Reading Behaviors

Leveled Literacy Intervention Lesson Record: 3-Student Version — **Even-Numbered Lesson**

Date: 10/21 — Green

Teacher: Mrs. Leone — Grade: 1 — Lesson: 12

1 — REREADING BOOKS AND ASSESSMENT / Rosa

Flying A – Rosa

Very Busy Hen D

Will	Rosa	Vanessa
strong 1:1 good s-mon. recognized many h-f words	strong 1:1 good s-mon Tpoint: self s-mon locates h-f words	reads puppet strong 1:1 uses dialogue recog. many h-f words

2 — PHONICS/WORD WORK

ABC Chart

initial s, t, p PX

M/moon My ABC Book

W	R	V
good letter recog. needs vocab. support	fast letter rec. good 1→s	good phonol s, t, p

Fountas & Pinnell *Leveled Literacy Intervention*. Copyright © 2009 by Irene C. Fountas and Gay Su Pinnell.
This page may be photocopied.

LESSON RECORD 3-STUDENT

Leveled Literacy Intervention Lesson Record: 3-Student Version — **Even-Numbered Lesson (cont.)**

3 — WRITING ABOUT READING / Dictated

c/a/n s/ee d/o/u

W	R	V
says words slowly quick I, a	needs spacing I, a quickly	self. mon spacing rereads confuses b/d form.

4 — NEW BOOK

Woof A

W	R	V
independent easy 1:1	strong 1:1 uses pix	engaged w/(m) uses pix strong 1:1

Fountas & Pinnell *Leveled Literacy Intervention*. Copyright © 2009 by Irene C. Fountas and Gay Su Pinnell.
This page may be photocopied.

LESSON RECORD 3-STUDENT

FIGURE 6.13 Sample Lesson Record, page 1 and 2

Intervention Record

This form is critical for monitoring the number of *LLI* lessons administered and the amount of small-group instruction in the classroom each week. Accurate record keeping will help you determine the effect of *LLI* on student achievement. Note that if you are using the *Online Data Management System*, this same data is collected electronically so you will not need to print the form. (See Figure 6.14.)

Student Achievement Log

This form can be used to document children's performance as they enter or exit *LLI*. Use the categories of information that apply to your assessments and add any others in the final two columns. (See Figure 6.15.) Note that if you are using the *Online Data Management System*, this same data is collected electronically so you would not need to print the form.

Intervention Record

Student Name: Stephen Year: Teacher: Ms. Samuels

Group: Grade One System: Orange (X Green) Blue School: Parkman

Attendance Record							Weekly Reading Record							
Date	Week	M	T	W	Th	F	Lesson	Reading Record Book Title	Level	Acc. %	Comp.	SC	Fluency	#SGI
9/6	1		G-1	G-2	G-3	G-4	4							3
9/13	2	G-5	G-6	G-7	G-8	G-9								4
9/20	3	G-10	G-11	G-12	TA	G-13	10							4
9/27	4	G-14	G-15	CA	G-16/G-17	G-18	16	Jesse	A	100%	6	–	–	4
10/4	5	G-19	G-20	G-21	G-22	G-23	22	Orson's Tummy	B	97%	6	1:2	–	4
10/11	6	G-24	G-25	G-26	G-27	G-28	28	Our Garden	B	96%	6	1:3	–	4
10/18	7	G-29	G-30	G-31	G-32	G-33								3
10/25	8	G-34	G-35	G-36	G-37	G-38	34	Looking for Tazo	C	98%	6	1:3	2	3
11/1	9	G-39	G-40	G-41	G-42	G-43	40	Clouds	C	96%	5	1:3	2	4
11/8	10	G-44	G-45	G-46	G-47	G-48	46	Time for Lunch	D	95%	7	1:4	3	3
11/15	11	G-49	G-50	G-51	TA	G-52	52	Three Bears	E	95%	6	1:3	3	4

NOTES:
steady progress
consistent self-monitoring

KEY:
Acc. % = Accuracy
Comp. = Comprehension Total Score
SC = Self-Correction
#SGI = Small Group Instruction (in addition to LLI)
TA = Teacher Absent
CA = Child Absent
TN = Teacher Not Available
CN = Child Not Available
SH = School Holiday

PROGRAM RECORD

FIGURE 6.14 Intervention Record

FIGURE 6.15 Student Achievement Log

Leveled Literacy Intervention Student Achievement Log: 3-Student Version

School Year: Teacher: Mrs. Phillips Assessment Used: F and P Benchmark 1

School: Windsor District/State:

GROUP ENTRY DATA

Student	Grade	Entry Date	Level	Accuracy %	Comp.	SC	Fluency	Notes
Sammantha	1	9/10	A	67%	6	1:10	n/a	no 1:1
Ronny	1	9/10	A	83%	5	1:10	n/a	no 1:1
Ethan	1	9/10	A	87%	6	1:8	n/a	inventing

GROUP EXIT DATA

Student	Grade	Exit Date	Level	Accuracy %	Comp.	SC	Fluency	Notes
Sammantha	1	12/23	G	95%	6	1:3	3	strong self-mon.
Ronny	1	12/23	G	97%	7	1:3	3	strong self-mon.
Ethan	1	12/23	G	98%	6	1:2	3	expressive strong 1:1

STUDENT ACTIVITY LOG: 3-STUDENT VERSION

Communication Sheet—Individual

This optional form can be used to communicate with the classroom teacher about a child's weekly progress. You may want the classroom teacher to share the same kind of information with you. (See Figure 6.16.)

Communication Sheet—Group

This is an additional optional form that can be used to communicate with the classroom teacher about a group's weekly progress. Write notes in each area that you feel will be helpful. (See Figure 6.17.)

FIGURE 6.16 Communication Sheet—Individual

FIGURE 6.17 Communication Sheet—Group

section 6 — Assessment and Record Keeping in the *LLI* System

Letter/Word Record

The Letter/Word Record is an optional form to keep track of specific letter learning and high-frequency words the group almost knows or controls consistently. (See Figure 6.18.) You may want to note whether each child knows the name of the letter, its sound, or how to form it. The lines in each box can be used to show the child's knowledge of the letter name (N), sound (S), or formation (F).

When you introduce a new word to the group, write it under the correct letter. You may want to check it off when the children can read it easily and place an *x* when they can write it easily.

Flip Record

An informal alternative form of record keeping is the Flip Record, which you can quickly make using index cards and a sheet of paper or stiff card stock. (See Figure 6.19.) Holding a sheet of 8.5" x 11" paper or card stock lengthwise, tape 5" x 8" index cards to the paper so that the cards overlap down the sheet. If you use a sheet of paper, you can place the Flip Record on a clipboard for stability. Have one card for each child, and write each child's name at the bottom of a card so the names will be visible when the cards overlap. Flip up the cards to write anecdotal notes on each child's progress; words, letters, or patterns that are challenging to the child; or any other notes you wish to make on the child's reading and writing behaviors. As each card is filled, peel it off the sheet and place it in the child's Student Folder.

Writing Samples in *My Writing Book*

My Writing Book also serves as a record of progress. Children generally do their writing on right-hand pages. The left-hand page can be used to work on letters and words. Have children practice letter formation, writing a word quickly, or saying words using (Elkonin) sound or letter boxes. The writing book serves as a record of the learning you are supporting in writing. Be sure to write the lesson number in the top corner. The samples in the book show the child's progress over time in learning about letters, sounds, words, and the ability to compose and write sentences.

FIGURE 6.18 Letter/Word Record Form

FIGURE 6.19 Flip Record

Reading Records for Progress Monitoring

There is no substitute for the information you gain from taking systematic reading records of children's behavior as they process continuous text. During the Rereading Books and Assessment section of the even-numbered standard lessons, you take a reading record on one child using a Recording Form or the *Fountas & Pinnell LLI Reading Record App* if you choose to do so electronically (see Reading Record App, page 17). This will mean that with a group of three children, you will take one reading record about once per week for each child (or once in a six-day cycle). Remember that for children reading the short books at levels A, B, and C, the record will take only the five minutes allotted (or less). Your F&P Calculator/Stopwatch will help you be very time efficient.

If you opt for taking reading records with paper and pencil instead of using the app, print the Recording Forms in advance from the Online Resources site and store them in the hanging folder for that lesson. You will also need a copy of the book and your F&P Calculator/Stopwatch.

When you take a reading record, code the reading behavior using the standardized system for coding (see Coding and Scoring Errors-at-a-Glance, page 90, and the *LLI* Professional Development and Tutorial videos), have a brief comprehension conversation, and make a teaching point. Score and analyze the record (see Administering the Reading Record Using the Recording Form, pages 87–89, and the Professional Development and Tutorial videos) to get important information on how the reader is using sources of information, initiating strategic actions, and comprehending the book.

Following the reading, look quickly at the evidence to provide insights about the way the child processed the text. Select one teaching point—something you can teach for, prompt for, or reinforce to improve the child's reading (see *When Readers Struggle: Teaching That Works*, Chapter 14: "Processing Texts: Teaching for Problem Solving" and *Prompting Guide, Part 1*).

Reading Graph and Reports

It can be helpful to keep a graph of progress for each reader. (See Figure 6.20.) If you are using the *Online Data Management System* (see page 16) you can do so electronically. If not, establish regular intervals

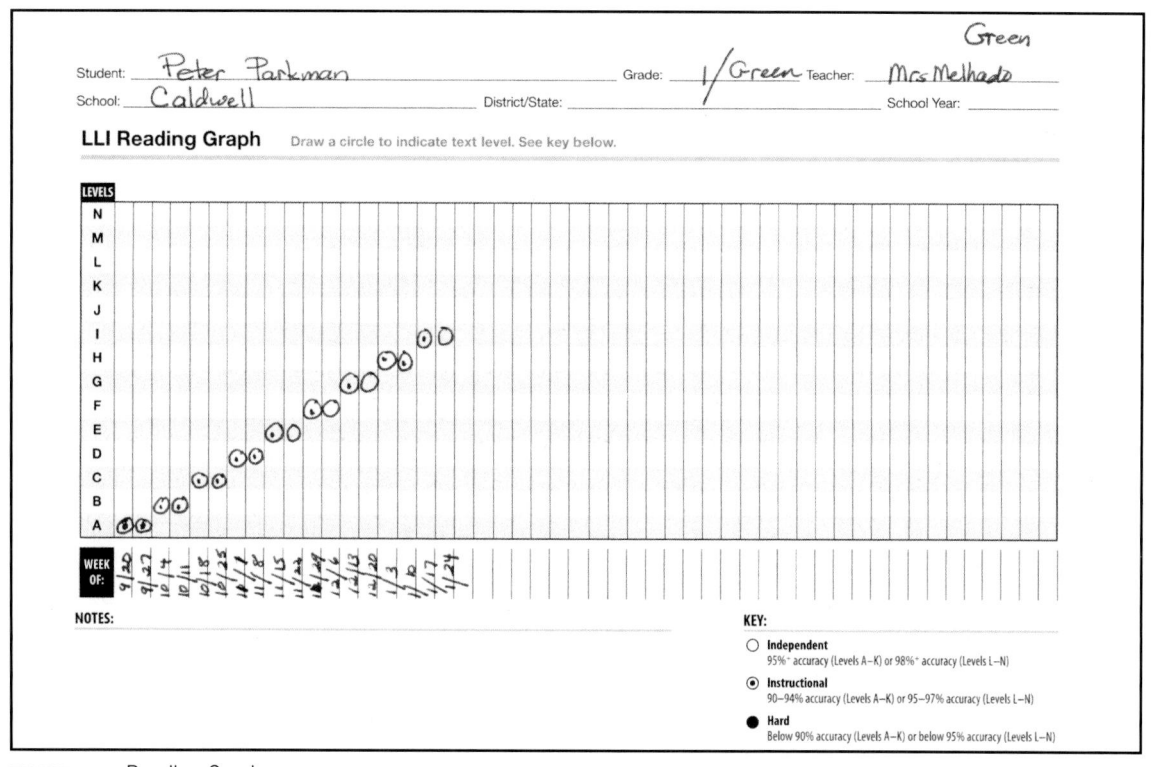

FIGURE 6.20 Reading Graph

for recording reading levels obtained through reading records on the Reading Graph (from Online Resources and on the interior of each Student Folder). Record the reading level by drawing a circle with a dot in it for reading at the instructional level (90–94 percent for levels A through K) and satisfactory comprehension. Use an open circle for reading at the independent level (100 percent) and satisfactory comprehension. If the reading is below those levels, fill in the circle to make it black. If comprehension is unsatisfactory, make the circle black regardless of accuracy. This tool allows you to enter the information from the child's reading record each week to document the child's progress on a graph. You can share the information on the graph with the classroom teacher.

Student Folder

The *LLI System* includes a Student Folder for each child. The color corresponds to the system you are using. On the inside of the folder is the Reading Graph described earlier. On the outside of the folder is space to note program entry data and program exit data. Keep important forms within the folder, and pass it on with student records from grade to grade.

▶ Change over Time in Children's Progress

The reading records, writing books, and Lesson Records provide evidence of children's growth over time. For a detailed description of three *LLI* children and their progress in building effective processing systems across time, see *When Readers Struggle: Teaching That Works, A–N*, Chapter 5: "Change over Time: Processing Systems in the Making." Note how the children began at the same instructional level but built their processing systems differently from each other over time.

section 7

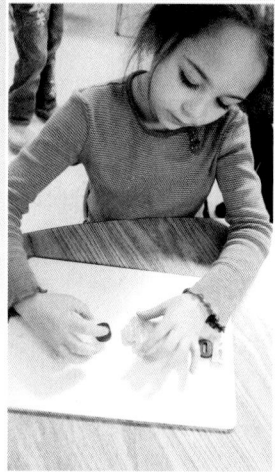

Professional Development for *LLI*

▶ Resources to Support Your Teaching

- ❏ *System Guide*—Offers guidance and suggestions for implementing *LLI*, explains each of the components and many of the forms you'll use, and contains a bibliography of professional books.

- ❏ **Professional Development and Tutorial videos**—To support your work individually or with a study group of professionals. The first video provides an overview of the system and model lessons. The second contains a tutorial on coding, scoring, and analyzing reading records and using the information to inform your teaching.

- ❏ **When Readers Struggle: Teaching That Works, A–N**—A comprehensive tool for learning about the difficulties readers face and how you can move them forward.

- ❏ *Fountas & Pinnell Leveled Literacy Intervention* website (www.fountasandpinnell.com/intervention)—Frequently asked questions and other information to use in implementing lessons.

- ❏ **Reflection Guide with a Recorded Lesson**—Use the Reflection Guide, Figure 7.1, to think about your own recorded lesson, or you can record your lesson and discuss it with colleagues. Then, share the insights each of you gained that will influence your own teaching. Downloadable from the Online Resources.

- ❏ **Professional Development Calendar**—Monthly suggestions for your continued growth as an *LLI* teacher. Work with your *LLI* colleagues in your school or district to set up meeting times once per month for approximately one and a half to two hours. You can also use the suggested professional readings at the end of each lesson for discussion. Your monthly *LLI* Calendar starts on the next page. It assumes lessons begin in August, but you can adjust the calendar as needed.

- ❏ Contact Heinemann's Professional Development group for customized onsite, offsite, or online professional development (www.heinemann.com/PD/default.aspx).

Leveled Literacy Intervention Reflection Guide

EVEN NUMBERED LESSON: LESSON #: _____

Rereading • How did I teach for, prompt for, or reinforce effective use of reading strategies (fluency and phrasing, searching for and using information, solving words, self-monitoring, or self-correcting)?	
Phonics/Word Work • How clearly did I state the principle? • How clearly did I help the children understand how to apply the principle to other words? • What was the evidence of new learning?	
Writing • How did I engage children in composing sentences (interactive or independent writing)? • What were the characteristics of the sentences children composed (language complexity, vocabulary, word difficulty, accuracy, etc.)? • How did I help the children learn how to form letters efficiently? • How did I help the children learn how to use sound analysis or visual analysis? • How did I help children use writing conventions? • How did I draw children's attention to strategies for the construction of words? • What links did I make to the children's previous knowledge? • How did I use rereading to help children consider changes they needed to make? • What did children learn how to do as writers?	
New Book *Before Reading:* • How did I help the children expand their knowledge of language structures and vocabulary? • What print or text features did I help them notice? • How did I help the children understand how the book works and understand critical aspects of the text meaning? *During Reading* • How did I teach for, prompt for, or reinforce effective processing strategies? • What were the children able to do independently? *After Reading* • What was the evidence of the children's understanding of the text? • How did I support processing strategies through my teaching points? • What did the children learn how to do as readers?	

Leveled Literacy Intervention Reflection Guide

ODD NUMBERED LESSON: LESSON #: _____

Rereading • How did I teach for, prompt for, or reinforce effective use of reading strategies (fluency and phrasing, searching for and using information, solving words, self-monitoring, or self-correcting)?	
Phonics/Word Work • How clearly did I state the principle? • How clearly did I help the children understand how to apply the principle to other words? • What was the evidence of new learning?	
New Book *Before Reading:* • How did I help the children expand their knowledge of language structures and vocabulary? • What print or text features did I help them notice? • How did I help the children understand how the book works and understand critical aspects of the text meaning? *During Reading* • How did I teach for, prompt for, or reinforce effective processing strategies? • What were the children able to do independently? *After Reading* • What was the evidence of the children's understanding of the text? • How did I support processing strategies through my teaching points? • What did the children learn how to do as readers?	
Letter/Word Work • How did I organize my materials so that children could work on words independently? • How fluent were the children in recognizing letters/words or taking words apart? • What were the children noticing about words? • What did the children learn about how words work?	

FIGURE 7.1 Reflection Guide

Monthly Professional Development Calendar

AUGUST	SEPTEMBER	OCTOBER
Knowing Your Readers	**Organizing and Making Transitions**	**Supporting Effective Reading**
You have collected important benchmark data on your children. Use the reading records from your assessment to talk with your colleagues about your groups and the starting levels. Use the Guide for Observing and Noting Reading Behaviors to discuss the specific behaviors you observed in one group and the areas of *Prompting Guide, Part 1* you will want to use as you start lessons. With a partner and the appropriate-level book, role-play how you will demonstrate the reading behaviors you have identified.	You have had a few weeks to get to know the children in your groups and to help them get used to the predictability of the lessons. Select one of the lessons on the Professional Development and Tutorial videos to watch. Observe the teacher's organization and the transition from one part of the lesson to the next. Discuss what you notice about her organization for teaching and how she was organized for smooth transitions and a quick-paced lesson.	Focus on the reading segment of your lesson. Think about how your introduction to the new text supports children's effective processing. Prepare for your meeting by making careful notes of the problem-solving difficulties children had as they read the new book during the last three lessons. Bring the book and share your observations with each other. Talk about what you might have done in the introduction to the text that would have prevented the processing difficulties.

NOVEMBER	DECEMBER	JANUARY
Using Ongoing Assessment to Inform Your Teaching	**Using the *Continuum* to Guide Teaching Decisions**	**Developing Phonics/Word Work Skills**
You have been taking a reading record on each child approximately every six days. Bring the last three reading records for one child from one of your groups. Have enough copies for your colleagues. Use the Guide for Observing and Noting Reading Behaviors (Figure 6.12) to discuss the three records. Talk about areas of strength and need indicated for each child. Also, talk about the change in the reader across the three records and what will be important to focus on next in your teaching.	At the end of each level in your Lesson Guides are excerpts from *The Literacy Continuum*. Bring a set of Lesson Records, reading records, and writing books for one group of children. Focus on the level at which you are teaching the children now. Refer to the *Continuum* at this level and the next level. Discuss what you feel the children control and what you will need to attend to so the children have good control of most of the competencies at the level and are ready to move on to the next level.	Bring a set of records from your *LLI* group to your meeting as well as a copy of the Master Plan for Word Work. Notice what principles you have taught so far. Look for evidence in your records that children are using those principles in reading and writing. Share your observations with your colleagues. Think about prompts from *Prompting Guide, Part 1* that will move children forward.

FIGURE 7.2 Monthly Professional Development Calendar

continues

Monthly Professional Development Calendar, continued

FEBRUARY	MARCH	APRIL
Observing Change in Writing	**Supporting Writing Development**	**Supporting Fluent, Phrased Reading**
Bring the writing book and Lesson Records for one of your children. Discuss the changes you see in the writing. Notice places where the child used correction tape. Look under the tape at the child's first attempt. Discuss: <ul><li>letter formation</li><li>letter spacing</li><li>complexity of language structures</li><li>amount of writing</li><li>ability to hear sounds and record the letters that represent them</li><li>ability to use high-frequency words</li><li>the content or kinds of thinking the child is sharing about text</li></ul> Look at the *Prompting Guides* for ideas that you find useful.	Bring the interactive writing pieces you created with one group of children. Share them with your colleagues and discuss your teaching decisions. <ul><li>What do you notice about the sentences you and the children composed?</li><li>What writing did you do and why?</li><li>Where did you share the pen and what did you help the children learn at these selected points?</li><li>What do you think the children learned how to do as writers?</li><li>What might you have done differently?</li></ul> Look at the *Prompting Guides* for ideas that you find useful.	Bring one of each book at a level you are using with a group to your meeting. With a partner, look through the books for characteristics that provide opportunities to teach for fluent, phrased reading in each. Consider: <ul><li>print layout (including phrase layout)</li><li>punctuation</li><li>use of dialogue</li><li>use of repetition</li><li>naturalness of language structures</li><li>use of bold letters or speech bubbles</li></ul> Share your insights with the group. Talk about the implications for introducing the texts and supporting the reading of the texts with your children. Look at the *Prompting Guides* for ideas that you find useful.

MAY	JUNE
Expanding Language Across the Lesson	**Supporting Comprehension Across the Lesson**
There are numerous opportunities to support children's use of language and expansion of their language across the lesson. With a partner in your group, look at each element of two consecutive lessons. Talk about: <ul><li>the opportunities for children to use language in each element</li><li>ways to increase the amount of language children use</li><li>opportunities to model and expand the children's language</li><li>opportunities for children to use book language</li><li>opportunities to expand the children's vocabulary</li></ul> Share your insights with the group. Talk about changes you want to make in your teaching of the lesson to provide stronger support for language development.	Bring two books you are using in *LLI* lessons. With a partner, look at the books and discuss how they work. Use the Analysis of New Book Characteristics in the corresponding lessons. Look at the Key Understandings and Author's Message. Refer to the New Book segment of the lesson as well as the Writing segment on the following day. Ask yourself: <ul><li>How can you support the children's attention to the meaning of the text in each element?</li><li>What aspects of the texts may be tricky for your readers?</li><li>How do you want to strengthen their understanding through the use of these books?</li></ul> Use *Prompting Guide, Part 2* to find language that will deepen children's understanding.

FIGURE 7.2 Monthly Professional Development Calendar, *continued*

▶ Frequently Asked Questions About Using *LLI*

Implementing the *LLI Green System*

How do I know whether to use Getting Started in the Orange and Green systems?

If your assessment indicates that level A is hard for the children and they know very little about print, then use Getting Started. If children come into *LLI* at level A or B but demonstrate inconsistent behaviors, they may still benefit from some Getting Started lessons. You will find that Getting Started lessons provide a stretch and help the children learn how to work together in a group.

Can LLI be used before or after school?

LLI can be successfully implemented in before- or after-school programs. The goal would be to group children so that they are on appropriate levels. Ideally, you would continue to work with a group size of three children.

Can LLI be used for tutoring?

The lessons can be used for tutoring with excellent results, although in a one-on-one situation, the child would not benefit from the important social interactions a group provides.

Does LLI replace Guided Reading?

Absolutely not. *LLI* is intended to be *supplementary instruction*. That means that the power of the program is in the extra help children get in addition to good classroom teaching that includes small-group reading instruction. Some classroom teachers have had successful results using *LLI* for a short time with their lowest-achieving readers. These children also have guided reading with their peers at least two or three times per week.

Is LLI the same as Guided Reading?

No, *LLI* is a much more intensive framework of components designed to support the accelerated progress of low-achieving children. It is highly systematic and sequential. The books are designed to build on one another. Although word work is provided in guided reading, *LLI* provides more intensive and longer work in phonics and word study. Most children do not need such an intensive approach.

If after eighteen weeks I'm not satisfied that a child is making enough progress, should I extend her?

Yes. If needed, a child can be regrouped with others and stay in *LLI* longer. Of course, you would want to do careful progress monitoring to be sure that the intervention is working. In extreme cases, you may want a thorough assessment of the child's learning needs by a psychologist.

Can I teach LLI lessons in the classroom, or do I need to pull children out?

The *LLI* lesson materials are portable enough to be used as a push-in or pull-out program. What's important is that you work with small groups. Work with the classroom teacher to find a small space that is far enough away from the guided reading table that the two groups will not interfere with each other. Be sure you have a table and a small easel. This is a very efficient way to work because children will have very little transition time.

Do I have to complete all of the lessons within each level?

No, but be cautious. Look at *The Literacy Continuum* for the level to be sure children control most of the behaviors. If your readers are finding the books very easy and they seem to understand the phonics and word work principles, you can skip to the next level. (Sometimes teachers spend a lesson doing a "read in" just to experience all the good books on the level. Or, they send the books back to the classroom for children to read.)

Scheduling

How can I make the schedule work when there are so many conflicts during a typical week?

A meeting of all the teachers at the grade level can be very helpful. Classroom teachers want children to have extra help but also have to consider all the demands on their time. Review the schedule and go over the different groups you are trying to convene to find a compromise.

Does a four-day week (or an otherwise short week) count as a week of intervention?

Yes. You should be counting both days and weeks. Even a short week counts as a week.

Do all children need to finish the intervention at the same time?

No. If one child is clearly accelerating, you can assess the child and move him out of the group (or into a group reading at a higher level) at any time. If a child needs more time in the intervention, have her join a lower group. It is fine for the child to reread, talk about, and write about some of the books in the collection. You can also "borrow" books and lessons from another system to provide new material. Remember, there is no repetition of titles among *LLI Systems*.

Selection

Can a child who has an IEP participate in **LLI**?

It depends on what services the district provides under the label of "special education." If the educational specifications parallel the specific teaching opportunities provided in *LLI*, then it is an excellent option.

Can I use **LLI** *with all my children?*

LLI was designed to supplement small-group instruction that children receive in the classroom. Most children do not need such a structured approach, and teachers prefer more decision making in sequencing texts. Also, *LLI* does not provide enough lessons for daily group instruction across an entire year.

Can children who have been in Reading Recovery® go into **LLI**?

Children should not be in both Reading Recovery® and *LLI* at the same time. Children who reach grade level and exit Reading Recovery® should not need *LLI*, but for children who have made progress but have not reached grade level and still need more support, *LLI* is an ideal option. If a child begins in *LLI*, she should enter Reading Recovery® when a slot becomes available if she is the lowest achieving child in grade 1.

How do you decide to group children who are at the same reading level but have different needs?

No group of children will have identical needs. For *LLI*, you are trying to place three children whose instructional level is the same or close to the same. You can fine-tune your interactions with children during the lesson to account for their different needs. For example, within a group reading at level A, one child may need more interactions around word solving and another around fluency. Most of the time, however, children have multiple needs that change from week to week. As with all teaching, observation is the key.

Attendance/Exiting the Intervention

What should I do when children are absent?

There will always be the problem of a child missing a lesson here and there. One suggestion would be to introduce the new book(s) the child missed while the other children in the group are involved with the rereading portion of the lesson. Often, the child can simply join in with the others on what they are doing. Or, you can send the missed book back to the classroom or home for the child to read and catch up. If attendance is spotty across the group, you can stop and have a "catch-up" day to read and reread books they have missed and to review phonics principles. If a child has an extended absence, reassess him and make a decision as to the level he should be reading.

How do you handle evidence of recurring attendance issues?

In the case of a child with frequent absences, first enlist the help of the parent, classroom teacher, or administrator to see if there is a problem and to underscore the importance of attendance for the child's progress. If there are health issues, work out a system for sending materials home. If the child falls far enough behind it may warrant re-assessment.

What do I do if a child moves out of the school before the intervention is complete?

If possible, conduct a final assessment to get an ending level and record it on the child's Student Folder. Send the folder with copies of your assessments on to the new school. Look at reading records and reflect on your observation of the children remaining in the group. Work with classroom teachers to select another child reading at the same instructional level to join the group. It should not be necessary to "catch the child up" by reading all of the previous books.

Can a child leave LLI *to enter Reading Recovery®?*

Yes, as soon as a slot in Reading Recovery is available, the neediest *LLI* child should be transferred to it and a new child entered into the *LLI* group. A child should not be in both *LLI* and Reading Recovery at the same time.

Grouping

Do I have to limit group size to three?

We strongly recommend three children for best results. Where it is impossible to limit the groups to three, just try to keep the groups as small as possible. Keep in mind that the larger the group, the slower the progress.

Is it possible to have an LLI *group with only two children?*

Yes. There will always be variations because children's needs are so diverse. But, in general, you want the interaction that comes from having a group of three.

What if one child in the group consistently lags behind the others?

You cannot expect all children in a group to perform in exactly the same way. Assess the child using a reading record to be sure her instructional level is in line with the others. It is a good idea to sit the child closest to you (so she can see charts). Try giving more individual support to this child to help the processing go a little faster as fluent reading is important. Also, suggest that she reread the books in the classroom or at home. If the level is really too hard, try regrouping to place the child with a group at a lower level.

Should I regroup children as I notice differences?

Group members need to get to know each other and learn how to behave as a group. But if a child is clearly not placed at the right level, then you should move him right away. If you are working with several groups and you notice some children seem misplaced, adjust your groupings as best you can to meet their needs. If there are small differences and no other grouping options, you may need to provide a bit more challenge or extra support for some.

What happens if one child in a group is making faster progress than the other two?

Look for another group and move the child if you are able. It is not necessary to have her read all the books the children have read prior to entry. If there is no group and the child still needs intervention, keep him or her in the *LLI* group and provide some extra writing or word work. Select other leveled books from the other collections to provide extra challenge. Most word work allows for children to go beyond the specific lesson.

What should I do if one child in the group is not moving along as quickly as the other two?

This problem will almost always exist when you are working with a group—even a small one. You have three choices: (1) Give the child some extra help when possible. Enlist the classroom teacher or any school helper in doing some extra reading, word work, or writing with the child and, if possible, have a conference with parents. (2) Slow the group down a bit by having a few "reading" or "writing" days to consolidate learning. (Be cautious with this option. It may not help and could slow the others down.) (3) Reassess the child and move him to another group.

Lesson Time

What if I have time left after I finish lesson activities?

This is a good problem to have if you covered all of the elements thoroughly. Use the time to work with high-frequency words, read *My Poetry Book*, read *My ABC Book*, or reread books that were introduced in previous lessons.

What should I do if the teaching time is cut short and I do only half of a lesson?

Start the same lesson again the next day for coherence. Or, do the second half and some extra reading of *My Poetry Book* or *My Writing Book*. Children can also work with high-frequency words or sort letters if needed.

What if my lessons are always too long and I find it hard to finish?

The 30-minute time frame is important, as we have found that young children start to lose attention after that. As you and your children get used to the routines, you will find it easier to keep the pace. Teach children to be aware of time and help you manage it. For example, encourage them to put word cards and other materials away quickly and transition smoothly from one activity to another. Organization will help. Keep the letter, picture, or word cards together in a plastic bag or small covered tub for a lesson. Keep all children's materials in one accordion file or hanging file and teach them to take them out and put them back quickly. Use a timer to divide the sections into 10-minute intervals. Finally, check children's reading fluency to make sure they are not reading too slowly. If that is the case, concentrate on fluency (see *Prompting Guide, Part 1*). You will notice that in the even-numbered lessons there is a suggestion for "Optional Letter/Word Work." This is always a review of a previously introduced principle.

Levels

Why are there only ten lessons on a level?

In our experience, with the intensive support you provide in *LLI* lessons, children can move up the levels at the designated pace. If you believe children need more time at a level, borrow books from another *LLI* system. Alternatively, you can select books from the level that you have in your school and create your own lessons using the framework. Be cautious about staying too long on a level. Teach hard for the behaviors and understandings listed on *The Literacy Continuum*.

What if my group reaches the end of a level and I am not sure they are ready to move to the next level?

Look carefully at the recent reading records. Then look at the first lesson for the next higher level. If you think they need more time, "borrow" from the same level in one of the other *LLI* systems. If you don't have the other systems, then find more books on the same level and create your own lessons using the same lesson framework. Review the phonics and word work from the level you are just finishing. Be sure you are teaching hard for areas that are holding them back. When children are ready to move up in the text level, recent reading records should show (1) high accuracy rates, (2) evidence of fluent reading (after level C), and (3) good comprehension.

Is it all right to move to the next level without teaching all the lessons?

Yes, but be cautious. If children are finding the reading and writing very easy, then you can skip the rest of the lessons at a level or even an entire level. Be sure to look at *The Literacy Continuum* for the level, and think about evidence that children have strong control of most of the behaviors and understandings required for the level.

What do you do about children whose reading might be at one level, but their writing is well below that level?

Go with the reading level for instruction in *LLI*. Be sure to give emphasis and attention to writing in the even-numbered lessons. Use the Classroom Connection option, which often involves more writing. Work closely with the classroom teacher to provide extra classroom writing opportunities.

Teaching Decisions

How much can I vary the lesson?

We encourage you to adjust the lesson in any way justified by information from your ongoing assessment and observation of learners' strengths and needs. No lesson plan can be written to fit all children. Your decision making across the lesson is critical. It would not make sense to consistently eliminate lesson components or to drastically slow down instruction, but you should tailor lessons to meet children's needs.

If children are finding the new text too difficult, should I read it to them first?

No. If the text is so difficult you need to read it to the children (or provide a very long introduction), then it is probably too hard. They need to experience independent processing of a new text that allows them to build their reading power. Move down to an easier level.

When should children stop pointing?

At level C they should begin to drop the finger and let the eyes take over the process. They may bring the finger back in at difficulty, but should gradually become less dependent on it. Remind children to "read it with your eyes." (See *Prompting Guide, Part 1*, "Early Reading Behaviors.") If they cannot do it, teach hard for it, or reassess the child. Some children may find this transition difficult and will need to practice on very easy texts.

When should children start to read silently?

At about level H or I, the voice should start to drop to a very soft level. Children should be discovering that they can read more quickly when they read silently. By about levels I and J, the reading should be silent so the children can learn to read silently with competence. Of course, you will still be sampling oral reading from individual children, one at a time. Some children may find this transition difficult and will need to practice on very easy texts.

If children are finding the new text very easy, should I cut back on the information in the introduction?

You can cut back a little bit, but remember that the introduction is designed to start readers thinking. It may be that children can move a little faster through the level or that your placement is too low.

What do you do about children who have low vocabulary (usually English language learners) when you get to books that have lots of concepts and new vocabulary?

You need a richer introduction and perhaps a longer discussion after reading to be sure children are gaining the vocabulary and book language structures they need. After rereading, you can revisit a few words just to use them and talk about their meaning. Talk with the classroom teacher to be sure that children are being exposed to new vocabulary daily through interactive read-aloud. Another way to help is to go to previous levels (for example, books that those children have not read) in any of the strands and give children some "extra" books to read that are easy for them. They can do this in the classroom and will build vocabulary in the process. Finally, work into the lesson some word "collections," where you write words that are connected with each other in some way—names of pets, names of animals, words about weather, and so on.

What do you do when children have gaps in phonics/word analysis? Do you keep giving them extra practice? Do you stay longer on a level to make up for the gaps? Do you go back and teach previous concepts that they don't have?

These are complex issues and will depend a great deal on teacher decision making. If children can read texts at a level (meeting the criteria for instructional level), then usually they have the phonics skills. But it would be a good idea to look at *The Literacy Continuum* and at the Word Work Master Plan for that level and the previous level. It may be that you need to spend a day or two tidying up some phonics knowledge that will be essential as they move into higher texts. Work closely with the classroom teacher to identify areas of support needed.

How do you help children take on high-frequency words, as there isn't enough practice time in the thirty-minute lesson?

Throughout the lessons you show children how to look closely at the words, connect them with other words, and learn them; so, their ability to take on new words should speed up. Children will be doing a great deal of reading, and many new words will be acquired in this activity. Not all words have to be learned in isolation from word cards because the system for learning words is being established.

Here are some ways to get in some extra word learning: (1) Print out an extra copy of high-frequency words from Online Resources and show them how to cut them apart and take them home. Spend some lesson time "practicing" what they can do with their words at home. For example, they can lay them out and find connections. They can play Concentration. They can just turn them over and make piles of "easy words" and "words I'm still learning." (2) Have an extra "word bag" in the classroom and arrange with the classroom teacher for children to go over the words during independent work time. (3) Invite family members to a conference and show them a couple of easy games to play with their children at home.

How much flexibility do I have with regard to word work? Do I have to work with the suggested words?

The suggested words are there only for your convenience. You can select others that fit the principle you are teaching. If you feel a different principle is needed, make the decision to use the principle that fits your children's needs.

What should I do if children are not learning words quickly enough?

Visit the section on instructional procedures in this guide (see Section 5) and reflect on whether you are being explicit enough in your teaching. Also, look at Chapter 2, "Building and Using a Repertoire of Words," in *When Readers Struggle: Teaching That Works, A–N.*

Should all the words in My Writing Book *be spelled conventionally?*

Yes, because children need to read their books at school and after they take them home. Use white correction tape to help children write conventional spellings and write some words in for them. Also, they may be using sound and letter boxes to help them write some words. There may be an occasional difficult word on which a particular child has made an excellent attempt and you do not want to intervene to make the spelling conventional. In those cases, you may decide to ignore a few temporary spellings.

If the lesson specifies interactive writing, can I use independent writing instead?

That is your decision. If you think children need a strong demonstration and to focus their attention on one text, then use interactive writing. If you think each child needs to write rather than observe some of the time, use independent writing. Sometimes, you can write one sentence interactively for children to copy (or you can write it quickly for them) and they can go on to write another sentence independently.

How do I support English language learners?

On the last page of every *LLI* lesson, you will find suggestions for fine-tuning the lesson to support English language learners. Also, see Appendix C in this guide for other suggestions.

What if I started on a level that is proving to be too difficult for the group?

As a general practice, begin at a level that you are confident will allow the children to read successfully. Stop where you are and move down to an easier level if you find you started at the wrong place. As children go up the levels, they may meet texts that they previously read and found hard. It will be a confidence booster to encounter them again and find them within reach.

Assessment

Why do I need to take reading records when I have the benchmark data from the beginning of the intervention?

The literacy levels of children, especially younger ones, change very rapidly with effective teaching. You need up-to-date objective information to inform your decision making and use of *Prompting Guides, Parts 1 and 2*. Your weekly reading records will provide important information for teaching individuals in the group. Also, this information will help you in planning introductions to the text, phonics, and writing.

How often should I take a reading record?

With a group size of three, we recommend taking a reading record every other day with one child. Your daily observations and this procedure will provide enough specific information to guide your teaching.

Do I have to use the Recording Form to take reading records?

If you know how to take running records and prefer a blank form, you can use one. (This may be more difficult at levels K through N because there are so many words on a line and children read quickly.) The other option is the *LLI Reading Record App*, available through Apple iTunes.

Do you recommend administering a Benchmark Assessment before moving to the next reading level?

No. That would be too much assessment. If you are observing and taking reading records once every six days on each child, then you should have a good idea of how the group is performing at the present level. If they are reading at instructional level on the first reading and at solid instructional level or independent level on the second reading, then they are probably ready to go on to the next level. Look at *The Literacy Continuum* for the present level to be sure that you are seeing evidence of the needed behaviors and understandings for thinking within, beyond, and about the text.

Parents

How can I support children who do not do their homework?

You have three ways to support the home option: (1) Make it special. Use the brightly colored Take-Home Bag. Spend some lesson time having children "practice" what they will do when they get home (taking out their book and other activities, doing them, putting them back in the bag, and putting the bag by the door so they won't forget it). Make it an event the first week when they bring back their bags and talk about what they did at home. (2) Enlist the classroom teacher in reminding children to take home their bags with books and activities and to do the work at home. (3) Schedule a conference to walk family members through the kinds of activities their children will be bringing home. Remember, it is important that children have extra practice reading. Sometimes family members are not available to listen to a child read. Some teachers have had good luck sending home a stuffed animal as a "reading buddy."

How can I keep families involved?

Make good use of the Take-Home books and Home/School Connection options. Help families understand how to use them by sending home the daily letters. Also, invite a parent or guardian to observe a lesson and talk with them afterward.

Should I send the LLI *books home with children?*

LLI provides take-home versions of the books that are designed for children to read and keep in a basket at home. This is important for low-achieving readers who may not have access to books they can read at home. Readers need large amounts of practice. You have the option to purchase more Take-Home books at a very reasonable price so that children benefit from rereading.

Should I tell families the level I am working on?

We don't believe it's necessary to share levels with families; rather you should focus on the continuous progress children are making. Show them the books their child was reading at the beginning of *LLI* and what he or she is reading now. Help them look at the books to understand progress. Explain that the level helps you to monitor progress and teach the child. Try to avoid the "level" being something that parents and caregivers focus on too much.

appendix

A	*LLI Green System* Book Chart	118
B	*LLI* Series Books	121
C	Text Analyses for Books in the *LLI Green System*	128
D	Master Plan for Word Work in the *LLI Green System*	129
E	New High-Frequency Words in the *LLI Green System*	155
F	F&P Calculator/Stopwatch Directions	158
G	*LLI* as a Complement to Reading Recovery®	159
H	Glossary	160
I	Bibliography	175

appendix A

System Book Chart

Book/Lesson	1	2	3	4	5
Getting Started	Waking Up	Frog Food	The New Puppy	Friends	Sam and Papa
Book/Lesson	6	7	8	9	10
Getting Started	Too Much Stuff	Ant Can't	Eggs	Where Things Grow	The Very Busy Hen
Book/Lesson	11	12	13	14	15
Level A	Flying	Woof!	The Painter	Smells	Jesse
Book/Lesson	16	17	18	19	20
Level A	Monkey	Oh No!	Getting Dressed	Family Pictures	My Bath

Level B Begins

Book/Lesson	21	22	23	24	25
Level B	Orson's Tummy Ache	At the Park	Bubbles	The Farmers	Mom and Kayla
Book/Lesson	26	27	28	29	30
Level B	My Puppy	Our Garden	My New School	Boots and Shoes	Traffic

Level C Begins

Book/Lesson	31	32	33	34	35
Level C	A Day at the Park	Jump	Looking for Taco	Swim!	Meli on the Stairs
Book/Lesson	36	37	38	39	40
Level C	The Sky	Homes	The Picnic	Clouds	Look!

Level D Begins

Book/Lesson	41	42	43	44	45
Level D	The Three Pigs	Snap!	Up in a Tree	Apple Pie	Time for Lunch
Book/Lesson	46	47	48	49	50
Level D	A Rainy Day	The Good Dog	My Friend	What Am I?	Trucks

Level E Begins

Book/Lesson	51	52	53	54	55
Level E	The Three Bears	The Puppets	The Surprise	Play Ball!	Talent Show
Book/Lesson	56	57	58	59	60
Level E	Kate's Truck	Baby Pictures	A Visit to the City	A Walk with Meli	Pets

Shaded Box = Independent books at easier level.

System Book Chart, *continued*

Level F Begins

Book/Lesson	61	62	63	64	65
Level F	The Three Little Pigs and a Big Bad Wolf	The Box	The Soccer Game	Books	Bunny and the Monster
Book/Lesson	66	67	68	69	70
Level F	The Pool	Pictures of Hugs	Farmer Dan's Ducks	The Big Storm	My Five Senses

Level G Begins

Book/Lesson	71	72	73	74	75
Level G	Goldie and the Three Bears	Helping Mom	Papa's Birthday	The Storm	Baby Bird
Book/Lesson	76	77	78	79	80
Level G	Lizzy	The Goat in the Garden	A Surprise for Mom	How Frogs Grow	Brave Taco

Level H Begins

Book/Lesson	81	82	83	84	85
Level H	The Skunk with No Stripes	The Tree House	The Gingerbread Man	Out for Lunch	Dinner for Maisy
Book/Lesson	86	87	88	89	90
Level H	Just Wait and See	In Winter	All About Animal Babies	The Gecko That Came to School	Grandma's Glasses

Level I Begins

Book/Lesson	91	92	93	94	95
Level I	Fun for Hugs	Home Sweet Home	Bear's Birthday	The Bossy Pig	Stone Soup
Book/Lesson	96	97	98	99	100
Level I	Best New Friends	The Missing Cat	The Lucky Penny	All About Honeybees	A Walk at Night

Level J Begins

Book/Lesson	101	102	103	104	105
Level J	Too Tall	Two Teams	All About Dolphins	The Cherries	The Lion and the Mouse
Book/Lesson	106	107	108	109	110
Level J	All About Boats	The Three Billy Goats	All About Chimps	Bad-Luck Day	A Trip to the Laundromutt

Shaded Box = Independent books at easier level.

APPENDIX A

System Book Chart, *continued*

Level K Begins

Book/Lesson	111	112	113	14	115
Level K	A Visit from Sweetie	The Grumpy Bears	A Hawk Hunts	More Pie!	The House by the River
Book/Lesson	**116**	**117**	**118**	**119**	**120**
Level K	Elephant Moms	Moving In	Firefighters at Work	The Spaceship	Let Me Play
Book/Lesson	**121**	**122**	**123**	**124**	**125**
Level K	Ouch!	Fireflies	The Climbing Party	Pickle's Nose	The Fox and the Goose
Book/Lesson	**126**	**127**	**128**	**129**	**130**
Level K	The Missing Eggs	Ants at Work	Under Your Feet	Hold Your Nose!	Mason's Fishing Trip

Shaded Box = Independent books at easier level.

appendix B

LLI Series Books

Series Title	Description	Book Titles	Level	System O	System G	System B
Meli Nonfiction	Meli, an adorable little West Highland terrier, gets care, training, and lots of love from her owner, Ron.	The New Puppy	A		X	
		Meli on the Stairs	C		X	
		A Walk with Meli	E		X	
		Meli at the Pet Shop	E			X
		Meli at the Vet	E			X
		Taking Care of Meli	F			X
		Meli at School	G			X
		The Problem with Meli	J			X
Big Machines Nonfiction	Dynamic photographs and interesting facts about cranes, fire trucks, bulldozers, road rollers, and more.	Trucks	B		X	
		Police Car	B			X
		Fighting Fires	G			X
		Road Builders	I			X
		Cranes	I			X
Fun Club Fiction with a factual element	Miss Dimple takes the After-School Fun Club on fun-filled field trips to a post office, an aquarium, a vet clinic, and a dairy farm.	The Fun Club Goes to a Dairy Farm	H			X
		The Fun Club Goes to the Post Office	I			X
		The Fun Club Goes to the Vet Clinic	I			X
		The Fun Club Goes to the Aquarium	K			X

continues

LLI Series Books, *continued*

Series Title	Description	Book Titles	Level	System O	System G	System B
All About Nonfiction	A collection of interesting, factual books about everything from honeybees to volcanoes. Stunning photographs, diagrams, and other nonfiction text features make these books highly accessible.	All About Animal Babies	F		X	
		All About Chimps	H		X	
		All About Honeybees	I		X	
		All About Dolphins	J		X	
		All About Boats	H		X	
		All About Penguins	C			X
		All About Snakes	C			X
		All About Sharks	F			X
		All About Bugs	F			X
		All About Sled Dogs	H			X
		All About Spiders	H			X
		All About Dinosaurs	I			X
		All About Redwood Trees	I			X
		All About Bats	J			X
		All About the Sonoran Desert	J			X
		All About African Elephants	K			X
		All About Astronauts	N			X
		All About Volcanoes	N			X
		All About Robots	K			X

LLI Series Books, continued

Series Title	Description	Book Titles	Level	System O	System G	System B
Orson and Taco Fiction	Big, easy-going Orson and feisty little Taco are canine friends whose adventures will touch your heart and tickle your funny bone.	Friends	A		X	
		Oh No!	A		X	
		Woof!	A		X	
		Orson's Tummy Ache	B		X	
		Looking for Taco	C		X	
		The Good Dog	D		X	
		Brave Taco	E		X	
		The Big Storm	F		X	
		A Trip to the Laundromutt	H		X	
		A Visit from Sweetie	K		X	
Fixit Family Fiction	The Fixit Family doesn't have a lot of luxuries, but they do have a lot of know-how. And that's a good thing, because something always seems to need fixing around their place.	The Drip	D			X
		Billy's Pen	D			X
		The Broken Clock	E			X
		Pinky the Pig	C			X
		The New Roof	G			X
		The Bird Feeders	H			X

APPENDIX B

continues

LLI Series Books, continued

Series Title	Description	Book Titles	Level	System O	System G	System B
Froggy and Friends Fiction	Artistic and fun-loving Froggy likes nothing better than spending time with his friends—with the possible exception of eating bugs!	Frog Food	A		X	
		The Painter	A		X	
		Baby Pictures	E		X	
		The Cherries	H		X	
		The Red Pajamas	D			X
		The Trip	E			X
		Frog Songs	J			X
		Good Friends	L			X
Fox Family Fiction	This loving family of foxes includes a rambunctious big sister and a slightly less secure little brother. Children will relate to the familiar situations, including trying to play quietly in the house, being wide awake at bedtime, and not liking what's for dinner.	A Surprise for Roxy	D			X
		Andy Fox at School	E			X
		A Fast Fox	F			X
		Super Fox	G			X
		Wide Awake!	H			X
		The Perfect Picnic	G			X
		Puddle Play	K			X

LLI Series Books, continued

Series Title	Description	Book Titles	Level	System O	System G	System B
Sam and Jesse Fiction	These realistic stories feature two cousins with very different interests. Still, the boys get along well most of the time, and they have one important thing in common—they both adore their grandfather.	Jesse	A		X	
		Sam and Papa	B		X	
		A Day at the Park	C		X	
		The Soccer Game	F		X	
		Papa's Birthday	G		X	
		At the Beach	G			X
		The Pirates	L			X
		The Hot Day	N			X
Bunny Rabbit Fiction	Bunny is a happy-go-lucky little rabbit from a big, extended family who finds fun in ordinary days—and manages to solve a couple of problems, too.	My Family	B	X		
		Hop, Hop, Hop	B	X		
		Out to Play	C	X		
		The Storm	E		X	
		Bunny and the Monster	F		X	
Meg and Hugs Fiction	These gentle stories tell of the relationship between Meg, a little girl who lives with her grandparents, and Hugs, her lovable but slightly contrary cat.	Up in a Tree	D		X	
		Pictures of Hugs	F		X	
		Fun for Hugs	I		X	
		The Missing Cat	I		X	

continues

LLI Series Books, *continued*

Series Title	Description	Book Titles	Level	System O	G	B
Moosling Fiction	The young moose hero of these books cannot be described as the brightest or most experienced animal in the forest. Still, his positive, helpful approach to life somehow always makes him a winner.	A Picnic in the Rain	D			X
		The Hug	E			X
		Moosling the Babysitter	G			X
		Footprints	H			X
		Hide and Seek	J			X
		Moosling in Winter	K			X
		Moosling the Hero	L			X
		The Costume Party	M			X
Family Fiction	Photographs lend realism to these simple stories of family members playing, working, going out to lunch, and planting a garden.	Playing Dress Up	A	X		
		My Big Brother	B	X		
		Family Pictures	A		X	
		Helping Mom	E		X	
		Out for Lunch	F		X	
		Grandma's Glasses	F		X	
Kim and Lizzy Fiction	Kim and Lizzy are best friends who live close to one another in the city and who share everything—even colds.	The Cold	D			X
		Kim's New Shoes	G			X
		The Play Date	G			X
		The Scream	K			X

LLI Series Books, *continued*

Series Title	Description	Book Titles	Level	System O	System G	System B
Classic Tales Fiction	The Classic Tales are updated versions of the familiar stories and themes that children have been enjoying for decades. At the end of each story, there is a readers' theater for rereading or dramatization. The books are oversized to accommodate their rich artwork.	The Hat	B	X		
		The Three Pigs	D		X	
		The Three Bears	E		X	
		Three Little Pigs and a Big Bad Wolf	F		X	
		Goldie and the Three Bears	G		X	
		The Goat in the Garden	G		X	
		The Gingerbread Man	H		X	
		Stone Soup	I		X	
		The Lion and the Mouse	J		X	
		The Three Billy Goats	J		X	
		The Little Red Hen	C			X
		The Mitten	D			X
		Chicken Little	E			X
		The Wind and the Sun	I			X
		The Great Big Enormous Turnip	H			X
		The Coyote and the Rabbit	H			X
		The Hare and the Tortoise	J			X
		The City Mouse and the Country Mouse	K			X
		Jack and the Beanstalk	L			X
		The Fox and the Gulls	M			X

APPENDIX B

appendix C

▶ Text Analyses for Books in the *LLI Green System*

On the first page of every lesson, you will see an analysis of the new book that covers the ten text factors we have found helpful in determining the challenges in a text. These factors are described in the chart below.

The text analysis will provide valuable information to guide your introduction and teaching of the new text. Additionally, in this section, we provide a detailed analysis of the word challenges of the new text. Next, you will find this analysis for each title. This information is helpful to us as teachers because it helps us to understand the kinds of word-solving challenges young readers are facing. You will not want to attend to all of these word features in teaching any one lesson. Instead, you will find some selected features in the text factor analysis. These features have been selected because they are key to the text *and* appropriate for the learning needs that children typically have when reading at these levels. We are always thinking about what the children need to know next.

Factors Related to Text Difficulty

Factor	Definition
Genre	The "genre" is the type of text and refers to a system by which fiction and nonfiction texts are classified. Each genre has characteristic features.
Text Structure	The "structure" is the way the text is organized and presented. It may be *narrative*, as in most fiction and biographical texts. Factual texts are organized categorically or topically and may have sections with headings. Writers of factual texts use several underlying structural patterns to provide information to readers: *enumeration, chronological sequence, temporal sequence, question/answer, compare/contrast, cause/effect,* and *problem/solution.* The presence of these structures, especially in combination can increase the challenge for readers.
Content	The "content" refers to the subject matter of the text—the concepts that are important to understand. In fiction, content may be related to the setting or to the kinds of problems characters have. In factual texts, content refers to the topic of focus. Content is considered in relation to the prior experience of readers.
Themes and Ideas	The "themes and ideas" are the big ideas that are communicated by the text. A text may have multiple themes or a main theme and several supporting themes or ideas. The themes and ideas are larger than the content of the text.
Language and Literary Features	Written language is qualitatively different from spoken language. Fiction writers use dialogue, figurative language, and other kinds of literary structures. Factual writers use description and technical language. In hybrid texts you may find a wide range of literary language.
Sentence Complexity	Meaning is mapped out onto the syntax of language. Texts with simpler, more natural sentences are easier to process. Sentences with embedded and conjoined clauses make a text more difficult.
Vocabulary	"Vocabulary" refers to the meaning of the words in our oral language. The more the words are accessible to readers in terms of meaning, the easier a text will be. The individual's *reading and writing vocabularies* refer to words that they understand and can also read or write.
Words	"Words" refer to recognizing and solving the printed words in the text. The challenge in a text partly depends on the number and the difficulty of the words that the reader must solve by recognizing them or decoding them. Having a great many of the same high-frequency words makes a text more accessible to readers.
Illustrations	The "illustrations" include drawings, paintings, or photographs that accompany the text and add meaning and enjoyment. In factual texts, illustrations also include graphics that provide a great deal of information that readers must integrate with the text. Illustrations are an integral part of a high-quality text. Increasingly, fiction texts are including a range of graphics.
Book and Print Features	The "book and print features" are the physical aspects of the text—what readers cope with in terms of length, size, and layout. Book and print features also include tools like the table of contents, glossary, pronunciation guides, indices, and sidebars.

appendix D

Master Plan for Word Work in the *LLI Green System*

	Lesson 1	Lesson 2	Lesson 3	Lesson 4	Lesson 5
Rhyming Words	[PWW] Rhyming Words Some words have parts that sound the same at the end. They rhyme. (*corn, morn*) [Phonological Awareness #1]	[PWW] Rhyming Words Some words have parts that sound the same at the end. They rhyme. (*hop, stop*) [Phonological Awareness #1]	[PWW] Rhyming Words You can hear and connect words that rhyme. (*hot, pot; cold, old*) [Phonological Awareness #2]	[PWW] Rhyming Words You can hear and connect words that rhyme. (*tree, bee; cat, hat; car, star; fish, dish; fan, van; snake, rake*) [Phonological Awareness #2]	[PWW] Rhyming Words You can hear and connect words that rhyme. (*cat, hat; car, star; fish, dish; fan, van; snake, rake*) [Phonological Awareness #2]
Names as Words **Letter Forms and Shapes** **High-Frequency Words**	[LWW] Your name is a word. There are two kinds of letters One is uppercase (or capital) and the other is lowercase (or small). You see some words many times when you read and use them many times when you write. You need to learn these words because they help you read and write. (*up, the, and*) [Early Literacy Concepts #6] [Letter Knowledge #3] [High-Frequency Words #1]	[LWW] Your name is a word. Each letter is different. You need to learn words that you see many times because they help you read and write. (*I, on*) [Early Literacy Concepts #6] [Letter Knowledge #14] [High-Frequency Words #1]	[LWW] Make the shape of a letter. You see some words many times when you read and use them many times when you write. You need to learn these words because they help you read and write. (*a, got*) [Letter Knowledge #14] [High-Frequency Words #1]	[LWW] Some letters have long straight lines. Some letters have short straight lines. You see some words many times when you read and use them many times when you write. You need to learn these words because they help you read and write. (*is*) [Letter Knowledge #1] [High-Frequency Words #1]	[LWW] Some letters have long straight lines. Some letters have short straight lines. You need to learn words that you see many times because they help you read and write. (*to, my, me*) [Letter Knowledge #1] [High-Frequency Words #1]

continues

Master Plan for Word Work in the *LLI Green System*, continued					
	Lesson 6	**Lesson 7**	**Lesson 8**	**Lesson 9**	**Lesson 10**
Syllables **Rhyming Words** **Beginning Consonants**	[PWW] Syllables You can hear, say, and clap the parts in a word. Words can have one or more parts. (*cat, dog, bird, bus, ball; turtle, monkey, balloon, spider, carrot, pizza; butterfly, umbrella, tricycle*) [Phonological Awareness #6]	[PWW] Syllables You can hear, say, or clap the parts in a word. Words can have one or more parts. (*dog, bird goat, bus, balloon, carrot, spider, ball, snake, toothbrush, butterfly, tricycle, elephant, umbrella*) [Phonological Awareness #6] [Word Structure #2]	[PWW] Rhyming Words You can make rhymes by thinking of words that sound the same at the end. (*man, fan, pan; pat, sat; dad, had; sit, kit; by, my; go, so; run, bun; stop, pop; boo, zoo; got, pot*) [Phonological Awareness #3]	[PWW] Syllables You can break a word into parts. You can blend the parts in a word. (*baby, candy, haircut, letter, cupcake, teapot, paper, kitten, butterfly, elephant, banana*) [Phonological Awareness #8] [Phonological Awareness #7]	[PWW] Beginning Consonant Sounds You can say a word slowly and hear the sound at the beginning of a word. You can match the sound and the letter at the beginning of a word. (*bear, cat, dog, leaf, mouse, nest, pig, ring, socks, turtle, vacuum, violin*) [Letter-Sound Relationships #1]
Letter Shapes **High-Frequency Words**	[LWW] Some letters have long straight lines. Some letters have short straight lines. Some letters have curves. You need to learn words that you see many times because they help you read and write. (*his, he, it, in, no*) [Letter Knowledge #1] [High-Frequency Words #1]	[LWW] Each letter is different. (*you, yes*) [Letter Knowledge #1]	[LWW] Letters can have long straight lines, short straight lines, or curves. You need to learn words that you see many times because they help you read and write. (*out*) [Letter Knowledge #5] [High-Frequency Word #1]	[LWW] Some words have two or three letters. You see some words many times when you read. Look at the shape of a letter and say the letter's name. (*we, too*) [High-Frequency Words #4] [Letter Knowledge #2]	[LWW] Each letter is different. You need to learn words that you see many times because they help you read and write. (*play, am*) [Letter Knowledge #1] [High-Frequency Words #1, #4]

Master Plan for Word Work in the *LLI Green System*, continued

	Lesson 11	**Lesson 12**	**Lesson 13**	**Lesson 14**	**Lesson 15**
Beginning Consonants	[PWW] Beginning Consonants (*s, t, h*) You can say a word slowly and hear the sound at the beginning of a word. You can match the sound and the letter at the beginning of a word. (*sail, socks, slide, snowman, tacks, tail, top, hand, horse, house, mouse*) [Letter-Sound Relationships #2]	[PWW] Beginning Consonants (*p, f, m*) You can say a word slowly and hear the sound at the beginning of a word. You can match the sound and the letter at the beginning of a word. (*pail, pear, pencil, fan, fork, four, man, mat, mouse*) [Letter-Sound Relationships #2]	[PWW] Beginning Consonants (*b, c, n*) You can hear the sound at the beginning of a word. You can match the sound and the letter at the beginning of a word. (*ball, banana, boy, cake, can, cup, net, nose, nut*) [Letter-Sound Relationships #2]	[PWW] Beginning Consonants (*g, l, w*) You can say a word slowly and hear the sound at the beginning of a word. You can match the sound and the letter at the beginning of a word. (*goat, girl, goose, lamp, lion, log, wagon, web, worm*) [Letter-Sound Relationships #2]	[PWW] Beginning Consonants (*d, j, r*) You can say a word slowly and hear the sound at the beginning of a word. You can match the sound and the letter at the beginning of a word. (*doll, drum, duck, jam, jar, jeep, rake, ring, rose*) [Letter-Sound Relationships #2]
Letter Forms and Shapes **High-Frequency Words**	[LWW] Some words have three or more letters. You see some words many times when you read and use them many times when you write. You need to learn these words because they help you read and write. (*see*) [High-Frequency Words #4]	[Optional LWW] There are two kinds of letters. One is uppercase (or capital), and the other is lowercase (or small). (*and; And; the, The; it, It; he, He; my, My*) [Letter Knowledge #3]	[LWW] You need to learn words that you see many times because they help you read and write. (*can*) [High-Frequency Words #1]	[Optional LWW] You can notice how letters look. Letters can have long straight lines, short straight lines, or curves. [Letter Knowledge #5]	[LWW] You see some words many times when you read and use them many times when you write. You need to learn these words because they help you read and write. (*like, love*) [High-Frequency Words #4]

continues

APPENDIX D

Master Plan for Word Work in the *LLI Green System*, continued

	Lesson 16	**Lesson 17**	**Lesson 18**	**Lesson 19**	**Lesson 20**
Beginning Consonants **Onsets and Rimes** **Phonemes**	[PWW] Beginning Consonants (*k, v, y, z*) You can say a word slowly and hear the sound at the beginning of a word. You can match the sound and the letter at the beginning of a word. (*kangaroo, kite, key, van, vest, yawn, yo-yo, zebra, zero*) [Letter-Sound Relationships #2]	[PWW] Onsets and Rimes You can hear and say the first and last part of a word. You can blend parts of a word. You can match the sound and the letter at the beginning of a word. (*bear, cat, dog, fish, goat, hat, kite, leaf, boat, cow, rose, tooth, zoo, toy, doll*) [Phonological Awareness #10] [Phonological Awareness #11] [Letter-Sound Relationships #2]	[PWW] Words with Three Phonemes You can say a word slowly. You can hear each sound in a word. You can match the sound and the letter. (*got, can, red, fun, man, ran, top, pig, fit, bat*) [Phonological Awareness #14] [Letter-Sound Relationships #1]	[PWW] Adding a Phoneme You can add a sound to the beginning of a word to make a new word. (*at/sat, in/pin, am/ham, it/sit; in, am, at, up*) [Phonological Awareness #20]	[PWW] Deleting a Phoneme You can say a word without the first sound to make another word. (*band/and, ham/am, cup/up, fat/at, tin, sand, his, bit, rat, fin, hit, pat, hand*) [Phonological Awareness #27]
High-Frequency Words **Phonemes** **Letter Forms**	[Optional LWW] You see some words many times when you read and use them many times when you write. You need to learn these words because they help you read and write. [High-Frequency Words #4]	[LWW] You see some words many times when you read and use them many times when you write. You need to learn these words because they help you read and write. (*at, look; no, in, it, am*) [High-Frequency Words #4]	[Optional LWW] You need to learn words that you see many times because they help you read and write. [High-Frequency Words #4]	[LWW] You see some words many times when you read and use them many times when you write. You need to learn these words because they help you read and write. (*this; the, is*) [High-Frequency Words #4]	[Optional LWW] There are two kinds of letters. One is uppercase (or capital) and the other is lowercase (or small). [Letter Knowledge #3]

Master Plan for Word Work in the *LLI Green System*, continued

	Lesson 21	**Lesson 22**	**Lesson 23**	**Lesson 24**	**Lesson 25**
VC Patterns	[PWW] Phonograms with a VC Pattern (*-an*) You can look at the part (pattern) to read a word. You can make new words by putting a letter or a letter cluster before the part (pattern). (*can, man, fan, ran, plan*) [Spelling Patterns #3]	[PWW] Phonograms with a VC Pattern (*-it*) You can look at the part (pattern) to read a word. You can make new words by putting a letter or a letter cluster before the part (pattern). (*sit, hit, fit, pit, kit*) [Spelling Patterns #3]	[PWW] Phonograms with a VC Pattern (*-am*) You can look at the part (pattern) to read a word. You can make new words by putting a letter or a letter cluster before the part (pattern). (*ham, Sam, jam, ram, clam*) [Spelling Patterns #3]	[PWW] Phonograms with a VC Pattern (*-in*) You can look at the part (pattern) to read a word. You can make new words by putting a letter or a letter cluster before the part (pattern). (*fin, tin, pin, spin, grin*) [Spelling Patterns #3]	[PWW] Phonograms with a VC Pattern (*-at*) You can look at the part (pattern) to read a word. You can make new words by putting a letter or a letter cluster before the part (pattern). (*cat, bat, rat, sat, flat*) [Spelling Patterns #3]
High-Frequency Words	[LWW] Some words have one, two, or three letters. You see some words many times when you read and use them many times when you write. You need to learn these words because they help you read and write. (*big*) [High-Frequency Words #1]	[Optional LWW] You see some words many times when you read and use them many times when you write. You need to use these words because they help you read and write. [High-Frequency Words #1]	[LWW] Some words have two letters. Some words have three or more letters. You need to learn words that you see many times because they help you read and write. (*a, at, am, and; he, his; I, is, it, in; me, my*) [High-Frequency Words #1]	[Optional LWW] You need to learn words that you see many times because they help you read and write. [High-Frequency Words #1]	[LWW] You need to learn words that you see many times because they help you read and write. (*Mom, has*) [High-Frequency Words #4]

continues

Master Plan for Word Work in the *LLI Green System*, continued

	Lesson 26	Lesson 27	Lesson 28	Lesson 29	Lesson 30
Short Vowel Sounds at the Beginning of Words **Short Vowel Sounds Between Two Consonants**	[PWW] Short Vowel Sounds Some words have a vowel at the beginning. You can hear a short vowel sound. (*at, am, and; egg; is, it, in; on; up*) [Letter-Sound Relationships #21]	[PWW] Short Vowel Sounds Some words have a vowel between two consonants. You can hear a short vowel sound. (*can, has, cat, Dad, ham*) [Letter-Sound Relationships #22]	[PWW] Short Vowel Sounds Some words have a vowel between two consonants. You can hear a short vowel sound. (*yes, red, bed, hen, jet*) [Letter-Sound Relationships #22]	[PWW] Short Vowel Sounds Some words have a vowel between two consonants. You can hear a short vowel sound. (*his, this, sit, pin, hit*) [Letter-Sound Relationships #22]	[PWW] Short Vowel Sounds Some words have a vowel between two consonants. You can hear a short vowel sound. (*Mom, got, hot, hop, top*) [Letter-Sound Relationships #22]
Consonants and Vowels **High-Frequency Words**	[Optional LWW] Some letters are consonants. Some letters are vowels. Every word has at least one vowel. [Letter Knowledge #7]	[LWW] You need to learn words that you see many times because they help you read and write. (*have, some, our*) [High-Frequency Words #4]	[Optional LWW] Some letters are consonants. Some letters are vowels. Every word has at least one vowel. [Letter Knowledge #7]	[LWW] You need to learn words that you see many times because they help you read and write. (*with*) [High-Frequency Words #4]	[Optional LWW] Some letters are vowels. Every word has at least one vowel. [Letter Knowledge #7]

Master Plan for Word Work in the *LLI Green System*, continued

	Lesson 31	Lesson 32	Lesson 33	Lesson 34	Lesson 35
Short Vowel Sounds Between Two Consonants **Ending Phonemes** **Ending Consonant Sounds**	[PWW] Short Vowel Sounds Some words have a vowel between two consonants. You can hear a short vowel sound. (*cut, bus, pup, but, sun*) [Letter-Sound Relationships #22]	[PWW] Ending Phonemes Some words sound the same at the end. You can connect words that sound the same at the end. (*bag, bell, cup, dog, drum, fan, goat, hem, jam, jeep, net, wall*) [Phonological Awareness #18]	[PWW] Ending Phonemes Some words sound the same at the end. You can connect words that sound the same at the end. (*tub, bib; fan, sun; clock, pack; car, pear; cave, hive; elf, knife*) [Phonological Awareness #18]	[PWW] Ending Consonant Sounds You can hear the sound at the end of a word. You can match the sound and the letter at the end of a word. (*n, p, m, l, d, t, g*) (*pin, ten*) [Letter-Sound Relationships #4]	[PWW] Ending Consonant Sounds You can hear the sound at the end of a word. You can match the sound and the letter at the end of a word. (*s, b, n, r, k, f, v*) (*bus, horse*) [Letter-Sound Relationships #4]
Consonants and Vowels **Letter Shapes** **High-Frequency Words** **Phonemes**	[LWW] Some letters are consonants. Some letters are vowels. Some letters have parts that look the same. (*want, wants*) [Letter Knowledge #7] [Letter Knowledge #5]	[Optional LWW] Each letter is different. Some letters have tails and some have tunnels. There are two kinds of letters. One is uppercase, and the other is lowercase. [Phonological Awareness #1] [Phonological Awareness #3]	[LWW] You need to learn words that you see many times because they help you read and write. (*come, here, not*) [High-Frequency Words #4]	[Optional LWW] You can hear the sound at the end of a word. You can match the sound and the letter at the end of a word. [Letter-Sound Relationships #4]	[LWW] You need to learn words that you see many times because they help you read and write. (*down; big, bit, bug, black, but, back*) [High-Frequency Words #4]

continues

Master Plan for Word Work in the *LLI Green System*, continued

	Lesson 36	**Lesson 37**	**Lesson 38**	**Lesson 39**	**Lesson 40**
Phonemes **Beginning and Ending Consonant Sounds** **Short Vowel Sounds** **Phonograms with a VC Pattern**	[PWW] Words with Three Phonemes You can say a word slowly. You can hear each sound in a word. You can match letters and sounds in words. (*run, cap, sit, pot, leg, fan, him*) [Phonological Awareness #14] [Letter-Sound Relationships #2, #4]	[PWW] Words with Three Phonemes You can say a word slowly. You can hear each sound in a word. You can match consonant sounds and letters at the beginning of a word and at the end of a word. Some words have one vowel between two consonants. (*tag, bug, men, rip, hot*) [Phonological Awareness #14] [Letter-Sound Relationships #2, #4, #22]	[PWW] Phonograms with a VC Pattern (-*ad*) You can look at a word part (pattern) to read a word. You can use the word part (pattern) to write a word. (*dad, had, bad, mad, glad*) [Spelling Patterns #3]	[PWW] Phonograms with a VC Pattern (-*ip*) You can look at a word part (pattern) to read a word. You can make new words by putting a letter or a letter cluster before the part (pattern). (*sip, hip, lip, tip, trip*) [Spelling Patterns #3]	[PWW] Phonograms with a VC Pattern (-*ap*) You can look at a word part (pattern) to read a word. You can make new words by putting a letter or a letter cluster before the part (pattern). (*cap, sap, tap, rap, clap*) [Spelling Patterns #3]
High Frequency Words **Consonants and Vowels** **Phonemes**	[Optional LWW] You can say a word slowly. You can hear each sound in a word. You can match consonant sounds and letters at the beginning of a word and at the end of a word. Some words have a vowel between two consonants. The sound of the vowel is short. (*fun, peg, ham, lot*) [Phonological Awareness #14] [Letter-Sound Relationships #2, #4, #22]	[LWW] You see some words many times when you read and use them many times when you write. You need to learn these words because they help you read and write. (*for, an*) [High-Frequency Words #1]	[Optional LWW] You can say a word slowly and hear each sound in a word. (*fun, peg, ham, not*) [Phonological Awareness #12]	[LWW] You see some words many times when you read and use them many times when you write. You need to learn these words because they help you read and write. (*said; had, bad, sad*) [High-Frequency Words #4]	[Optional LWW] You can say a word slowly. You can hear each sound in a word. You can change the first letter in a word to make a new word. (*big, pig, dig, wig*) [Phonological Awareness #14, #21]

Master Plan for Word Work in the *LLI Green System, continued*

	Lesson 41	Lesson 42	Lesson 43	Lesson 44	Lesson 45
Spelling Patterns (*-et, -ag*) **Short and Long Vowel Sounds** **Phonograms with a VC*e* Pattern**	[PWW] Phonograms with a VC Pattern (*-et*) You can look at a word part (pattern) to read a word. You can make new words by putting a letter or a letter cluster before the part (pattern). (*net, met, pet, let, get*) [Spelling Patterns #3]	[PWW] Phonograms with a VC Pattern (*-ag*) You can look at a word part (pattern) to read a word. You can make new words by putting a letter or a letter cluster before the part (pattern). (*bag, tag, rag, flag, sag*) [Spelling Patterns #3]	[PWW] Long Vowel Sounds Some words have a long a vowel sound as in *lake* and *paint*. Some words have a long *e* vowel sound as in *eat* and *tree*. Some words have a long *i* vowel sound as in *ice* and *right*. Some words have a long *o* vowel sound as in *go* and *oak*. Some words have a long *u* vowel sound as in *use* and *true*. (*rake, jeep, bike, rope, mule*) [Letter-Sound Relationships #23]	[PWW] Short and Long Vowel Sounds A vowel can stand for a sound that is different from its name. It is a short vowel sound. A vowel can stand for a sound like its name. It is a long vowel sound. (*can, cane; not, note; bit, bite; cub, cube; pan, pane; hop, hope; rip, ripe; hug, huge*) [Letter-Sound Relationships #25]	[PWW] Phonograms with a Vowel-Consonant-Silent *e* (VC*e*) Pattern Some words have a vowel, a consonant, and silent *e* at the end. The vowel sound is usually the name of the first vowel. (*take, make, wake, lake; came, game, same, tame; sale, male, pale, tale*) [Spelling Patterns #5]
High-Frequency Words **Phonological Awareness** (*Change Beginning Phoneme, Long and Short Vowels*) **Short and Long Vowel Sounds**	[LWW] You need to learn words that you see many times because they help you read and write. (*let, two, did, but*) [High-Frequency Words #4]	[Optional LWW] You can change the first letter in a word to make a new word. (*ten, pen, men, hen*) [Phonological Awareness #21]	[LWW] You need to learn words that you see many times because they help you read and write. (*was, get, went, will*) [High-Frequency Words #4]	[Optional LWW] A vowel can stand for a sound that is different from its name. It is a short vowel sound. A vowel can stand for a sound like its name. It is a long vowel sound. (*pin, pine; can, cane; not, note*) [Letter-Sound Relationships #25]	[LWW] You see some words many times when you read and use them many times when you write. You need to learn these words because they help you read and write. [High-Frequency Words #4]

continues

APPENDIX D

Master Plan for Word Work in the *LLI Green System*, continued

	Lesson 46	**Lesson 47**	**Lesson 48**	**Lesson 49**	**Lesson 50**
Phonograms with a VC*e* Pattern **Short and Long Vowel Sounds** **Phonemes**	[PWW] Phonograms with a Vowel-Consonant-Silent *e* (VC*e*) Pattern Some words have a vowel, a consonant, and silent *e* at the end. The vowel sound is usually the name of the first vowel. A vowel can stand for a sound that is different from its name. It is a short vowel sound. (*like, bike, pike, Mike; side, ride, tide, wide; five, dive, hive*) [Spelling Patterns #5] [Letter-Sound Relationships #25]	[PWW] Phonograms with a Vowel-Consonant-Silent *e* (VC*e*) Pattern Some words have a vowel, a consonant, and silent *e* at the end. The vowel sound is usually the name of the first vowel. (*bone, cone, tone, lone; rope, hope, mope, nope; nose, rose, hose, pose*) [Spelling Patterns #5]	[PWW] Phonograms with a Vowel-Consonant-Silent *e* (VC*e*) Pattern Some words have a vowel, a consonant, and silent *e* at the end. The vowel sound is usually the name of the first vowel. [Spelling Patterns #5]	[PWW] Short and Long Vowel Sounds A vowel can stand for a sound that is different from its name. It is a short vowel sound. A vowel can stand for a sound like its name. It is a long vowel sound. (*five, alive, nine, bite; fish, six, him, did, bit*) [Letter-Sound Relationships #25]	[PWW] Deleting a Beginning Phoneme You can say a word without the first sound. (*can, an, band, task, bend, pin, sit, his, pat, bus, cup*) [Phonological Awareness #27]
Onsets and Rimes **High-Frequency Words** **Phonemes** **Consonants and Vowels**	[Optional LWW] You can say and listen for the first and last parts of a word. You can blend the parts of a word. (*l-ike, b-ike, s-ide, f-ive, b-one, r-ope, w-ore; hike, wide, dive, cone, hope, tore*) [Phonological Awareness #10, #11]	[LWW] You see some words many times when you read and use them many times when you write. You need to learn these words because they help you read and write. (*good, put*) [High-Frequency Words #1, #4]	[Optional LWW] You need to learn words that you see many times because they help you read and write. (*review*) [High-Frequency Words #1, #4]	[LWW] You need to learn words that you see many times because they help you read and write. (*what; wide, hide, ride, tide*) [High-Frequency Words #4]	[Optional LWW] You can add a sound to the beginning of a word to make a new word. You can match the sound and the letter at the beginning of a word. (*in, pin, it, sit, at, cat*) [Phonological Awareness #20] [Letter-Sound Relationships #2]

Master Plan for Word Work in the *LLI Green System*, continued

	Lesson 51	**Lesson 52**	**Lesson 53**	**Lesson 54**	**Lesson 55**
Phonemes	[PWW] Deleting a Beginning Phoneme You can say a word without the first sound. (*fit, it, tan, send, bat, pup, land, tin, bit, for, mask*) [Phonological Awareness #27]	[PWW] Changing a Beginning Phoneme You can change the first letter in a word to make a new word. When you know the sound, you can find the letter. (*can, man, ran, pan, fan, tan; not, pot, hot, cot, got; big, fig, pig, rig; get, pet, bet, net*) [Phonological Awareness #21] [Letter-Sound Relationships #2]	[PWW] Changing a Beginning Phoneme You can change the first letter in a word to make a new word. When you know the sound, you can find the letter or letters. (*like, bike, hike; look, book, hook, took; went, bent, sent; will, bill, mill, hill*) [Phonological Awareness #21] [Letter-Sound Relationships #2]	[PWW] Deleting an Ending Phoneme You can say a word and then take away the last sound to make a new word. (*seed, see, bust, bus, ramp, ram, fort, for, farm, far, barn, bar, band, ban, pant, pan, zoom, zoo*) [Phonological Awareness #28]	[PWW] Deleting an Ending Phoneme You can say a word and then take away the last sound to make a new word. (*seen, see, cart, tool, beet, hump, bark, form, team*) [Phonological Awareness #28]
High-Frequency Words **Inflectional Endings** **Plurals**	[LWW] You need to learn words that you see many times because they help you read and write. (*she, saw, all, then*) [High-Frequency Words #4]	[Optional LWW] You can add a letter to the beginning of a word to read or write another word. When you know the sound, you can find the letter. (*and, land; am, ham; up, cup*) [Phonological Awareness #21] [Word-Solving Actions #24]	[LWW] Some words have three or more letters. You need to learn words that you see many times because they help you read and write. (*are, going, they*) [High-Frequency Words #4]	[Optional LWW] You can add -*ing* to the end of some words to show that something is happening now. (*go, going, see, seeing, look, looking, play, playing*) [Word Structure #46]	[LWW] You need to learn words that you see many times because they help you read and write. (*your, very; hills*) [High-Frequency Words #4]

continues

Master Plan for Word Work in the *LLI Green System*, continued

	Lesson 56	**Lesson 57**	**Lesson 58**	**Lesson 59**	**Lesson 60**
Phonemes **Consonant Clusters**	[PWW] Change Ending Phonemes You can change the last sound in a word to make a new word. When you know the sound, you can find the letter or letters. (*can, cat, cap, cab; big, bit, bin; has, had, hat*) [Phonological Awareness #22] [Letter-Sound Relationships #4]	[PWW] Change Ending Phonemes You can change the last sound in a word to make a new word. When you know the sound, you can find the letter or letters. (*pig, pin, pit; but, bus, bun; mom, mop, mob*) [Phonological Awareness #22] [Letter-Sound Relationships #4]	[PWW] Initial Consonant Clusters (*pl*) A group of two or three consonant letters is a consonant cluster. You can usually hear each sound in a consonant cluster. (*play, plan, plot, plate*) [Letter-Sound Relationships #7]	[PWW] Initial Consonant Clusters (*cl*) A group of two or three consonant letters is a consonant cluster. You can usually hear each sound in a consonant cluster. (*clip, clap, clue, clay*) [Letter-Sound Relationships #7]	[PWW] Initial Consonant Clusters (*fl*) A group of two or three consonant letters is a consonant cluster. You can usually hear each sound in a consonant cluster. (*fly, flop, flip, flag*) [Letter-Sound Relationships #7]
Inflectional Endings **Contractions** **High-Frequency Words**	[Optional LWW] You can add *-ed* to the end of some words to show that something already happened. (*look, looked, want, wanted, play, played*) [Word Structure #47]	[LWW] Some contractions are made with *will*. Some contractions are made with *is* (*I'll, he'll, she'll, we'll, you'll, they'll; it's, he's, she's*) [Word Structure #23, #22]	[Optional LWW] Sometimes you need to add *-s* to the end of a verb to make it sound right in a sentence. (*looks, puts, sees, likes, plays, wants*) [Word Structure #44]	[LWW] You need to learn words that you see many times because they help you read and write. (*says, now, that*) [High-Frequency Words #4]	[Optional LWW] You need to learn words that you see many times because they help you read and write. [High-Frequency Words #4]

Master Plan for Word Work in the *LLI Green System*, continued

	Lesson 61	Lesson 62	Lesson 63	Lesson 64	Lesson 65
Consonant Clusters and Digraphs	[PWW] Initial Consonant Clusters (*gl*) A group of two or three consonant letters is a consonant cluster. You can usually hear each sound in a consonant cluster. (*glad, glue, glass, glide*) [Letter-Sound Relationships #7]	[PWW] Initial Consonant Clusters (*bl*) A group of two or three consonant letters is a consonant cluster. You can usually hear each sound in a consonant cluster. (*blue, black, blow, blot*) [Letter-Sound Relationships #7]	[PWW] Initial Consonant Digraphs (*th, sh*) A consonant digraph has two consonant letters that stand for one sound. You can hear the sound of a consonant digraph at the beginning of a word. (*the, that, then, they, this; she, ship shot, shut, shop*) [Letter-Sound Relationships #8]	[PWW] Final Consonant Digraphs (*th, sh*) A consonant digraph has two consonant letters that stand for one sound. You can hear the sound of a consonant digraph at the end of a word. (*with, path, moth, cloth, bath; fish, wash, cash, dish, rush*) [Letter-Sound Relationships #9]	[PWW] Initial and Final Consonant Digraphs (*th, sh*) A consonant digraph has two consonant letters that stand for one sound. You can hear the sound of a consonant digraph at the beginning and end of a word. (*the, then, them; ship, shop, shot; fish, dish, dash*) [Letter-Sound Relationships #8, #9]
High-Frequency Words **Consonant Clusters and Digraphs** **Contractions**	[LWW] You need to learn words that you see many times because they help you read and write. (*were, made, her, came*) [High-Frequency Words #4]	[Optional LWW] A group of two or three consonant letters is a consonant cluster. You can usually hear each sound in a consonant cluster. (*play, clay, clap, flap, flat, plot, blot, blow, flow, glow*) [Letter-Sound Relationships #7]	[LWW] You need to learn words that you see many times because they help you read and write. (*could, yell, help*) [High-Frequency Words #4]	[Optional LWW] A consonant digraph has two consonant letters that stand for one sound. You can hear the sound of a consonant digraph at the beginning or end of a word. (*fish, dish, dash, cash, mash, math, ship, shin, thin, then, them, they*) [Letter-Sound Relationships #8, #9]	[LWW] To write a contraction with *not*, leave out the letter *o* and put an apostrophe in place of that missing letter. (*who; can not/can't, do not/don't, does not/ doesn't, could not/ couldn't*) [Word Structure #20]

continues

APPENDIX D

Master Plan for Word Work in the *LLI Green System*, continued

	Lesson 66	Lesson 67	Lesson 68	Lesson 69	Lesson 70
Consonant Clusters	[PWW] Initial Consonant Clusters (*fr, gr, cr*) A group of two or three consonant letters is a consonant cluster. You can usually hear each in a consonant cluster. (*frog, from, friend; grass, green, grip; crib, crow, crust*) [Letter-Sound Relationships #7]	[PWW] Initial Consonant Clusters (*pr, br, dr*) A group of two or three consonant letters is a consonant cluster. You can usually hear each sound in a consonant cluster. (*print, prune, pretzel; bridge, brick, broke; drum, drop, drink, prince, press, brain, brake, drag, dress*) [Letter-Sound Relationships #7]	[PWW] Initial Consonant Clusters (*sl, sm, sn*) A group of two or three consonant letters is a consonant cluster. You can usually hear each sound in a consonant cluster. (*slide, slip, slow; smoke, small, smile; snake, snow, snail, slam, slap, smell, smart, snap, snout*) [Letter-Sound Relationships #7]	[PWW] Initial Consonant Clusters (*sp, sk, st*) A group of two or three consonant letters is a consonant cluster. You can usually hear each sound in a consonant cluster. (*spoon, spell, spot; skeleton, skate, sky; star, stop, stand, spin, spit, ski, skunk, still, stone*) [Letter-Sound Relationships #7]	[PWW] Consonant Clusters A group of two or three consonant letters is a consonant cluster. You can usually hear each sound in a consonant cluster. (*block, bridge, skunk, stairs, smile, sled, tree, grasshopper, crayon, snail, blanket, dress, plant, princess*) [Letter-Sound Relationships #7]
High-Frequency Words **Consonant Clusters**	[Optional LWW] You need to learn words that you see many times because they help you read and write. [High-Frequency Words #4]	[LWW] You need to learn words that you see many times because they help you read and write. (*took, him, when*) [High-Frequency Words #4]	[Optional LWW] A group of two or three consonant letters is a consonant cluster. You can usually hear each sound in a consonant cluster. (*stick, brother, shop*) [Letter-Sound Relationships #7]	[LWW] A group of two or three consonant letters is a consonant cluster. You can usually hear each sound in a consonant cluster. [Letter-Sound Relationships #7]	[Optional LWW] A group of two or three consonant letters is a consonant cluster. You can usually hear each sound in a consonant cluster. (*block, bridge, slow, flip, bring, clothes, smell, plate, glue, snail, spark, dream, crash, storm*) [Letter-Sound Relationships #7]

Master Plan for Word Work in the *LLI Green System*, *continued*

	Lesson 71	**Lesson 72**	**Lesson 73**	**Lesson 74**	**Lesson 75**
Final Consonant Clusters	[PWW] Final Consonant Clusters (*nd*) Some words end with a consonant cluster. You can hear each sound in a consonant cluster at the end of a word. (*and, land, band, bend, send, end*) [Letter-Sound Relationships #15]	[PWW] Final Consonant Clusters (*nt*) Some words end with a consonant cluster. You can hear each sound in a consonant cluster at the end of a word. (*want, went, sent, bent, ant, pant*) [Letter-Sound Relationships #15]	[PWW] Final Consonant Clusters (*sk*) Some words end with a consonant cluster. You can hear each sound in a consonant cluster at the end of a word. (*ask, mask, task, tusk, dusk, husk*) [Letter-Sound Relationships #15]	[PWW] Final Consonant Clusters (*st*) Some words end with a consonant cluster. You can hear each sound in a consonant cluster at the end of a word. (*fast, past, last, list, mist, must*) [Letter-Sound Relationships #15]	[PWW] Final Consonant Clusters (*ld*) Some words end with a consonant cluster. You can hear each sound in a consonant cluster at the end of a word. (*old, told, fold, bold, bald, held*)
High-Frequency Words **Consonant Clusters and Digraphs** **Contractions**	[LWW] You need to learn words that you see many times because they help you read and write. (*gone, walk*) [High-Frequency Words #4]	[Optional LWW] A consonant digraph has two consonant letters that stand for one sound. (*the, then, they, this, that, them, these, there*) [Letter-Sound Relationships #8]	[LWW] You need to learn words that you see many times because they help you read and write. (*give, ask, make*) [High-Frequency Words #4]	[Optional LWW] To write a contraction with *is*, leave out the letter *i* and put an apostrophe in place of that missing letter. (*he's, she's, it's, that's*) [Word Structure #22]	[LWW] You need to learn words that you see many times because they help you read and write. (*had*) [High-Frequency Words #4]

continues

APPENDIX D

143

Master Plan for Word Work in the *LLI Green System*, continued

	Lesson 76	**Lesson 77**	**Lesson 78**	**Lesson 79**	**Lesson 80**
Final Consonant Digraphs **Spelling Patterns**	[PWW] Final Consonant Digraph (*ck*) A consonant digraph has two consonant letters that stand for one sound. You can hear the sound of a consonant digraph at the end of a word. (*duck, deck, dock, rock, rack, sack, sick, suck*) [Letter-Sound Relationships #9]	[PWW] Final Consonant Digraph (*ng*) A consonant digraph has two consonant letters that stand for one sound. You can hear the sound of a consonant digraph at the end of a word. (*king, ring, sing, song, sung, hung, hang, rang*) [Letter-Sound Relationships #9]	[PWW] Phonograms with Double Consonants Some words have a double consonant at the end. The sound of the vowel is usually short. You can change the first letter of a word to make a new word. (*will, off, pass, buzz, bell, puff, mess*) [Spelling Patterns #6] [Phonological Awareness #21]	[PWW] Common Phonograms with a VC Pattern (*-ay*) You can look at a part (pattern) to read a word. You can make new words by putting a letter or a letter cluster before the part (pattern). (*play, say, way, day, gray*) [Spelling Patterns #3]	[PWW] Common Phonograms with a VC Pattern (*-ow*) You can look at a part (pattern) to read a word. Make new words by putting a letter or a letter cluster before the part (pattern). (*now, cow, how, plow, wow*) [Spelling Patterns #3]
Consonant Clusters **High-Frequency Words** **Letter-Sound Relationships**	[Optional LWW] A group of two or three consonant letters is a consonant cluster. You can hear each sound in a consonant cluster. (*block, bridge, snow, green, play, drink, smile, skin, plug, drag, grow, skunk, spider*) [Letter-Sound Relationships #7]	[LWW] You need to learn words that you see many times because they help you read and write. (*stop, away, soon, how*) [High-Frequency Words #4]	[Optional LWW] You need to learn words that you see many times because they help you read and write. [High-Frequency Words #4]	[LWW] *Y* can stand for a long *i* vowel sound or a long *e* vowel sound. (*my, by, fly, sky, cry; baby, happy, funny, silly, daddy*) [Letter-Sound Relationships #26]	[Optional LWW] Some consonants or consonant clusters at the beginning of a word stand for two different sounds. (*slide/sled, clap/cloud, fly/flower, ship/shoe, skeleton/skate, truck/train*) [Letter-Sound Relationships #12]

Master Plan for Word Work in the *LLI Green System*, continued

	Lesson 81	**Lesson 82**	**Lesson 83**	**Lesson 84**	**Lesson 85**
Phonograms **Letter-Sound Relationships** **Consonants**	[PWW] Common Phonograms with a VC Pattern (-ow) You can look at a part (pattern) to read a word. You can make new words by putting a letter or a letter cluster before the part (pattern). (*row, low, grow, crow, snow*) [Spelling Patterns #3]	[PWW] Consonants That Represent Different Beginning Sounds (c) Some consonants or consonant clusters at the beginning of a word stand for two different sounds. (*can, cat, came, come, could; city, cent, circus, circle, celery*) [Letter-Sound Relationships #12]	[PWW] Consonants That Represent Different Beginning Sounds (g) Some consonants or consonant clusters at the beginning of a word stand for two different sounds. (*go, got, get, good, gone; gym, germ, giant, gel, giraffe*) [Letter-Sound Relationships #12]	[PWW] Consonants That Represent Different Ending Sounds (c) Some consonants or consonant clusters stand for two different sounds at the end of a word. (*attic, comic, magic, music, picnic; dance, face, ice, nice, race*) [Letter-Sound Relationships #13]	[PWW] Consonants That Represent Different Ending Sounds (g) Some consonants or consonant clusters at the end of a word stand for two different sounds. (*big, rug, plug, frog, twig; age, large, huge, page, orange*) [Letter-Sound Relationships #13]
Phonological Awareness **High-Frequency Words** **Syllables**	[LWW] You can break a word into parts. You can blend the parts of a word. (*a/way, a/go, a/gain, a/bout, a/round*) [Phonological Awareness #8] [Phonological Awareness #11]	[Optional LWW] You can look at a word part (pattern) to read a word. You can make new words by putting a letter or a letter cluster before the part (pattern). (*day, say, way, play, gray; now, cow, how, plow*) [Spelling Patterns #3]	[LWW] You need to learn words that you see many times because they help you read and write. (*after, laugh, end*) [High-Frequency Words #4]	[Optional LWW] You can hear, say, and clap the parts in a word. Words can have one or more parts. (*mon/key, pic/nic, bas/ket, be/hind, pea/nut*) [Phonological Awareness #6]	[LWW] You need to learn words that you see many times because they help you read and write. (*every*) [High-Frequency Words #4]

APPENDIX D

continues

Master Plan for Word Work in the *LLI Green System*, continued

	Lesson 86	**Lesson 87**	**Lesson 88**	**Lesson 89**	**Lesson 90**
Phonemes	[PWW] Four or More Phonemes in Sequence You can say a word slowly. You can hear each sound in a word. You can match the letters and the sounds in words. The letters in a word are always in the same order. (*plot, clam, sled, stub*) [Phonological Awareness #25] [Letter Knowledge #11]	[PWW] Four or More Phonemes in Sequence You can say a word slowly. You can hear each sound in a word. You can match the letters and the sounds in words. (*spin, drop, club, frog*) [Phonological Awareness #14] [Letter-Sound Relationships #1]	[PWW] Four or More Phonemes in Sequence You can say a word slowly. You can hear each sound in a word. You can match the letters and the sounds in words. (*lamp, band, send, bump*) [Phonological Awareness #25] [Letter Knowledge #11]	[PWW] Four or More Phonemes in Sequence You can say a word slowly. You can hear each sound in a word. You can match the letters and and the sounds in words. (*crush, black, trash, brick*) [Phonological Awareness #25]	[PWW] Four or More Phonemes in Sequence You can say a word slowly. You can hear each sound in a word. You can match the letters and the sounds in words. (*stung, track, sling, click*) [Phonological Awareness #25]
High-Frequency Words **Phonological Awareness** **Letter-Sound Relationships**	[Optional LWW] You can read and write words you know quickly. [High-Frequency Words #8]	[LWW] You can break a word into parts. You can blend the parts in a word. (*keep; some/thing, some/where, some/one, some/time, some/body*) [Phonological Awareness #8] [Phonological Awareness #7]	[Optional LWW] You can change the first letter in a word to make a new word. You can change the last letter in a word to make a new word. (*fast, last, past, cast, mast, vast; slid, sip, slim, slit*) [Phonological Awareness #21] [Phonological Awareness #22]	[LWW] Some consonants or consonant clusters at the beginning of a word stand for two different sounds. (*them; the, then, they, them, this, that; thick, thing, thank, thirty, think thorn*) [Letter-Sound Relationships #12]	[Optional LWW] You need to learn words that you see many times because they help you read and write. [High-Frequency Words #4]

Master Plan for Word Work in the *LLI Green System*, continued

	Lesson 91	**Lesson 92**	**Lesson 93**	**Lesson 94**	**Lesson 95**
Inflectional Endings	[PWW] Inflectional Ending (-*ed*) You can add -*ed* to the end of some verbs to show that something already happened. When you add -*ed* to a verb, it can sound like /d/, /ed/, or /t/. (*played, yelled, called, stayed; looked, walked, jumped, asked; wanted landed, ended, listed*) [Word Structure #47] [Word Structure #48]	[PWW] Inflectional Ending (-*ing*) You can add -*ing* to the end of some verbs to show that something is happening now. (*playing, looking, yelling, asking, saying*) [Word Structure #46]	[PWW] Inflectional Ending (-*ing*) Think about how to write words correctly when you add the ending -*ing*. (*coming, liking, making, giving, having*) [Word Structure #46]	[PWW] Inflectional Ending (-*ing*) Think about how to write words correctly when you add the ending -*ing*. (*stopping, getting, letting, patting, hopping*) [Word Structure #46]	[PWW] Inflectional Ending (-*ing*) Think about how to write words correctly when you add the ending -*ing*. (*looking, seeing, going, coming, taking, biking, stopping, tapping, batting*) [Word Structure #46]
High-Frequency Words **Inflectional Endings**	[LWW] You need to learn words that you see many times because they help you read and write. (*over, off*) [High-Frequency Words #4]	[Optional LWW] Add -*ing* to the end of some verbs to show that something is happening now. Think about how to write words correctly when you adding the ending -*ing*. (*going, seeing*) [Word Structure #46]	[LWW] Some words have three or more letters. You need to learn words that you see many times because they help you read and write. [High-Frequency Words #4]	[Optional LWW] Think about how to write words correctly when you add the ending -*ing*. (*giving, having*) [Word Structure #46]	[LWW] Some words have three or more letters. You need to learn words that you see many times because they help you read and write. (*very, any, first, next*) [High-Frequency Words #4]

continues

Master Plan for Word Work in the *LLI Green System*, continued

	Lesson 96	**Lesson 97**	**Lesson 98**	**Lesson 99**	**Lesson 100**
Inflectional Endings **Homophones** **Synonyms** **Antonyms** **Homographs**	[PWW] Inflectional Ending (*-ed*) Add *-ed* to the end of some verbs to show that something already happened. Think about how to write words correctly when you add the ending *-ed*. (*stopped, patted, hopped, batted, kidded*) [Word Structure #47]	[PWW] Homophones Some words sound the same, but they look different and mean something different. (*here/hear, see/sea, be/bee, to/two, for/four*) [Word Meaning/ Vocabulary #6]	[PWW] Synonyms Some words mean the same. They are synonyms. (*big/large, small/little, over/above, cool/cold, laugh/giggle*) [Word Meaning/ Vocabulary #4]	[PWW] Antonyms Some words mean the opposite. They are antonyms. (*good/bad, up/down, on/off, come/go, big/little*) [Word Meaning/ Vocabulary #5]	[PWW] Homographs Some words are spelled the same, but they mean something different. Sometimes they are pronounced differently. (*bat, bow, close, duck, tear*) [Word Meaning/ Vocabulary #7]
Inflectional Endings **High-Frequency Words** **Homophones**	[Optional LWW] Add *-ed* to the end of some verbs to show that something already happened. [Word Structure #47]	[LWW] You need to learn words that you see many times because they help you read and write. (*gave, just*) [High-Frequency Words #4]	[Optional LWW] Some words sound the same, but they look different and mean something different. (*hear, here; be, bee; two, to; see, sea; for, four; beet, beat; break, brake; son, sun*) [Word Meaning/ Vocabulary #6]	[LWW] You need to learn words that you see many times because they help you read and write. (*of, from, many*) [High-Frequency Words #4]	[Optional LWW] You can change the first letter in a word to make a new word. (*is-as-us; in-on-an; it-at*) [Phonological Awareness #21] [Letter Knowledge #7]

Master Plan for Word Work in the *LLI Green System*, continued

	Lesson 101	**Lesson 102**	**Lesson 103**	**Lesson 104**	**Lesson 105**
Phonological Awareness **Vowels** **Letter/Sound Relationships** **Consonant Digraphs** **Spelling Patterns**	[PWW] Change Middle Phonemes You can change a sound in the middle of a word to make a new word. Some words have one vowel between two consonants. The sound of the vowel is short. (*sat, sit, set; bat, it, bet, but; cap, cup, cop; pet, pot, pat, pit*) [Phonological Awareness #30] [Letter-Sound Relationships #22]	[PWW] Change Middle Phonemes You can change a sound in the middle of a word to make a new word. Some words have one vowel between two consonants. The sound of the vowel is short. (*led, lad, lid; dog, dig, dug; big, bug, beg, bog, bag; top, tap, tip*) [Phonological Awareness #30] [Letter-Sound Relationships #22]	[PWW] Consonant Digraphs (*th, sh, ch, wh*) A consonant digraph has two consonant letters that make one sound. (*thing, she, chip, when; three, thorn, throne, shovel, ship, shirt, child, chick, chin, wheel, whistle, whale*) [Letter-Sound Relationships #8]	[PWW] Phonograms with a Double Vowel (*-eed, -eek*) Some words have a double vowel followed by a consonant. Sometimes a double vowel sounds like the name of the vowel (long sound). (*weed, seed, feed, bleed, greed; seek, peek, week, creek, cheek*) [Spelling Patterns #7]	[PWW] Phonograms with a Double Vowel (*-eep, -eed*) Some words have a double vowel followed by a consonant. Sometimes a double vowel sounds like the name of the vowel (long sound). (*jeep, deep, keep, sheep, steep; feet, meet, beet, greet, sheet*) [Spelling Patterns #7]
High-Frequency Words **Contractions**	[LWW] You need to learn words that you see many times because they help you read and write. (*right, shout, thought*) [High-Frequency Words #4]	[Optional LWW] Some contractions are made with *are*. To write a contraction with *are*, leave out the letter *a* and put an apostrophe in its place. (*you're, we're, they're*) (*they're, there, their*) [Word Structure #21]	[LWW] You need to learn words that you see many times because they help you read and write. (*live, even, through*) [High-Frequency Words #4]	[Optional LWW] Some contractions are made with *not*. To write a contraction with *not*, leave out the letter *o* and put an apostrophe in its place. (*couldn't, wouldn't, shouldn't*)	[LWW] You need to learn words that you see many times because they help you read and write. (*ever; even, every, very*) [High-Frequency Words #4]

continues

Master Plan for Word Work in the *LLI Green System*, continued

	Lesson 106	Lesson 107	Lesson 108	Lesson 109	Lesson 110
Spelling Patterns *(Double Vowels: oo)* **Letter/Sound Relationships** *(Two Medial Vowels: ay, ai, ea, ee, ie, oa,*	[PWW] Phonograms with a Double Vowel (*-oon, -oot*) Some words have a double vowel followed by a consonant. Sometimes a double vowel sounds like the name of the vowel (long sound). Sometimes a double vowel stands for other vowel sounds. (*moon, noon, soon, loon, spoon; root, boot, toot, hoot, shoot*) [Spelling Patterns #7]	[PWW] Phonograms with a Double Vowel (*-ool, -ook*) Some words have a double vowel followed by a consonant. Sometimes a double vowel sounds like the name of the vowel (long sound). Sometimes a double vowel stands for other vowel sounds. (*tool, pool, fool, stool, school; look, cook, book took, shook*) [Spelling Patterns #7]	[PWW] Letter Combinations That Represent Long Vowel Sounds (*ay, ai*) In some words, two vowels together stand for one sound. When there are two vowels, they usually stand for the sound of the name of the first vowel. (*pay, play, day, today, say; sail, pail, paid, wait, rain*) [Letter-Sound Relationships #27]	[PWW] Letter Combinations That Represent Long Vowel Sounds (*ea, ee*) In some words, two vowels together stand for one sound. When there are two vowels, they usually stand for the sound of the name of the first vowel. (*treat, beat, seat, real, meat; meet, beet, feel, greet, sleet*) [Letter-Sound Relationships #27]	[PWW] Letter Combinations That Represent Long Vowel Sounds (*ie, oa*) In some words, two vowels together stand for one sound. When there are two vowels, they usually stand for the sound of the name of the first vowel. (*pie, tied, die, lie, cried; boat, goat, toast, roast, float*) [Letter-Sound Relationships #27]
High-Frequency Words *(must, nice)* **Word Structure** *(Compound Words)* **Letter/Sound Relationships** *(ai, ay)*	[Optional LWW] Some words have three or more letters. You need to learn words that you see many times because they help you read and write. [High-Frequency Words #4]	[LWW] You see some words many times when you read and use them many times when you write. You need to learn these words because they help you read and write. (*must, nice*) [High-Frequency Words #4]	[Optional LWW] In some words, two vowels together stand for one sound. When there are two vowels, they usually stand for the sound of the name of the first vowel. (*train, brain, braid, laid; tray, bay, stay, stray*) [Letter-Sound Relationships #27]	[LWW] Some words are made of two smaller words. They are compound words. Each smaller word helps you think about the meaning of the whole word. (*into, inside, outside, everyone, today; upset, myself, maybe, inside, someone, something, yourself, without*) [Word Meaning/Vocabulary #10]	[Optional LWW] Some words are made of two smaller words. They are compound words. Some smaller words appear in many compound words. (*everyone, everything, everywhere, everybody; anyone, anything, anywhere, anybody*) [Word Meaning/Vocabulary #10] [Word Meaning/Vocabulary #11]

Master Plan for Word Work in the *LLI Green System,* continued

	Lesson 111	Lesson 112	Lesson 113	Lesson 114	Lesson 115
Letter/Sound Relationships *(ue, ui, oy, oi, ou, ow; Consonant Clusters: dr, tr)* **Word Structure** *(Plurals Using es)*	[PWW] Letter Combinations That Represent Long Vowel Sounds (*ue, ui*) In some words, two vowels together stand for one sound. When there are two vowels, they usually stand for the sound of the name of the first vowel. (*cue, due, blue, true, clue; suit, fruit, juice, cruise, bruise*) [Letter-Sound Relationships #27]	[PWW] Letter Combinations That Represent Unique Vowel Sounds (*oi, oy*) Some letters together stand for a special vowel sound. (*boy, toy, royal, enjoy, oyster; boil, soil, join, voice, toilet*) [Letter-Sound Relationships #28]	[PWW] Letter Combinations That Represent Unique Vowel Sounds (*ou, ow*) Some letters together stand for a special vowel sound. (*our, out, house, ouch, flour; cow, how, tower, howl, crowd*) [Letter-Sound Relationships #28]	[PWW] Plurals Ending in -*es* Add -*es* to words that end with *ch, sh, s, x,* and *z* to make them mean more than one. (*hat/hats, book/books, pot/pots, dish/dishes. Inch/inches, fox/foxes, gas/gases, buzz/buzzes*) [Word Structure #29]	[PWW] Initial Consonant Clusters (*dr, tr*) A group of two or three consonant letters is a consonant cluster. You can usually hear each sound in a consonant cluster. (*drop, drink, draw, drum, drag; trap, truck, tree, trim, true*) [Letter-Sound Relationships #7]
High-Frequency Words *(why, began, by, much)* **Word Structure** *(Plurals Using es)*	[LWW] You need to learn words that you see many times because they help you read and write. (*why, began*) [High-Frequency Words #4]	[Optional LWW] You need to learn words that you see many times because they help you read and write. [High-Frequency Words #4]	[LWW] In some words, one or more vowels together with one or more consonants can stand for one vowel sound. (*high, sigh, light, right, might, bright; flight, tight, sight, fright*) [Letter-Sound Relationships #27]	[Optional LWW] Add -*es* to words that end with *ch, sh, s, x,* and *z* to make them mean more than one. (*hat/hats, book/books, pot/pots, dish/dishes. Inch/inches, fox/foxes, gas/gases, buzz/buzzes*) [Word Structure #29]	[LWW] You need to learn words that you see many times because they help you read and write. (*by, much*) [High-Frequency Words #4]

continues

Master Plan for Word Work in the *LLI Green System*, continued

	Lesson 116	Lesson 117	Lesson 118	Lesson 119	Lesson 120
Letter/Sound Relationships *(Consonant Clusters: scr, str, spr, spl, er, ar, ir, or)* **Word Structure** *(Compound Words)*	[PWW] Initial Consonant Clusters (*scr, str*) A group of two or three consonant letters is a consonant cluster. You can hear each sound in a consonant cluster. (*scrap, scram, screw, scream, scrub; string, strap, strong, stray, stroll*) [Letter-Sound Relationships #7]	[PWW] Initial Consonant Clusters (*spr, spl*) A group of two or three consonant letters is a consonant cluster. You can hear each sound in a consonant cluster. (*spring, sprout, spray, spree, sprang; splash, splat, split, splint, spleen*) [Letter-Sound Relationships #7]	[PWW] Compound Words The word parts in a compound word help you think about the meaning of the whole word. (*toothbrush, airplane, homework, highchair, sidewalk, popcorn, football*) [Word Structure #16]	[PWW] Vowel Sounds with *r* (*er, ar*) When the letter *r* follows a vowel or a pair of vowels, blend the sound of the vowel with *r*. (*her, jerk, germ, fern, herd; are, car, park, farm, start*) [Letter-Sound Relationships #31]	[PWW] Vowel Sounds with *r* (*ir, or*) When the letter *r* follows a vowel or a pair of vowels, blend the sound of the vowel with *r*. (*sir, third, shirt, birth, stir; for, short, storm, corn, more*) [Letter-Sound Relationships #31]
Word Structure *(Compound Words)* **Word Meaning/ Vocabulary** *(Antonyms)* **Letter/Sound Relationships** *(Aught, Ought)* **Recognize and Use High-Frequency Words**	[Optional LWW] Some words mean the opposite. They are antonyms. (*hot/cold, big/little, up/down, top/bottom, in/out, day/night, win/lose*) [Word Meaning/ Vocabulary #5]	[LWW] Some letters together stand for the vowel sound you can hear in *saw*. (*thought, bought, brought; caught, daughter, naughty*) [Letter-Sound Relationships #29]	[Optional LWW] The word parts in a compound word help you think about the meaning of the whole word. (*toothbrush, airplane, homework, highchair, sidewalk, popcorn, football*) [Word Structure #16]	[LWW] Some words have three or more letters. You need to learn words that you see many times because they help you read and write. [High-Frequency Words #4]	[Optional LWW] You need to learn words that you see many times because they help you read and write. [High-Frequency Words #4]

Master Plan for Word Work in the *LLI Green System*, continued

	Lesson 121	Lesson 122	Lesson 123	Lesson 124	Lesson 125
Letter/Sound Relationships *(ur, o, aw, au, aught, aught, al)* **Word Structure** *(Change y to i and add -es or -ed)*	[PWW] Vowel Sounds with *r* (*ur*) When the letter *r* follows a vowel or a pair of vowels, blend the sound of the vowels with *r*. (*fur, hurt, turn, burn, purr; art, bird, born, card, curb, curl, dirt, ever, girl, over, part, sore, surf, tore, verb*) [Letter-Sound Relationships #31]	[PWW] Vowel Sound /ȯ/ (as in *saw*) Some letters together stand for the vowel sound you can hear in *saw*. (*song, soft, cost, cloth, moth; saw, paw, crawl, draw, straw*) [Letter-Sound Relationships #29]	[PWW] Vowel Sound /ȯ/ (as in *saw*) Some letters together stand for the vowel sound you can hear in *saw*. (*cause, pause, sauce, fault, haunt; taught, caught, daughter, naughty*) [Letter-Sound Relationships #29]	[PWW] Vowel Sound /ȯ/ (as in *saw*) Some letters together stand for the vowel sound you can hear in *saw*. (*bought, brought, fought; all, call, walk, talk, bald*) [Letter-Sound Relationships #29]	[PWW] Inflectional Endings on Words Ending with *y* (*-es, -ed*) Add *-es* to the end of some verbs to show that something is happening now. Add *-ed* to the end of some verbs to show that something already happened. For verbs that end with *y*, change the *y* to *i* before adding *-es* or *-ed*. (*cry, cries, cried; fry, fries, fried; marry, marries, married; dry, dries, dried; try, tries, tried; copy, copies, copied*)
High-Frequency Words *(Other, Until, Along, While)* **Word Structure** *(Comparisons: -er, -est)*	[LWW] You need to learn words that you see many times because they help you read and write. (*other, until*) [High-Frequency Words #4]	[Optional LWW] Add the ending *-er* or *-est* to the end of a base word to show you are comparing. Think about how to write words correctly when adding the endings *-er* and *-est*. (*fast, faster, fastest; tall, taller, tallest; old, older, oldest; slow, slower, slowest; small, smaller, smallest; kind, kinder, kindest*) [Word Structure #53]	[LWW] Add the ending *-er* or *-est* to the end of a base word to show you are comparing. (*cute, cuter, cutest; late, later, latest; wise, wiser, wisest; fine, finer, finest; ripe, riper, ripest; pale, paler, palest*) [Word Structure #53]	[Optional LWW] Add the ending *-er* or *-est* to the end of a base word to show you are comparing. (*bigger, biggest; redder, reddest; madder, maddest; sad, sadder, saddest; wet, wetter, wettest; fat, fatter, fattest*) [Word Structure #53]	[LWW] You need to learn words that you see many times because they help you read and write. (*along, while*) [High-Frequency Words #4]

continues

Master Plan for Word Work in the *LLI Green System*, continued

	Lesson 126	**Lesson 127**	**Lesson 128**	**Lesson 129**	**Lesson 130**
Spelling Patterns *(ain, ail, eat, ear, out)*	[PWW] Phonograms with Vowel Combinations (VVC) (-*ain*) Some words have two vowels together (vowel combination). Sometimes a vowel pair sounds like the name of the first vowel. (*rain, pain, train, drain, Spain*) [Spelling Patterns #9]	[PWW] Phonograms with Vowel Combinations (VVC) (-*ail*) Some words have two vowels together (vowel combination). Sometimes a vowel pair sounds like the name of the first vowel. (*pail, sail, mail, trail, fail, bail, jail, nail, snail, tail*) [Spelling Patterns #9]	[PWW] Phonograms with Vowel Combinations (VVC) (-*eat*) Some words have two vowels together (vowel combination). Sometimes a vowel pair sounds like the name of the first vowel. (*beat, bleat, treat, defeat, wheat, meat, seat, heat, cheat*) [Spelling Patterns #9]	[PWW] Phonograms with Vowel Combinations (VVC) (-*ear*) Some words have two vowels together (vowel combination). Sometimes a vowel pair sounds like the name of the first vowel. Sometimes a vowel pair stands for other sounds. (*near, fear, rear, year smear; dear, hear, gear, clear, spear*) [Spelling Patterns #9]	[PWW] Phonograms with Vowel Combinations (VVC) (-*out*) Some words have two vowels together (vowel combination). Sometimes a vowel pair sounds like the name of the first vowel. Sometimes a vowel pair stands for other sounds. (*pout, trout, shout, spout, about; scout, sprout, snout*) [Spelling Patterns #9]
High-Frequency Words **Spelling Patterns**	[Optional LWW] You see some words many times when you read and use them many times when you write. You need to learn these words because they help you read and write. (*what, why, going, all, that, are, right, over, away*) [High-Frequency Words #4]	[LWW] You see some words many times when you read and use them many times when you write. You need to learn these words because they help you read and write. (*really, busy*) [High-Frequency Words #4]	[Optional LWW] Some words have parts (patterns) that are the same. You can use the part (pattern) to read a word. Some consonants or consonant clusters stand for two different sounds in a word. (*convenient, face, place; caught, right; wake, hay, while, smile*) [Spelling Patterns #10] [Letter-Sound Relationships #12, #13, #14]	[LWW] You see some words many times when you read and use them many times when you write. You need to learn these words because they help you read and write. (*often*) [High-Frequency Words #4]	[Optional LWW] Some words have parts (patterns) that are the same. You can use the part (pattern) to read a word. [Spelling Patterns #10]

154

appendix E

New High-Frequency Words in the *LLI Green System*

lesson 1	lesson 2	lesson 3	lesson 4	lesson 5	lesson 6
up the and	I on	a got	is	to my me	his he it in no

lesson 7	lesson 8	lesson 9	lesson 10	lesson 11	lesson 12
you yes	out	we too	play am	see	and the it he my

lesson 13	lesson 14	lesson 15	lesson 16	lesson 17	lesson 18
can	\<review\>	like love	\<review\>	look at	\<review\>

lesson 19	lesson 20	lesson 21	lesson 22	lesson 23	lesson 24
this	\<none\>	big	\<review\>	\<review\>	\<review\>

lesson 25	lesson 26	lesson 27	lesson 28	lesson 29	lesson 30
Mom has	\<none\>	have some our	\<none\>	with	\<none\>

lesson 31	lesson 32	lesson 33	lesson 34	lesson 35	lesson 36
want, wants	\<none\>	come here not	\<none\>	down	\<none\>

lesson 37	lesson 38	lesson 39	lesson 40	lesson 41	lesson 42
for an	\<review\>	said	\<review\>	let two did but	\<review\>

continues

New High-Frequency Words in the *LLI Green System*, continued

lesson 43	lesson 44	lesson 45	lesson 46	lesson 47	lesson 48
was get went will	<none>	<review>	<none>	good put	<review>
lesson 49	**lesson 50**	**lesson 51**	**lesson 52**	**lesson 53**	**lesson 54**
what	<none>	she saw all then	<none>	are going they	<none>
lesson 55	**lesson 56**	**lesson 57**	**lesson 58**	**lesson 59**	**lesson 60**
your very	<none>	<none>	<none>	says now that	<review>
lesson 61	**lesson 62**	**lesson 63**	**lesson 64**	**lesson 65**	**lesson 66**
were made her came	<none>	could yell help	<none>	who	<review>
lesson 67	**lesson 68**	**lesson 69**	**lesson 70**	**lesson 71**	**lesson 72**
took him when	<review>	<none>	<none>	gone walk	<none>
lesson 73	**lesson 74**	**lesson 75**	**lesson 76**	**lesson 77**	**lesson 78**
give ask make	<none>	had	<review>	stop away soon how	<review>
lesson 79	**lesson 80**	**lesson 81**	**lesson 82**	**lesson 83**	**lesson 84**
<none>	<none>	<none>	<none>	after laugh end	<none>

New High-Frequency Words in the *LLI Green System*, continued

lesson 85	lesson 86	lesson 87	lesson 88	lesson 89	lesson 90
every	<review>	keep	<none>	them	<review>

lesson 91	lesson 92	lesson 93	lesson 94	lesson 95	lesson 96
over off	<none>	<review>	<none>	very any first next	<none>

lesson 97	lesson 98	lesson 99	lesson 100	lesson 101	lesson 102
gave just	<none>	of from many	<none>	right shout thought	<none>

lesson 103	through	lesson 104	lesson 105	lesson 106	lesson 107
live even		<none>	ever	<review>	must nice

lesson 108	lesson 109	lesson 110	lesson 111	lesson 112	lesson 113
<none>	<none>	<none>	why began	<review>	<none>

lesson 114	lesson 115	lesson 116	lesson 117	lesson 118	lesson 119
<none>	by much	<none>	<none>	<none>	<review>

lesson 120	lesson 121	lesson 122	lesson 123	lesson 124	lesson 125
<review>	other until	<none>	<none>	<none>	along while

lesson 126	lesson 127	lesson 128	lesson 129	lesson 130	
<review>	really busy	<none>	often	<none>	

appendix F

▶ F&P Calculator/ Stopwatch Directions

Using the F&P Calculator/Stopwatch will facilitate taking a reading record on each child. This device is easy to use in conjunction with the Recording Form, which can be printed from Online Resources. The following are the instructions for using the calculator/stopwatch in abbreviated form.

1. Press **RW** and enter the number of running words (RW) in the text on the calculator/stopwatch.
2. Press **Start Time** on the calculator as the child begins oral reading. Press **End Time** when the reading is complete.
3. Press **#Errors** and enter the number of errors on the calculator.
4. Press **#SC** and enter the number of self-corrections on the calculator.
5. Press **Time** to get **Elapsed Minutes or Seconds**.
6. Press **WPM** to see **Words per Minute**.
7. Press **Accur.%** for **Percentage of Accuracy**.
8. Press **SC** to get the **Self-Correction Ratio.**

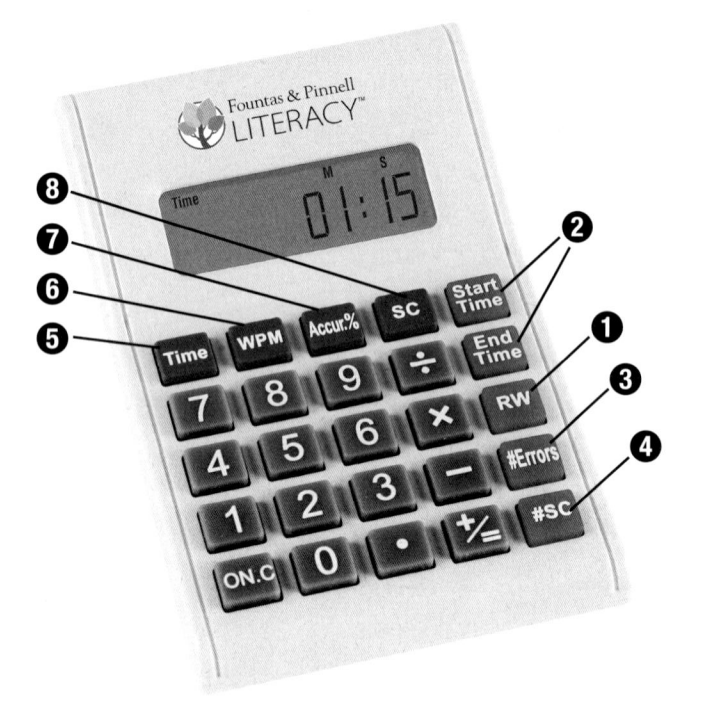

▶ *LLI* as a Complement to Reading Recovery®

Reading Recovery® is a one-to-one tutoring program for grade 1 children who are the lowest-achieving readers in their age cohorts. Selected using multiple assessments, Reading Recovery children receive attention at the developmental moment when one-to-one intervention can make the most difference in learning to read. A large body of research shows that children who receive one-to-one tutoring in Reading Recovery make accelerated progress, catch up with their peers, and become readers in a very short period of time. No other program has ever achieved the results of Reading Recovery. For some children, one-to-one instruction at a particular point in time is the only option that will have successful results. (See the What Works Clearinghouse Web site at www.whatworks.ed.gov.) Group instruction cannot replace Reading Recovery.

A single solution to reading difficulties, however, is seldom enough, even in schools with strong, broad-based, school-wide literacy initiatives. There is a need for a series of interventions so that many more children can benefit. Inevitably, schools will provide small-group instruction to address this need. *Leveled Literacy Intervention* seeks to make small-group interventions more effective.

Ideally, where Reading Recovery exists, *LLI* will complement one-to-one tutoring in the following ways:

- Children who are having difficulty engaging with reading and writing at mid- and late-kindergarten can have some very specific attention in the form of daily lessons. In our experience, many will develop basic competencies that will enable them to succeed in first grade. Those who do not can enter Reading Recovery immediately in the fall. They will likely enter with a greater level of competence.

- Children who are not the lowest achievers in reading but still need extra help can receive intensive instruction beginning in fall of grade one. Some children will not need extra help after the group intervention. If they still need extra help, they can enter Reading Recovery in the second round of children. Reading Recovery is a short-term intervention designed to provide 12–20 weeks of intensive individual tutoring, making room for at least 2 "rounds" of children in the available teaching slots over the school year.

- Children who are not at discontinuing status at the end of about 20 weeks of Reading Recovery can receive small-group support for the rest of the grade one year. Many, with this extended support, will reach expected grade levels.

- Children in grades 2 and 3 can receive supplemental instruction of a systematic nature to help them benefit from ongoing class instruction.

The above-described system, combining Reading Recovery and *Leveled Literacy Intervention*, represents a coherent, multi-layered approach to helping struggling readers. For schools that have Reading Recovery in place, we seek to extend the impact of those expert teachers over the entire school day to serve children in both one-to-one tutoring and small-group instruction. For schools that do not have Reading Recovery in place, *LLI* offers a more effective alternative to many current practices.

appendix H

▶ Glossary

The following is a glossary of the terms, materials, and Instructional Routines used in the *LLI System* and described briefly in this guide.

abbreviation Shortened form of a word that uses some of the letters: for example., *Mr., etc., NY*.

academic language The language needed to be successful in schools and in other scholarly settings. Academic language is often used in classroom lessons, assignments, presentations, and books. Another term for academic language is *academic vocabulary*.

accuracy (as in oral reading) or **accuracy rate** The percentage of words the child reads aloud correctly.

adjective suffix A suffix put at the end of a word root or base word to form an adjective. See also *suffix*.

adjusting (as a strategic action) Reading in different ways as appropriate to the purpose for reading and type of text.

adventure / adventure story A contemporary realistic or historical fiction or fantasy text that presents a series of exciting or suspenseful events, often involving a main character taking a journey and overcoming danger and risk.

adverb suffix A suffix put at the end of a word root or base word to form an adverb. See also *suffix*.

affix A letter or group of letters added to the beginning or ending of a base or root word to change its meaning or function (a *prefix* or a *suffix*).

alphabet book /ABC book A book that helps children develop the concept and sequence of the alphabet by pairing alphabet letters with pictures of people, animals, or objects with labels related to the letters.

Alphabet Linking Chart A chart containing upper- and lowercase letters of the alphabet paired with pictures representing words beginning with each letter (*a, apple*).

alphabetic principle The concept that there is a relationship between the spoken sounds in oral language and the graphic forms in written language.

analogy The resemblance of a known word to an unknown word that helps you solve the unknown word's meaning. Often an analogy shows the relationship between two pairs of words.

analyzing (as a strategic action) Examining the elements of a text in order to know more about how it is constructed, and noticing aspects of the writer's craft.

analyzing a reading record Looking at errors, self-corrections, and sources of information to plan instruction.

animal fantasy A modern fantasy text geared to a very young audience in which animals act like people and encounter human problems.

animal story A contemporary realistic or historical fiction or fantasy text that involves animals and that often focuses on the relationships between humans and animals.

antonym A word that has the opposite meaning from another word: for example, *cold* versus *hot*.

assessment A means for gathering information or data that reveals what learners control, partially control, or do not yet control consistently.

autobiography A biographical text in which the story of a real person's life is written and narrated by that person. Autobiography is usually told in chronological sequence but may be in another order.

automaticity Rapid, accurate, fluent word decoding without conscious effort or attention.

base word A word in its simplest form, which can be modified by adding affixes: for example, *read; reread, reading*. A base word has meaning, can stand on its own, and is easily apparent in the language. Compare to *word root*.

behaviors Observable actions.

biography A biographical text in which the story of a real person's life is written and narrated by another person. Biography is usually told in chronological sequence but may be in another order.

blend To combine sounds or word parts.

bold / boldface Type that is heavier and darker than usual, often used for emphasis.

book and print features The physical attributes of a text: for example, font, layout, length.

callout A nonfiction text feature, such as a definition, a quote, or an important concept, that is highlighted by being set to one side of a text or enlarged within the body of the text.

capitalization The use of capital letters, usually the first letter in a word, as a convention of written language (e.g., for proper names and to begin sentences).

categorization A structural pattern used especially in nonfiction texts to present information in logical categories (and subcategories) of related material.

cause and effect A structural pattern used especially in nonfiction texts, often to propose the reasons or explanations for how and why something occurs.

chapter book A form of early reading text that is divided into chapters, each of which narrates an episode in the whole.

choral reading Reading aloud in unison with a group.

chronological sequence A structural pattern used especially in nonfiction texts to describe a series of events in the order they happened in time.

circular story A fiction story in which a sense of completeness or closure results from the way the end of a piece returns to subject matter, wording, or phrasing found at the beginning of the story.

closed syllable A syllable that ends in a consonant: for example, *lem*-on.

code (a reading record) To record a child's oral reading errors, self-corrections, and other behaviors.

Coding and Scoring Errors at-a-Glance A chart containing a brief summary of how to code and score oral reading errors.

comparative ending A suffix (e.g., *-er, -est*) put at the end of a base word to show comparison between or among two or more things.

compare and contrast A structural pattern used especially in nonfiction texts to compare two ideas, events, or phenomena by showing how they are alike and how they are different.

compound word A word made of two or more smaller words or morphemes: for example, *play ground*. The meaning of a compound word can be a combination of the meanings of the words it is made of or can be unrelated to the meanings of the combined units.

comprehension (as in reading) the process of constructing meaning while reading text.

comprehension conversation The conversation that takes place in the Rereading and Assessment section of the lesson, in which the child shares his understanding of the text.

concept word A word that represents an abstract idea or name. Categories of concept words include color names, number words, days of the week, months of the year, seasons, and so on.

Conflict In a fiction text, a central problem within the plot that is resolved near the end of the story. In literature, characters are usually in conflict with nature, with other people, with society as a whole, or with themselves. Another term for conflict is *problem*.

connecting strategies Ways of solving words by using connections or analogies with similar known words (e.g., knowing *she* and *out* helps with *shout*).

connective A word or phrase that clarifies relationships and ideas in language. Simple connectives appear often in both oral and written language: for example, *and, but, because*. Sophisticated connectives are used in written texts texts but do not appear often in everyday oral language: for example, *although, however, yet*. Academic connectives appear in written texts but are seldom used in oral language: for example, *in contrast, nonetheless, whereas*.

consonant A speech sound made by partial or complete closure of the airflow that causes friction at one or more points in the breath channel. The consonant sounds are represented by the letters *b, c, d, f, g, h, j, k, l, m, n, p, q, r, s, t, v, w, y,* and *z*.

consonant blend Two or more consonant letters that often appear together in words and represent sounds that are smoothly joined, although each of the sounds can be heard in the word: for example, *trim*.

consonant cluster A sequence of two or three consonant letters: for example, *trim, chair*.

consonant clusters and digraphs charts A chart of common consonant clusters paired with pictures representing words beginning with each: for example, *bl, block*.

consonant digraph Two consonant letters that appear together and represent a single sound that is different from the sound of either letter: for example, *shell*.

consonant-vowel-consonant (CVC) A common sequence of sounds in a single syllable (for example, *hat*)

content (as a text characteristic) The subject matter of a text.

contraction A shortened form of one or more words. A letter or letters are left out, and an apostrophe takes the place of the missing letter or letters.

conventions In writing, formal usage that has become customary in written language. Grammar and usage, capitalization, punctuation, spelling, and handwriting and word-processing are categories of writing conventions.

counting book A book in which the structure depends on a numerical progression.

critiquing (as a strategic action) Evaluating a text based on the reader's personal, world, or text knowledge, and thinking critically about the ideas in the text.

cumulative tale A folktale in which story events are repeated with each new episode, giving them a rhythmic quality.

cursive A form of handwriting in which letters are connected.

decoding Using letter-sound relationships to translate a word from a series of symbols to a unit of meaning.

description A structural pattern used especially in nonfiction texts to provide sensory and emotional details so that readers can determine how something looks, moves, tastes, smells, or feels.

dialect A regional variety of a language. In most languages, including English and Spanish, dialects are mutually intelligible; the differences are actually minor.

dialogue Spoken words, usually set off with quotation marks in text. Dialogue is an element of a writer's style.

diary A record of events and observations written in the first person and kept regularly in sequential, dated entries.

dictated writing A teaching context in which the teacher reads aloud a sentence, and children write it in *My Writing Book* to learn how to go from oral to written language. The teacher provides support as needed.

diction Clear pronunciation and enunciation in speech.

dimension A trait, characteristic, or attribute of a character in fiction.

directionality The orientation of print (in the English language, from left to right).

distinctive letter features Visual features that make each letter of the alphabet different from every other letter.

draft An early version of a writer's composition.

drafting and revising The process of getting ideas down on paper and shaping them to convey the writer's message.

drawing In writing, creating a rough image (i.e., a sketch) or a finished image (i.e., a drawing) of a person, place, thing, or idea to capture, work with, and render the writer's ideas.

early literacy concepts Very early understandings related to how written language or print is organized and used—how it works.

editing and proofreading The process of polishing the final draft of a written composition to prepare it for publication.

English language learner A person whose native language is not English and who is acquiring English as an additional language.

error A reader's response that is not consistent with the text and that is *not* self-corrected.

expository text / expository nonfiction A nonfiction text that gives the reader information about a topic. Expository texts use a variety of underlying text structures such as description, temporal sequence, categorization, compare and contrast, problem and solution, and question and answer. Forms of expository text include reports, news articles, and feature articles.

F&P Calculator stopwatch A device that calculates the reading time, reading rate, accuracy rate, and self-correction ratio for a reading.

F&P Text Level Gradient™ A twenty-six-point (A–Z) text-rating scale of difficulty, in which each text level, from the easiest at level A to the most challenging at level Z, represents a small but significant increase in difficulty over the previous level. The gradient correlates these levels to grade levels.

fable A folktale that demonstrates a useful truth and teaches a lesson. Usually including personified animals or natural elements such as the sun, fables appear to be simple but often convey abstract ideas.

factual text See *informational text.*

fairy tale A folktale about real problems but also involving magic and magical creatures. Also called "wonder tales," fairy tales have been handed down through oral language over the years.

family, friends, and school story A contemporary realistic text focused on the everyday experiences of children of a variety of ages, including relationships with family and friends and experiences at school.

fantasy A fiction text that contains elements that are highly unreal. Fantasy as a category of fiction includes genres such as animal fantasy, fantasy, and science fiction.

fiction Invented, imaginative prose or poetry that tells a story. Along with nonfiction, fiction is one of two basic genres of literature.

figurative language Language that compares two objects or ideas to allow the reader to see something more clearly or understand something in a new way. An element of a writer's style, figurative language changes or goes beyond literal meaning. See also *simile, metaphor, personification.*

fluency In reading, this term names the ability to read continuous text with good momentum, phrasing, appropriate pausing, intonation, and stress. In word solving, this term names the ability to solve words with speed, accuracy, and flexibility.

fold sheet A tool for classroom and home practice that involves having children work with letters or words by writing and illustrating, folding the sheet if necessary, and writing their name on the cover.

folktale A traditional fiction text about a people or "folk," originally handed down orally from generation to generation. Folktales are usually simple tales and often involve talking animals.

font In printed text, the collection of type (letters) in a particular style.

form A kind of text that is characterized by particular elements. Short story, for example, is a form of fiction writing.

genre A kind of category of text or artistic work or a class of artistic endeavor (including music, drama, and studio arts) that has a characteristic form or technique.

gradient of reading difficulty (see **F&P Text Level Gradient**™

grammar Complex rules by which people can generate an unlimited number of phrases, sentences, and longer texts in that language. *Conventional grammar* refers to the accepted grammatical conventions in a society.

grapheme A letter or cluster of letters representing a single sound, or phoneme: for example, *a, eigh, ay*.

graphic feature In fiction texts, graphic features are usually illustrations. In nonfiction texts, graphic features include photographs, paintings and drawings, charts, diagrams, tables and graphs, maps, and timelines.

graphophonic relationship The relationship between the oral sounds of the language and the written letters or clusters of letters. See also *semantic system, syntactic system*.

Guide for Observing and Noting Reading Behaviors Lists questions a teacher should ask herself about the ways a child is processing or problem-solving texts.

hard reading level The level at which the child reads the text aloud with less than 90 percent accuracy (levels A–K) or less than 95 percent accuracy (levels L–Z).

have a try To write a word, notice that it doesn't look quite right, try it two or three other ways, and decide which construction looks right; to make an attempt and self-check.

high-frequency words Words that occur often in the spoken and written language.

historical fiction A fiction text that takes place in a realistically (and often factually) portrayed setting of a past era. Compare to *realistic fiction*.

homograph One of two or more words spelled alike but different in meaning, derivation, or pronunciation: for example, the *bat* flew away, he swung the *bat*; take a *bow, bow* and arrow.

homonym One of two or more words spelled and pronounced alike but different in meaning: for example, we had *quail* for dinner; I would *quail* in fear. A homonym is a type of homograph.

homophone One of two or more words pronounced alike but different in spelling and meaning: for example, *meat, meet; bear, bare*.

humorous story A realistic fiction text that is full of fun and meant to entertain.

hybrid / hybrid text A text that includes at least one nonfiction genre and at least one fiction genre blended in a coherent whole.

illustration Graphic representation of important content (for example, art, photos, maps, graphs, charts) in a fiction or nonfiction text.

imagery The use of language—descriptions, comparisons, and figures of speech—that helps the mind form sensory impressions. Imagery is an element of a writer's style.

independent reading level The level at which the child reads the text with 95 percent or higher accuracy and excellent or satisfactory comprehension (levels A–K) or 98 percent or higher accuracy with excellent or satisfactory comprehension (levels L–Z).

independent writing Children write a text independently with teacher support as needed.

individual instruction A type of instruction in which the teacher works with just one child.

inferring (as a strategic action) Going beyond the literal meaning of a text and thinking about what is not stated but is implied by the writer.

inflectional ending A suffix added to a base word to show tense, plurality, possession, or comparison: for example, dark-*er*.

informational text A nonfiction text in which a purpose is to inform or give facts about a topic. Informational texts include the following genres—biography, autobiography, memoir, and narrative nonfiction, as well as expository texts, procedural texts, and persuasive texts.

Insertion (as an error in reading) A word added during oral reading that is not in the text.

instructional reading level At levels A–K, the level at which the child reads the text with 90–94 percent accuracy and excellent or satisfactory comprehension; or 95 percent or higher accuracy and limited comprehension. At levels L–Z, the level at which the child reads the text with 95–97 percent accuracy and excellent or satisfactory comprehension; or 98 percent or higher accuracy and limited comprehension.

interactive read-aloud A teaching context in which students are actively listening and responding to an oral reading of a text.

interactive writing A teaching context in which the teacher and students cooperatively plan, compose, and write a group text; both teacher and students act as scribes (in turn).

intervention Intensive additional instruction for children not progressing as rapidly as expected; usually one-on-one tutoring or small-group (one teacher to three students) teaching.

intonation The rise and fall in pitch of the voice in speech to convey meaning.

italic / italics A type style that is characterized by slanting letters.

key understandings Important ideas within (literal), beyond (implied), or about (determine through critical analysis) the text that are necessary to comprehension.

label A written word or phrase that names the content of an illustration.

label book A picture book consisting of illustrations with brief identifying text.

language and literary features (as text characteristics) Qualities particular to written language that are qualitatively different from those associated with spoken language: for example, dialogue, setting, description, mood.

language structure See *syntax*.

language use The craft of using sentences, phrases, and expressions to describe events, actions, or information.

layout The way the print and illustrations are arranged on a page.

letter and word games Games that require children to look carefully at words, letters, and parts of words.

letter combination Two or more letters that appear together and represent vowel sounds in words: for example, *ea* in *meat*, *igh* in *sight*.

letter knowledge The ability to recognize and label the graphic symbols of language.

Letter Minibooks Short books, each of which is focused on a particular letter and its relation to a sound.

letters Graphic symbols representing the sounds in a language. Each letter has particular distinctive features and may be identified by letter name or sound.

letter-sound correspondence The correspondence of letter(s) and sound(s) in written or spoken language.

letter-sound relationships (See **letter-sound correspondence**.)

leveled books Texts designed along a gradient from level A (easiest) to level Z (hardest).

lexicon Words that make up language.

long vowel The elongated vowel sound that is the same as the name of the vowel. It is sometimes represented by two or more letters: for example, c*a*ke, *ei*ght, m*ai*l. Another term for long vowel is *lax vowel*.

lowercase letter A small letter form that is usually different from its corresponding capital or uppercase form.

M (meaning) One of the sources of information that readers use (MSV: meaning, language structure, visual information). Meaning, the semantic system of language, refer to meaning derived from words, meaning across a text or texts, and meaning from personal experience or knowledge.

magnetic letters Multicolored upper- and lowercase letters that children manipulate to learn to read and form words.

maintaining fluency (as a strategic action) Integrating sources of information in a smoothly operating process that results in expressive, phrased reading.

making connections (as a strategic action) Searching for and using connections to knowledge gained through personal experiences, learning about the world, and reading other texts.

memoir A biographical text in which a writer takes a reflective stance in looking back on a particular time or person. Usually written in the first person, memoirs are often briefer and more intense accounts of a memory or set of memories than the accounts found in biographies and autobiographies.

mentor texts Books or other texts that serve as examples of excellent writing. Mentor texts are read and reread to provide models for literature discussion and student writing.

message An important idea that an author conveys in a fiction or nonfiction text. See also *main idea, theme*.

modeled writing An instructional technique in which a teacher demonstrates the process of composing a particular genre, making the process explicit for students.

monitoring and self-correcting (as a strategic action) Checking whether the reading sounds right, looks right, and makes sense, and solving problems when it doesn't.

My ABC Book A book containing upper- and lowercase letters on each page, along with a key word and a picture to develop chiildren's knowledge of the alphabet, upper- and lowercase letters, features of letters, and letter/sound relationships.

My Poetry Book A book containing all of the poems used in lessons in the particular system in which you are working.

My Writing Book A consumable blank book that children can use for writing. The books are filled as children write and draw for activities in *LLI* lessons. When the book is filled, he child takes it home and begins a new book for subsequent lessons. Complete pages in *My Writing Book* are excellent for reading practice either in school or at home.

multisyllable word A word that contains more than one syllable.

name chart A tool for helping children learn about letters, sounds, and words. It is a list of names, usually in alphabetical order by the first letter. Some teachers write the first letter of each name in red and the rest of the name in black. The print should be clear, and names should not be jammed together.

name puzzle Using a set of letters, each child forms a puzzle of his or her own name in order to notice letters and their distinguishing characteristics.

narrative text A fiction or nonfiction text that uses a narrative structure and tells a story.

narrative text structure A method of organizing a text. A simple narrative structure follows a traditional sequence that includes a beginning, a problem, a series of events, a resolution of the problem, and an ending. Alternative narrative structures may include devices such as flashback or flash-forward to change the sequence of events or allow for multiple narrators. See also *organization, text structure,* and *nonnarrative text structure.*

new word learning A variety of ways children learn new words, including looking at the first letter and running a finger left to write as they scan the word with their eyes.

nonfiction Prose or poetry that provides factual information. According to their structures, nonfiction texts can be organized into the categories of narrative and nonnarrative. Along with fiction, nonfiction is one of the two basic genres of literature.

nonnarrative text structure A method of organizing a text. Nonnarrative structures are used especially in three genres of nonfiction—expository texts, procedural texts, and persuasive texts. In nonnarrative nonfiction texts, underlying structural patterns include description, cause and effect, chronological sequence, temporal sequence, categorization, compare and contrast, problem and solution, and question and answer. See also *organization, text structure,* and *narrative text structure.*

nursery rhyme A short rhyme for children, usually telling a story.

omission (as in error) A word left out or skipped during oral reading.

Online Data Management System **(ODMS)** A Heinemann resource that enables teachers and administrators to track and print reports on entry/exit data and progress-monitoring data for individuals or groups of children.

Online Resources A password-protected website that provides the specific resources needed for each lesson as well as general resources used in many lessons. It includes Recording Forms for taking reading records on instructional-level books, word and picture cards, Letter Minibooks, Alphabet Linking Charts, Parent Letters, and other record-keeping and observation forms and resources used in *LLI*.

onset In a syllable, the part (consonant, consonant cluster, or consonant digraph) that comes before the vowel: for example, the *cr* in *cream*. See also *rime*.

onset-rime segmentation The identification and separation of the onset (first part) and rime (last part, containing the vowel) in a word: for example, *dr-ip*.

open syllable A syllable that ends in a vowel sound: for example, *ho*-tel.

oral games Games teachers can play with children to help them learn how to listen for and identify words in sentences, syllables, onsets and rimes, and individual phonemes.

oral reading Reading out loud for others to hear.

organization The arrangement of ideas in a text according to a logical structure, either narrative or nonnarrative. Another term for organization is *text structure.*

orthographic awareness The knowledge of the visual features of written language, including distinctive features of letters as well as spelling patterns in words.

orthography The representation of the sounds of a language with the proper letters according to standard usage (spelling).

performance reading An instructional context in which the students read orally to perform for others; they may read in unison or take parts. Shared reading, choral reading, and readers' theater are kinds of performance reading.

phoneme The smallest unit of sound in spoken language. There are forty-four units of speech sounds in English.

phoneme addition To add a beginning or ending sound to a word: for example, /h/ + *and*; *an* + /t/.

phoneme blending To identify individual sounds and then to put them together smoothly to make a word: for example, /k/ /a/ /t/ = *cat*.

phoneme deletion To omit a beginning, middle, or ending sound of a word: for example, /k/ /a/ /s/ /k/ − /k/ = *ask*.

phoneme-grapheme correspondence The relationship between the sounds (phonemes) and letters (graphemes) of a language.

phoneme isolation The identification of an individual sound— beginning, middle, or end—in a word.

phoneme manipulation The movement of sounds from one place in a word to another.

phoneme reversal The exchange of the first and last sounds of a word to make a different word.

phoneme substitution The replacement of the beginning, middle, or ending sound of a word with a new sound.

phonemic (or phoneme) awareness The ability to hear individual sounds in words and to identify particular sounds.

phonemic strategies Ways of solving words that use how words sound and relationships between letters and letter clusters and phonemes in those words.

phonetics The scientific study of speech sounds—how the sounds are made vocally and the relation of speech sounds to the total language process.

phonics The knowledge of letter-sound relationships and how they are used in reading and writing. Teaching phonics refers to helping children acquire this body of knowledge about the oral and written language systems; additionally, teaching phonics helps children use phonics knowledge as part of a reading and writing process. Phonics instruction uses a small portion of the body of knowledge that makes up phonetics.

phonogram A phonetic element represented by graphic characters or symbols. In word recognition, words containing a graphic sequence composed of a vowel grapheme and an ending consonant grapheme (such as *an* or *it*) are sometimes called a word family.

phonological awareness The awareness of words, rhyming words, onsets and rimes, syllables, and individual sounds (phonemes).

phonological system The sounds of the language and how they work together in ways that are meaningful to the speakers of the language.

picture book A form of illustrated fiction or nonfiction text in which pictures work with the text to tell a story or provide information.

play A form of dramatic text written to be performed rather than just read. A play will include references to characters, scenery, and action, as well as stage directions, and usually consists of scripted (written) dialogue between characters. Plays can be realistic fiction, historical fiction, or fantasy, and they might also include elements of special types of fiction such as mystery or romance.

plot The events, actions, conflict, and resolution of a story presented in a certain order in a fiction text. A simple plot progresses chronologically from start to end, whereas more complex plots may shift back and forth in time.

plural Of, relating to, or constituting more than one.

poetry Compact, metrical writing characterized by imagination and artistry and imbued with intense meaning. Along with prose, poetry is one of the two broad categories into which all literature can be divided.

possessive Grammatical form used to show ownership; for example., *John's, his.*

predicting (as a strategic action) Using what is known to think about what will follow while reading continuous text.

prefix A group of letters placed in front of a base word to change its meaning: for example, *pre*plan.

principle In phonics, a generalization or a sound-spelling relationship that is predictable.

problem See *conflict.*

problem and solution A structural pattern used especially in nonfiction texts to define a problem and clearly propose a solution. This pattern is often used in persuasive and expository texts.

processing (as in reading) The mental operations involved in constructing meaning from written language.

prompt A question, direction, or statement designed to encourage the child to say more about a topic.

Prompting Guide, Part 1 and Part 2 A tool you can use in each lesson as a quick reference for specific language to teach for, to prompt for, or to reinforce effective reading and writing behaviors. The guide, which consists of two parts, is organized in categories and color-coded so that you can turn quickly to the area needed and refer to it as you teach.

Professional Development and Tutorial Video You can use the *LLI Professional Development and Tutorial Video* to support your work individually or with a study group of professionals. The video includes an overview of the program and mode as well as tutorial on coding, scoring, and analyzing reading records and information on using the data to inform your teaching.

punctuation Marks used in written text to clarify meaning and separate structural units. The comma and the period are common punctuation marks.

purpose A writer's overall intention in creating a text, or a reader's overall intention in reading a text. To tell a story is one example of a writer's purpose, and to be entertained is one example of a reader's purpose.

readers' theater A performance of literature—That is, a story, a play, or poetry—read aloud expressively by one or more persons rather than acted.

realistic fiction A fiction text that takes place in contemporary or modern times about believable characters involved in events that could happen. Contemporary realistic fiction usually presents modern problems that are typical for the characters, and it may highlight social issues. Compare with *historical fiction.*

related words Words that are related because of sound, spelling, category, or meaning. See also *synonym, antonym, homophone, homograph, analogy.*

repetition (in oral reading) The reader saying a word, phrase, or section of the text more than once.

resolution / solution The point in the plot of a fiction story when the main conflict is solved.

rhyme The repetition of vowel and consonant sounds in the stressed syllables of words in verse, especially at the ends of lines.

rime In a syllable, the ending part containing the letters that represent the vowel sound and the consonant letters that follow: that is., dr-*eam*. See also *onset*.

root word See *word root*.

rubric A scoring tool that relies on descriptions of response categories for evaluation.

running words The number of words read aloud and coded during the Rereading Books and Assessment part of even-numbered lessons.

S (Structure) One of the sources of information that readers use (MSV: meaning, language structure, visual information). Language structure refers to the way words are put together in phrases and sentences (syntax or grammar).

scoring a running record Counting coded errors and self-corrections, which allows you to calculate *accuracy rate* and *self-correction ratio* on the Recording Form. The form also provides space for a *fluency score* (levels C–N) and *reading rate* (levels J–N).

Scoring and Coding at-a-Glance A summary of the steps for scoring the three parts of a running record: oral reading, comprehension conversation, and writing about reading.

Searching The reader looking for information in order to read accurately, self-correct, or understand a text.

searching for and using information (as a strategic action) Looking for and thinking about all kinds of content in order to make sense of a text while reading.

segment To divide into parts: for example, *to/ma/to*.

self-correcting Noticing when reading doesn't make sense, sound right, or look right, and fixing it when it doesn't.

self-correction ratio The proportion of errors the reader corrects himself.

semantic system The system by which speakers of a language communicate meaning through language. See also *graphophonic relationship, syntactic system*.

sentence complexity (as a text characteristic) The complexity of the structure or syntax of a sentence. Addition of phrases and clauses to simple sentences increases complexity.

sentence strips Strips of card stock on which sentences have been written and then cut up and mixed up so children can put them back together.

series/series book A set of books that are connected by the same character(s) or setting. Each book in a series stands alone, and often books may be read in any order.

shared reading An instructional context in which the teacher involves a group of students in the reading of a particular big book in order to introduce aspects of literacy (such as print conventions), develop reading strategies (such as decoding or predicting), and teach vocabulary.

shared writing An instructional context in which the teacher involves a group of students in the composing of a coherent text together. The teacher writes while scaffolding children's language and ideas.

short vowel A brief-duration sound represented by a vowel letter: for example, the lal in *cat*.

silent *e* The final *e* in a spelling pattern that usually signals a long vowel sound in the word and that does not represent a sound itself: for example, *make*.

sketching and drawing (in writing) To create a rough (sketch) or finished (drawing) image of a person, a place, a thing, or an idea to capture, work with, and render the writer's ideas.

small books In the *LLI Green System*, learning takes place with the foundational support of 130 children's books called small books.

small-group reading instruction The teacher working with children brought together because they are similar enough in reading development to teach in a small group; guided reading.

solving words (as a strategic action) Using a range of strategies to take words apart and understand their meaning(s).

sound boxes/letter boxes (Elkonin boxes) A tool for helping children to learn about the sounds and letters in words.

sounding out Pronouncing the sounds of the letters in a word as a step in reading the word.

sources of information The various cues in a written text that combine to make meaning (for example, syntax, meaning, and the physical shape and arrangement of type).

speech bubble A shape, often rounded, containing the words a character or person says in a cartoon or other text. Another term for *speech bubble* is *speech balloon.*

spelling aloud Naming the letters in a word rather than reading the word.

spelling patterns Beginning letters (onsets) and common phonograms (rimes), which form the basis for the English syllable. Knowing these patterns, a student can build countless words.

split dialogue Written dialogue in which a "*said phrase*" divides the speaker's words: for example, "Come on," said Mom. "Let's go home."

standardized Remaining essentially the same over multiple instances.

strategic action Any one of many simultaneous, coordinated thinking activities that go on in a reader's head. See *thinking within, beyond, and about the text.*

stress The emphasis given to some syllables or words in pronunciation. See also *accented syllable.*

student folders A set of folders to keep reading records and other data for each child. These folders can be passed on each year as part of children's records. The inside of the folder includes a graph for tracking a child's initial level, progress throughout *LLI*, and exit information.

suffix A group of letters added at the end of a base word or word root to change its function or meaning: for example, hand*ful*, hope*less*.

summarizing (as a strategic action) Putting together and remembering important information, disregarding irrelevant information, while reading.

syllabication The division of words into syllables.

syllable A minimal unit of sequential speech sounds composed of a vowel sound or a consonant-vowel combination. A syllable always contains a vowel or vowel-like speech sound: for example, *pen/ny.*

synonym One of two or more words that have different sounds but the same meaning: for example, *high, tall.*

syntactic awareness The knowledge of grammatical patterns or structures.

syntactic system Rules that govern the ways in which morphemes and words work together in sentence patterns. This system is not the same as proper grammar, which refers to the accepted grammatical conventions. See also *graphophonic relationship, semantic system.*

syntax The way sentences are formed with words and phrases and the grammatical rules that govern their formation.

synthesizing (as a strategic action) Combining new information or ideas from reading text with existing knowledge to create new understandings.

table charts Charts the teacher constructs with the children, based on activities in the lessons, that are large enough for all the children in a group to see across a table.

Take-Home Bags Bags in which children take home items such as word bags, sentence strips, Take-Home Books, or other materials for Classroom and Home Connection activities.

Take-Home Books Black-and-white versions of the books children read in their lessons.

text structure The overall architecture or organization of a piece of writing. Another term for text structure is *organization*. See also *narrative text structure* and *nonnarrative text structure*.

theme The central underlying idea, concept, or message that the author conveys in a fiction text. Compare to *main idea*.

thinking within, beyond, and about the text Three ways of thinking about a text while reading. Thinking within the text involves efficiently and effectively understanding what's on the page, the author's literal message. Thinking beyond the text requires making inferences and putting text ideas together in different ways to construct the text's meaning. In thinking about the text, readers analyze and critique the author's craft.

thought bubble A shape, often rounded, containing the words (or sometimes an image that suggests one or more words) a character or person thinks in a cartoon or other text. Another term for *thought bubble* is *thought balloon*.

told The teacher telling the reader a word she cannot read.

topic The subject of a piece of writing.

traditional literature Stories passed down in oral or written form through history. An integral part of world culture, traditional literature includes folktales, tall tales, fairy tales, fables, myths, legends, epics, and ballads.

underlying structural pattern See *nonnarrative text structure*.

understandings Basic concepts that are critical to comprehending a particular area of content.

uppercase letter A large letter form that is usually different from its corresponding lowercase form. Another term for *uppercase letter* is *capital letter*.

(V) Visual Information One of three sources of information that readers use (MSV: meaning, language structure, visual information). Visual information refers to the letters that represent the sounds of language and the way they are combined (spelling patterns) to create words; visual information at the sentence level includes punctuation.

Verbal Path Language used to help children get the hand moving the right way to form letters efficiently.

visual strategies Ways of solving words that use knowledge of how words look, including the clusters and patterns of the letters in words.

vocabulary Words and their meanings. See also *word meaning / vocabulary*.

vowel A speech sound or phoneme made without stoppage of or friction in the airflow. The vowel sounds are represented by *a, e, i, o, u,* and sometimes *y*.

vowel combination See *letter combination*.

Ways to Sort and Match Letters Using magnetic letters or letter cards, children sort letters to learn their distinctive features.

word A unit of meaning in language.

word analysis To break apart words into parts or individual sounds in order to parse them.

word bags A collection of high-frequency word cards that are kept in a sealable, one-quart plastic bag.

word boundaries The white space that appears before the first letter and after the last letter of a word and that defines the letter or letters as a word. It is important for young readers to learn to recognize word boundaries.

word-by-word matching Usually applied to a beginning reader's ability to match one spoken word with one printed word while reading and pointing. In older readers, the eyes take over the process.

word family A term often used to designate words that are connected by phonograms or rimes (e.g., *hot, not, pot, shot*). A word family can also be a series of words connected by meaning (e.g., *baseless, baseline, baseboard*).

wordless picture book A form in which a story is told exclusively with pictures.

word meaning / vocabulary *Word meaning* refers to the commonly accepted meaning of a word in oral or written language. *Vocabulary* often refers to the words one knows in oral or written language.

word root A word part, usually from another language, that carries the essential meaning of and is the basis for an English word: for example, *flect, reflect*. Most word roots cannot stand on their own as English words. Some word roots can be combined with affixes to create English words. Compare to *base word*.

words (as a text characteristic) Decodability of words in a text; phonetic and structural features of words

word structure The parts that make up a word.

words in text Children use their eyes to locate known and unknown words in text.

word-solving actions The strategies a reader uses to recognize words and understand their meaning(s).

writing Children engaging in the writing process and producing pieces of their own writing in many genres.

writing about reading Children responding to reading a text by writing and sometimes drawing.

writing words fluently Children learning to write words fast by writing words several times each.

"You Try It" A prompt given by the teacher that directs a child to make an attempt at reading a word during oral reading.

appendix I

▶ Bibliography

Armbruster, B. B. F. Lehr, and J. Osborn. *Put Reading First: The Research Building Blocks for Teaching Children to Read.* Jessup, MD: Center for the Improvement of Early Learning Achievement, 2003.

Armbruster, B. B., F. Lehr, and J. Osborn. *Put Reading First: The Research Building Blocks for Teaching Children to Read: Kindergarten through Grade 1.* Jessup, MD: National Institute for Literacy, 2001.

Clay, Marie. *Becoming Literate: The Construction of Inner Control.* Portsmouth, NH, 1991.

Clay, Marie. *Change over Time in Children's Literacy Development.* Portsmouth, NH: Heinemann, 2001.

Clay, Marie. *By Different Paths to Common Outcomes.* York, ME: Stenhouse, 1998.

Clay, Marie. *The Observation Survey of Early Literary Achievement.* Chicago, IL: Heinemann Library, 2005.

Demers, L. (2012) *Leveled Literacy Intervention: Research and Data Collection Project 2010–2011.* Portsmouth, NH: Heinemann.

Fountas, Irene C., and Gay Su **Pinnell.** *Fountas and Pinnell Benchmark Assessment System 1: Grades K–2, Levels A–N.* Portsmouth, NH: Heinemann, 2007.

Fountas, Irene C., and Gay Su **Pinnell.** *Fountas & Pinnell Benchmark Assessment System 2: Grades 3–8, Levels L–Z.* Portsmouth, NH: Heinemann, 2007.

Fountas, Irene C., and Gay Su **Pinnell.** *Fountas & Pinnell Benchmark Assessment System 3: Grades 3–8, Levels L–Z.* Portsmouth, NH: Heinemann, 2016.

Fountas, Irene C., and Gay Su **Pinnell.** *Guided Reading: Responsive Teaching Across the Grades, Second Edition.* Portsmouth, NH: Heinemann, 2017.

Fountas, Irene C., and Gay Su **Pinnell.** *Teaching for Comprehending and Fluency: Thinking, Talking, and Writing About Reading, K–8.* Portsmouth, NH: Heinemann, 2003.

Goldenberg, C. N. "Promoting Early Literacy Development Among Spanish-Speaking Children: Lessons from Two Studies." *Getting Ready Right from the Start: Effective Early Literacy Interventions.* Needham, MA: Allyn & Bacon, 1994.

Hiebert, E. H., and B. M. Taylor (Eds.). "Promoting Early Literacy Development Among Spanish-Speaking Children: Lessons from Two Studies." *Getting Ready Right from the Start: Effective Early Literacy Interventions.* Needham, MA: Allyn & Bacon, 1994.

Juel, C. "Learning to Read and Write: A Longitudinal Study of 54 Children from First Through Fourth Grades." *Journal of Educational Psychology*, Vol. 80, No. 4 (1988), pp. 437–447.

McCarrier, A., I. C. Fountas, and G. S. Pinnell. *Interactive Writing: How Language & Literacy Come Together.* Portsmouth, NH, 1999.

Peterman, R., A. Grehan, S. Ross, B. Gallagher, & E. Dexter, *An Evaluation of the Leveled Literacy Intervention Program: A Small-Group Intervention for Students in K–2.* Paper presented at the annual meeting of the American Educational Research Association, San Diego, CA. (2009, April).

Pikulsky, John J. *Factors Common to Successful Early Intervention Programs.* Boston: Houghton Mifflin, 1997.

Pinnell, Gay Su, and Irene C. **Fountas**. *The Continuum of Literacy Learning, Grades K–2: A Guide to Teaching.* Portsmouth, NH: Heinemann, 2007.

Pinnell, Gay Su, and Irene C. **Fountas**. *The Fountas & Pinnell Literacy Continuum, Grades PreK–8; A Tool for Assessment, Planning, and Teaching.* Portsmouth, NH: Heinemann, 2016.

Pinnell, Gay Su, and Irene C. **Fountas**. *Phonics Lessons with CD-ROM, Grade K: Letters, Words, and How They Work.* Portsmouth, NH: Heinemann, 2003.

Pinnell, Gay Su, and Irene C. **Fountas**. *Phonics Lessons with CD-ROM, Grade 1: Letters, Words, and How They Work.* Portsmouth, NH: Heinemann, 2003.

Pinnell, Gay Su, and Irene C. **Fountas**. *Phonics Lessons with CD-ROM, Grade 2: Letters, Words, and How They Work.* Portsmouth, NH: Heinemann, 2003.

Pinnell, Gay Su, and Irene C. **Fountas**. *Sing a Song of Poetry, Kindergarten: A Teaching Resource for Phonemic Awareness, Phonics and Fluency.* Portsmouth, NH: Heinemann, 2004.

Pinnell, Gay Su, and Irene C. **Fountas**. *Sing a Song of Poetry, Grade 1: A Teaching Resource for Phonemic Awareness, Phonics and Fluency.* Portsmouth, NH: Heinemann, 2004.

Pinnell, Gay Su, and Irene C. **Fountas**. *Sing a Song of Poetry, Grade 2: A Teaching Resource for Phonemic Awareness, Phonics and Fluency.* Portsmouth, NH: Heinemann, 2003.

Pinnell, Gay Su, and Irene C. **Fountas**. *When Readers Struggle: Teaching That Works.* Portsmouth, NH: Heinemann, 2008.

Pinnell, Gay Su, and Irene C. **Fountas**. *Word Matters: Teaching Phonics and Spelling in the Reading/Writing Classroom.* Portsmouth, NH: Heinemann, 1998.

Ransford-Kaldon, C., C. Ross, C. Lee, E. Sutton Flynt, L. Franceschini, & T. Zoblot sky (2013). Efficacy of the Leveled Literacy Intervention System for K–2 Urban Students: An Empirical Evaluation of *LLI* in Denver Public Schools. Memphis, TN: Center for Research in Educational Policy, University of Memphis. 2013

Report of the National Reading Panel: Teaching Children to Read: An Evidence-Based Assessment of the Scientific Research Literature on Reading and Its Implications for Reading Instruction. Reports of the Subgroups. Washington, DC: National Institutes of Health and Human Development, 2001.

Snow, C. E., M. S. Burns and P. Griffin (Eds.). *Committee on the Prevention of Reading Difficulties in Young Children, National Research Council* Washington, DC: National Academy Press, 1998.

Stanovich, K. E. "Matthew Effects in Reading: Some Consequences of Individual Differences in the Acquisition of Literacy." *Reading Research Quarterly*, Vol. 21 (1986), 301–406.

Vygotsky, L. S. *Mind in Society: The Development of Higher Psychological Processes.* Cambridge, MA: Harvard University Press, 1978.

Ward, E. (2011). *Leveled Literacy Intervention: Research and Data Collection Project 2009–2010.* Portsmouth, NH: Heinemann.